DATE DUE

MAR 2 04	

DEMCO INC 38-2971

VIOLENCE
AT WORK

Second edition

Duncan Chappell and Vittorio Di Martino

International Labour Office · Geneva

Chappell, D.; Di Martino, V.
Violence at work. Second edition
Geneva, International Labour Office, 2000

Occupational safety, Violence, Aggression, Crime, Developed country, Developing country. 13.04.2
ISBN 92-2-110840-6

Also published in French: *La violence au travail*, Geneva, ILO, 2000

ILO Cataloguing in Publication Data

Confrontation and dialogue usually form part of the normal working environment. Workers and managers are confronted on a daily basis with their personal and work-related problems. They have to face the anxieties and frustration of co-workers, organizational difficulties, personality clashes, aggressive intruders from the outside, and problematic relations with clients and the public. Despite this, dialogue usually prevails over confrontation, and people manage to organize efficient and productive activities within the workplace. There are cases, however, where dialogue fails to develop in a positive way, where relationships between workers, managers, clients or the public deteriorate, and the objectives of working efficiently and achieving productive results are affected. Violence may enter the workplace and turn a previously benign environment into a hostile and hazardous setting.

Contemporary community awareness and concern about the issue of violence at work have been magnified to a significant degree by the attention given in the media to several tragic and dramatic workplace killings perpetrated by disturbed individuals, armed with powerful weapons. The study emphasizes, however, that workplace violence is not merely an episodic problem created by deranged persons, but it is a highly complex issue, rooted in wider social, economic, organizational and cultural factors. Thus instead of searching for simple, single solutions to deal with the entire problem, the full range of causes which generate violence must be analysed and a variety of intervention strategies applied. Recognizing and understanding the variety and complexity of the factors which contribute to violence must be a key precursor to the design and implementation of any effective anti-violence or control programme.

Workers, trade unions, employers, public bodies and experts on a broad international front are now expressing common concern about the issue of violence at work. Based on data, experiences and recent publications, it is intended both to provide a basis for understanding the nature of violence at work, and to suggest ways of preventing it in the future. The study stresses the importance of a preventive, systematic and targeted response to violence at work. For example, in many countries the scope of existing criminal, health and safety, labour, environmental and allied law is being extended progressively and adapted to deal with the issue of workplace violence. In several countries violence at work is emerging as a separate legal issue with legislative and regulatory provisions making for a focused rather than a diffuse response.

The study also identifies and discusses a large set of guidelines which is emerging from governments, trade unions, specialist study groups, workplace violence experts and employers' groups, most of which contain blueprints for action. Despite different approaches and methods, such guidelines reveal common themes: preventive action is possible and necessary; work organization and the working environment can provide important pointers to the causes and solutions to the problem; the participation of workers and their representatives is crucial both in identifying the problems and implementing solutions; the interpersonal skills of management and workers alike must not be underrated; there cannot be one formula for action because the uniqueness of each workplace situation must be considered; and continued review of policies and programmes is needed to keep up with the rapidly changing situation.

The ILO has been in the vanguard in addressing protection of workers' dignity and equality in the workplace. Its recent work on this important subject includes publications on occupational stress, sexual harassment, and workers' privacy, among others. This publication should be seen as part of its continuing work programme.

The publication is directed towards all those engaged in combating violence at work: policy-makers in government agencies, employers' and workers' organizations, health and safety professionals, personnel managers, trainers and workers. We hope that this study will promote dialogue, policies and initiatives "to repudiate violence and remove it from the workplace now".

F. J. Dy-Hammar,

Chief,
Conditions of Work and Welfare Facilities Branch,
International Labour Office

PREFACE TO THE SECOND EDITION

Almost a year has passed since the appearance of the first edition of *Violence at work*, a year of growing attention and awareness with regard to this alarming phenomenon worldwide. New information is emerging which shows that what we see is only the tip of the iceberg: the real size of the problem is still largely unknown. The enormous cost of violence at work for the individual, the workplace and the community at large is also becoming progressively more apparent.

Violence at work has consequently gained momentum as a priority issue. Governments, trade unions and employers are increasingly worried by what is emerging as one of the greatest concerns at the workplace today. Immediate action is being demanded by interested parties and public opinion, and is reflected and reinforced by the media.

The response at the national and international levels is taking shape. The European Commission is analysing the action necessary at the EU level on the prevention of workplace violence as part of its current programme on safety, hygiene and health at work. The ILO is preparing a manual of best practices and successful methods of prevention of violence at work, and is considering the topic as a major issue within its Programme on SafeWork for 2000-2001.

All around the world, further surveys and studies have been carried out to identify the main problem areas, and innovative experiments are underway to assess the feasibility and effectiveness of different solutions to the problem. However the new information and suggestions coming from these initiatives are just starting to become available, and this new edition mirrors the state of transition in this field.

A genuine effort has been made to integrate and update the original material, as well as to provide new cases and examples of successful responses to violence at work. It is hoped that this new edition meets the need to provide a fresh view on the subject, as well as triggering new publications and new preventive action in this area.

Vittorio Di Martino

CONTENTS

Tables

Violence at work

Figures

ACKNOWLEDGEMENTS

Special thanks are due to all those who contributed to different parts of this book, in particular, Michele Jankanish for input into the design and preparation of the chapter on legal issues; Janet Neubecker for searching and selecting from the vast documentation; Kristine Falciola for Internet research; Helen Wielander for the typing and processing of the manuscript; and John Myers for his support and involvement in the research and editorial work.

The ILO would like to thank the many individuals, governments, employers, trade unions, research institutes and other organizations that provided information, advice and comments on the issues of this publication.

Part I: Understanding violence at work

INTRODUCTION: A CATALYST FOR ACTION

1

The shootings at Dunblane Primary School on 13 March 1996

The school day had started at 9 a.m. for all primary classes. The school had 640 pupils, making it one of the largest primary schools in Scotland. On 13 March all primary 1, 2 and 3 classes had attended assembly from 9.10 a.m. to 9.30 a.m. They consisted of a total of about 250 pupils, together with their teachers and the school chaplain. They included Primary 1/13 which was a class of 28 pupils, along with their teacher Mrs. [M]. This class had already changed for their gym lesson before attending assembly; 25 members of the class were 5 years of age; and three were 6 years of age. Mrs. [M] was 47 years of age.

At the conclusion of assembly all those present had dispersed to their respective classrooms, with the exception of Primary 1/13 who with Mrs. [M] had made their way to the gymnasium...[Thomas Hamilton] entered the gym. He was wearing a dark jacket, black corduroy trousers and a woolly hat with ear defenders. He had a pistol in his hand. He advanced a couple of steps into the gym and fired indiscriminately and in rapid succession. [The report then goes on to detail the shooting by Hamilton of pupils and teachers, ending with Hamilton taking his own life.]

Mrs. [M] and 15 children lay dead in the gym and one further child was close to death. They had sustained a total of 58 gunshot wounds; 26 of these wounds were of such a nature that individually they would have proved fatal. While it is not possible to be precise as to the times at which the shootings took place, it is likely that they occurred within a period of 3-4 minutes, starting between 9.35 a.m. and 9.40 a.m.

The survivors of the incident were taken to Stirling Royal Infirmary. They consisted of the remaining 12 members of the class; two pupils aged 11 who were elsewhere than in the gym when they were injured; and [three teachers] Mrs. [H], Mrs. [B] and Mrs. [T]. Thirteen of them had sustained gunshot wounds, 4 being serious, 6 very serious and 3 minor.[1]

LEARNING FROM WORKPLACE TRAGEDIES

This report is about violence at work – its scope, causes and how it may be prevented. The tragedy which occurred at the Dunblane Primary School is an example,

---

[1] This edited description of the events which took place at the Dunblane Primary School in Scotland has been taken from the official inquiry into the shootings by the Hon. Lord W. Douglas Cullen. The results of the inquiry were presented to Parliament by the Secretary of State for Scotland in October 1996. See Cullen, 1996 – *The Public Inquiry into the Shootings at Dunblane Primary School on 13 March 1996* (hereafter the Cullen Report), Ch. 3, pp. 11-13. This excerpt, and others from the Cullen Report reproduced elsewhere in this book, are crown copyright, reproduced with the permission of the Controller of Her Majesty's Stationery Office.

fortunately both rare and extreme, of the intrusion of violence into one workplace which most would have believed to be entirely safe and secure.

The damage inflicted by one lone individual, armed with powerful modern weapons, upon the young pupils and their teachers at this Scottish school came as a profound shock to the British nation. The shootings prompted an official inquiry, conducted by Lord Cullen.

The Cullen Report, as it has become known, was published in October 1996. Among the recommendations made by Lord Cullen were a number relating to the possession and use of firearms, as well as measures to enhance the security and safety of British schools.[2] The firearms recommendations led, ultimately, to a decision by the British Government to place a complete ban on the possession and use of handguns in the United Kingdom.[3] In regard to the health and safety of teaching staff and pupils, the British Government has also acknowledged the need to prepare a safety strategy for the protection of the school population against violence, and to provide more comprehensive guidance to the school population as a whole about hazards arising in workplaces in the education sector.[4]

Hostage-taking at a nursery school in Neuilly-sur-Seine, 13 March 1993

"It was 9.30 a.m., and it was the usual morning routine in the youngest class (3-4 year-olds). After the children have sung or done language activities together, I start what we call 'workshops': the children go off to little tables to do an activity of their choice – pottery, painting, drawing. That day we were just starting to prepare Mothers' Day presents. I glanced up from the desk to see an armed man rush into the classroom. His head was partly covered by a hood and a balaclava. The man closed the door, and aimed at us with his gun. I was shocked and stunned – I hadn't seen him arrive, I didn't know how he had got into the class. I could feel that my legs were shaking, but I asked him 'What are you doing here? Who are you? What do you want?' With a sign, the man showed that he didn't want to talk to me, and handed me a typewritten sheet which started off with 'This is a hostage taking' in big letters. The rest of the text was a whole string of instructions written in excellent and well-structured French: 'Go and tell the headmistress... don't do anything which could put the children's lives in danger... in my bag I have all I need to blow up the classroom...' I didn't even finish reading it all, I just ran to tell the headmistress. She came straight to the classroom and tried to start a conversation with the man, but he interrupted her almost immediately and gave her the order, brandishing his gun, to go and phone the commissioner."

Statement by teacher L.D. to *Paris Match*, 27 March 1993.

---

[2] These recommendations are summarized in Ch. 12 of the Cullen Report. An official Government Response to each of the recommendations was provided at the time of the publication of the Report. See Scottish Office, 1996 – *The Public Inquiry into the Shootings at Dunblane Primary School on 13 March 1996: The Government Response.*

[3] See Cullen Report, Ch. 9 and the Government Response (Scottish Office, 1996, pp. 5-6). See also Associated Press, "Handguns surrender begins under new British law to ban ownership." Web site: http://customnews.cnn.com/cnews/protection-name=WorldPart_type=57682, retrieved 2 July 1997.

[4] Government Response (Scottish Office, 1997, pp. 6-7).

A tragedy like that occurring at Dunblane can on occasions act as a powerful catalyst for social action and reform. The ripples of anxiety and fear about the lethal reach of violence in this primary school have also spread far beyond the borders of Scotland and the United Kingdom. France had already been deeply affected by an incident in Neuilly-sur-Seine (Paris) in 1993, when a number of schoolchildren and their teachers were held hostage for several days by an armed man.[5]

Then only a few weeks after the events in Dunblane, a further mass murder took place at a national historic site on the small Australian island state of Tasmania. On 28 April 1996 a lone offender, armed with military style assault rifles, killed 35 people and wounded more than 30 others at the isolated rural community of Port Arthur.[6]

The Port Arthur site is a national park, visited each year by thousands of people from both Australia and overseas. Park employees were among those killed or injured, and many were witnesses to the shootings. As will be seen later in this book, the aftermath of such tragedies can be particularly devastating for those involved as witnesses or as members of emergency and other services. Members of the park staff who survived the massacre were among those deeply traumatized by the incident, as the following excerpt from the official inquiry indicates:

The Port Arthur massacre – The events of 28 April 1996

There can be no doubt that what happened at the Port Arthur Historic Site on Sunday, April 28, 1996, can best be described as horrific.

It is perhaps impossible for other than those 31 people of staff and helpers, plus the visitors present, to fully understand the amazement of the happening and the fright, hopelessness, bravery, heroism, stress, trauma, and the wonderful acts of thinking of others, planning, of sharing, and of loss and sadness that all took place in the space of that first 30 to 60 minutes of the shootings.

No one was fully aware of what was happening, there was uncertainty as to what to do and how to address the situation – no one had been trained for such a catastrophic happening as this one.

Yet, we are told of how certain staff took charge of the situation; how others acted without fully thinking of the consequences and led groups and individuals away to safety and to hide in trenches, ditches, in the scrub, and in isolated buildings:

- we hear of staff members thinking only of others, even though they were themselves injured or shot, and a trained nursing officer who was visiting a contractor on the site, doing wonderful work and comforting those injured;

---

[5] This incident prompted a major review of the security and safety of French schools. See: "Les dix-neuf mesures arrêtés. Le plan de prévention de la violence à l'école se présente en trois grands axes et dix-neuf mesures", in *Le Figaro*, 21 March 1996, p. 9.

[6] In February 1997 a Joint Parliamentary Group of the Parliament of Tasmania appointed a Special Commissioner, Mr. Max Doyle, to inquire into the ongoing traumas and problems facing the people of Port Arthur and its surrounding area following the shootings. The Special Commissioner presented his report to the Joint Parliamentary Group in June 1997. See Joint Parliamentary Group, 1997 – *Report of the Special Commissioner for Port Arthur, Mr. Max Doyle, into matters affecting the Port Arthur Historic Site and other associated matters* (hereafter the Doyle Report), Bellerive, Tasmania, Joint Parliamentary Group, 1997. Permission to quote the Doyle Report has been granted by the Department of Justice of Tasmania.

- we are told of a site concessionaire who left his business to render assistance and comfort to the injured and the dying at various places and in the Broad Arrow Café itself, and then organized refreshments and care for the assembled, shocked visitors;

- and of a local contractor who assisted with the injured, and helped organize sheets and blankets for bandages and the warmth of visitors, etc.;

- of some of these same people having to enter the café to inspect the carnage of that horrific scene within; of staff carrying on even though they were aware of relations and loved ones being victims of the tragedy;

- at about 1.30 p.m. on that fateful day, the entire management group of the site were at a destination near Swansea, therefore it was the rank and file members of that organization who acted so instantaneously to the emergency and who acquitted themselves so meritoriously under such horrifying and difficult conditions.

Let there be no doubt that what happened during that first hour after 1.30 p.m. on April 28 saw all these acts of heroism, love and care take place – but at a terrible toll on the lives of those who were then, and have been since, affected by these events. It must be also recorded that during the 60 minute period, some 500 visitors were within the site, and that so many lives were saved is a recognition of the bravery of so few who acted in their interests.

Source: Doyle Report, pp. 54-55.

The shootings at Dunblane and Port Arthur and the events at Neuilly had already been preceded by a number of other highly publicized workplace homicides in the United States dating from the mid-1980s onwards.[7] More recently schools have again been the scene of some of the most tragic episodes of violence.

The Thurston High School shooting incident in 1998 prompted immediate action by President Clinton – the United States Departments of Education and Justice were directed to develop a guide to help school personnel, parents, community members and others to identify early indicators of troubling and potentially dangerous student behaviour. Three months after the shooting, they jointly published *A guide to safe school* – see under "Published guidelines on violence – A selection", in Chapter 5.

The recent tragedy at the Columbine High School in Littleton, Colorado, where, on 20 April 1999, 14 students and one teacher were killed in yet another school shooting has, again, highlighted the dramatic importance of the problem.[8]

THE EMERGENCE OF VIOLENCE AT WORK AS AN ISSUE

There is no doubt that a series of recent tragedies like these has helped to focus international attention on violence at work as an issue of significant concern. The

---

[7] Criminologists in the United States have tended to date the current concern about workplace violence to an attack which took place by a lone gunman on an Oklahoma Post Office in 1986 which resulted in the deaths of 14 people and the wounding of six. Since that time a series of further murderous attacks at post offices, mainly by disgruntled employees, has resulted in the US postal system being put under sustained scrutiny. See Johnson and Indvik, 1996, p. 18.

[8] See Liberty Internet Magazine "Courage at Columbine High School", retrieved at http://www.doctorliberty.com/columbine.html, 7 July 1999.

The Thurston High School shooting: The events of 20 May 1998

On Wednesday, police confiscate what they think is a stolen .32-caliber hand-gun from the locker of Kipland P. Kinkel, 15 years of age. He is expelled from Thurston High School, taken to Skipworth Juvenile Detention Facility in Eugene, charged with possession of a stolen firearm and released to his parents, William and Faith Kinkel.

1. Kipland Kinkel drives to Thurston High School Thursday morning and parks several blocks away. The freshman has a .22-caliber semiautomatic rifle, a .22-caliber handgun and a 9 mm Glock handgun.

2. Kinkel walks into the school and enters the cafeteria through a side door, wearing a khaki-colored trench coat and hat. As many as 400 students are gathered there.

3. Kinkel raises the rifle to hip level, starts swiveling it slowly side to side and begins firing. Students think he is part of a skit related to school.

4. Kinkel starts to reload and is rushed by wrestler Jake Ryker, who has been shot. Jake is joined by his brother Josh. Students detain Kinkel until police arrive.

5. One student dead at scene. Twenty-three others are hit by gunfire. Some are in critical condition. There is a panicked rush for the cafeteria doors.

6. Ambulances take 12 of the injured to McKenzie-Willamette Hospital in Springfield. One dies later at the hospital.

7. Eleven of the injured are taken to Sacred Heart Medical Center in Eugene.

Police question Kinkel, whom they describe as having a "very calm de-meanor". During questioning, officers are dispatched to his home, where the bodies of William and Faith Kinkel are found. Anxious parents begin arriving at the school. They are gathered together in one location. At 8.45 a.m., names of the wounded are announced. Each name draws screams. Some parents sob uncontrollably.

Source: *Oregon Live*, retrieved at http://www.oregonlive.com/todaysnews/9805/sequence.html, on 1 July 1999.

---

workplace in general has been traditionally viewed as a relatively benign and vio-lence-free environment. It is also an environment in which confrontation and dia-logue can form a part of the normal operating milieu. Workers and managers are confronted on a daily basis with their personal and work-related problems. They may have to face the anxieties and frustration of co-workers, organizational difficul-ties, personality clashes, aggressive intruders from the outside, and problematic rela-tions with clients and the public. Despite this, dialogue usually prevails over con-frontation and people manage to organize efficient and productive activities within the workplace. There are cases, however, where this course of events fails to develop in a positive way; when relationships between workers, managers, clients or the pub-lic deteriorate, and the objectives of working efficiently and achieving productive re-sults are affected. When this situation occurs, and it would seem to be occurring with increasing frequency, violence may enter the workplace and transform it into a hostile and hazardous setting.

Some brief examples can assist at this stage in illustrating the scope, dimension and type of violence associated with workplaces in many parts of the world:

The United States

Workplace violence has been identified as the most important 1999 security threat to America's largest corporations, according to Fortune 1000 security executives interviewed in the annual Pinkerton survey.[9]

Homicide is the most dramatic and serious aspect of workplace violence. In the United States, official statistics show that homicide has become the second leading cause of occupational death overall and the first cause in relation to women.[10] Each week, an average of 20 workers are murdered while

18,000 are assaulted while at work or on duty. Non-fatal assaults result in millions of lost workdays and cost workers millions of dollars in lost wages.

Workplace violence is clustered in certain occupational settings: for example, the retail trade and service industries account for more than half of workplace homicides and 85 per cent of non-fatal workplace assaults. Taxicab drivers have the highest risk of workplace homicides of any occupational group. Workers in health care, community services, and retail settings are at increased risk of non-fatal assaults.[11]

South Africa

Workplace hostilities in South Africa are reported as "abnormally high". Preliminary results from a 1998-99 Internet survey indicate that 78 per cent of South Africans who took part in the survey had experienced hostile behaviour at the workplace during their working life.[12]

The United Kingdom

A survey conducted by the British Retail Consortium into crime and the retail sector found that more than 11,000 retail staff were the victims of physical violence, and more than 350,000 staff were the victims of threats and verbal abuse.[13] The survey, the third of its type, covered the 1994/95 financial year.[14]

As with last year, the majority of physical attacks occurred when staff were trying to prevent theft (59 per cent). Other causes of physical violence are dealing with troublemakers (16 per cent), robbery incidents (10 per cent), angry customers (5 per cent), drunk or drugged people (5 per cent) and other circumstances (5 per cent).

Whilst the survey questionnaire did not ask about the number of staff murdered during the course of business, it is unfortunate that retailers reported a number of such incidents, although this particular crime continues to be very rare in relation to the number of staff who work in the retail industry. However, it is encouraging to report a reduction in the number of

---

[9] Pinkerton mailed written questionnaires to 1,121 security directors and other executives having supervisory responsibility for corporate security at Fortune 1000 companies. Of these 269 (24 per cent) were returned and reflected in the results (press release from Pinkerton Incorporated, 17 March 1999 – "Workplace violence greatest security threat to corporate America: Pinkerton survey findings", retrieved at http://members.aol.com/endwpv/pinkerton-survey.html, 7 July 1999.

[10] Jenkins, 1996, p. iv. See also Kelleher, 1996.

[11] Jenkins, 1996.

[12] Information and statement provided to the ILO in June 1999 by S. Marais-Steinman, co-author (with M. Herman) of *Corporate hyenas at work*, Pretoria, Kagiso Publishers, 1997.

[13] Brooks and Cross, 1996, p. 17.

[14] These results are based on a detailed postal survey which drew results from companies trading through 53,000 outlets in the United Kingdom with an annual turnover of £81 billion. Respondents accounted for 44 per cent of total United Kingdom retail sales. See Brooks and Cross, 1996, p. 6.

physical attacks against staff, which may be attributed to better training emphasizing that staff safety comes first.

The risk of actual physical violence is 5 attacks per 1,000 staff, threats of violence 35:1,000 and verbal 81:1,000. Off-licences [shops in the United Kingdom selling alcoholic drink for consumption elsewhere – similar to late-night convenience stores in United States] continue to have the highest risk of actual physical violence 12:1,000, mixed business and DIY [Do It Yourself] 8:1,000.[15]

France

Acts of violence against transport personnel have been on the rise in the *Île-de-France* in 1998. RATP, Régie Autonome des Transports Parisiens, and SNCF, Société Nationale des Chemins de Fer, report an increase of 12 per cent and 34 per cent respectively in the number of attacks on their staff. According to RATP there were more than 2,000 attacks reported in 1998.[16]

Japan

A severe economic recession has resulted in major corporate downsizing, shattering certain long-held assumptions in that country about job and career stability. The loss of lifetime job security and seniority systems has been accompanied by alleged bullying of white-collar workers.[17] A "bullying hot-line" has been established by the Tokyo Managers' Union, and its counsellors reported more than 1,700 requests for consultation during two short periods in June and October 1996.[18] Issues raised included sexual harassment of women under the age of 30, while many older women felt they were being forced out of the workplace. Stress was common among all callers, with many indicating that they required urgent mental health treatment. Families whose members had committed or attempted suicide were among the callers, including the mother of an office worker in her twenties who said:

My daughter was bullied at work. Whenever she made a mistake it was pointed out in front of everybody and she felt very embarrassed. She resigned, but the company refused to accept it, so she committed suicide.[19]

The Philippines

Migration for work purposes has long been a feature of the Filipino employment market. More than half of all overseas Filipino contract workers are women (365,000 in 1995) and most were hired for work in Saudi Arabia, Hong Kong (China), Japan, Singapore and Malaysia, for employment in largely unprotected sectors of these foreign labour markets – domestic service and entertainment.[20] Research has shown that these Filipino women workers are frequently and disproportionately affected by violence associated with their employment:

For many women, the home and the workplace are one and the same. Violence at the workplace involves incidents where women are abused, threatened, or assaulted in circumstances involving an implicit or explicit challenge to their safety, well-being and health.

---

[15] Brooks and Cross, 1996, p. 17.

[16] *RATP et SNCF Île-de-France, Réunion mensuelle de sécurité, 11 janvier 1999.* Document provided to the ILO by the Ministère de l'Equipement, des Transports et du Logement.

[17] See Yamaji, 1997 and Coleman, 1996.

[18] Yamaji, 1997.

[19] Yamaji, 1997. For a more detailed description of the sexual harassment problems encountered by Japanese working women, see Japanese Trade Union Confederation, p. 63.

[20] Abrera-Mangahas, 1996, pp. 24-26.

Trapped in relative isolation, these women workers often suffer from a range of abusive situations, including but not limited to: verbal threats, bullying and insults; harassment (covering physical, sexual and racial harassment); long hours of work and multiple tasks in several households; and even extreme conditions of deliberate isolation. Many affected helpers report maltreatment, a general term that includes several of the following behaviours – pulling the hair, battering, beating the hands with any instrument, burning of the flesh of the victim, banging the head against the wall, throwing of toxic, chemically dangerous liquids. Employers commonly hold the worker's passport as a way of ensuring continued subservience.[21]

Germany

An extensive national survey conducted during 1991 by the Federal Institute of Occupational Health and Safety revealed that 93 per cent of the women questioned had been sexually harassed at the workplace during the course of their occupational life.[22] Cases of sexual harassment were not an "exceptional phenomenon" in the day-to-day working life of these women, with even those affected by serious incidents, including threatened professional disadvantage for failing to provide sexual favours, reporting multiple harassment.

These vignettes of violence occurring at workplaces around the globe suggest that this issue is truly one which transcends the boundaries of a particular country, work setting or occupational group. No country, work setting or occupation can claim realistically to be entirely free of this form of violence although some countries, like some workplaces and occupations, are undoubtedly at higher risk than others of experiencing such violence.

The state of our knowledge about current patterns and trends in violence at work is reviewed in the next chapter. However, there does appear to be evidence that both the incidence and prevalence of workplace violence is increasing in many jurisdictions. This trend may well reflect a growing community awareness and condemnation of this aspect of violence, resulting in increased reporting of incidents, as well as an actual rise in the total number of violent acts being committed in certain jurisdictions. A similar trend has been observed in recent years in the arena of family and domestic violence, where a "hidden issue" has rapidly become a very public one, and the subject of extensive attention and action.[23]

The real magnitude of domestic violence is only now being disclosed, as is its potential to have a negative impact on the workplace through the transfer of family conflicts to a work setting. It is also becoming clear that violence has a disproportionate impact on women, children and young people as well as socially and economically deprived groups both in developing and industrialized countries. The vulnerability to job loss and insecurity of a growing number of workers seems also to be mirrored by an increase in violence at work. Even in those countries and workplaces where violence still appears to be a "hidden issue", it is likely to reveal itself immediately upon closer analysis and investigation. Once violence has been identified, it often still remains largely under reported.

---

[21] ibid., p. 33. Research also shows that violence is a feature of the working conditions of domestic helpers within the internal labour market in the Philippines. See Gopalen, 1996.

[22] Beermann and Meschkutat, 1995, p. 21.

[23] According to a 1997 survey by Liz Claiborne Inc., 57 per cent of corporate leaders believe domestic violence is a major problem which affects their corporate balance sheet negatively. From Claiborne, 1997.

Given this situation it is not surprising that increasing concern is now being expressed by workers, trade unions, employers, public bodies and experts on a broad international front about the issue of violence at work.[24] This concern is being matched by calls for action to prevent such violence or, when it occurs, to deal with it in a way which alleviates the enormous social, economic and allied costs to the victims, their families, employers and the community at large. The question remains as to the nature and direction of the action which should be taken, and the identity of those who should be held responsible for its initiation.

THE CHANGING PROFILE OF VIOLENCE AT WORK

The variety of behaviours which may be covered under the general rubric of violence at work is so large, the border line with acceptable behaviours is often so vague, and the perception in different contexts and cultures of what constitutes violence is so diverse, that it becomes a significant challenge to both describe and define this phenomenon.

In practice, violence in the workplace may include a wide range of behaviours, often continuing or overlapping, as exemplified in the following box.

Examples of violent behaviours at work

homicide	mobbing
rape	victimizing
robbery	intimidation
wounding	threats
battering	ostracism
physical attacks	leaving offensive messages
kicking	aggressive posturing
biting	rude gestures
punching	interfering with work tools
spitting	and equipment
scratching	hostile behaviour
squeezing, pinching and	swearing
related actions	shouting
stalking	name-calling
harassment, including sexual	innuendo
and racial abuse	deliberate silence
bullying	

Attention has traditionally been focused on physical violence, and the typical profile of violence at work which has emerged has been largely one of isolated, major incidents of the kind referred to at the start of this chapter. In more recent years, however, new evidence has been emerging of the impact and harm caused by non-physical violence, often referred to as **psychological violence**. Thus a 1994 survey by the Canadian Union of Public Employees (CUPE) revealed that for almost 70 per cent of respondents, verbal aggression was stated to be the leading form of violence against employees.[25]

---

[24] Conclusions of the EURO-FIET/ETUC seminar on violence to workers, which took place in London in February 1993, in FIET, 1994, p. 21.

[25] Pizzino, 1994, p. 9.

Violence at work

Figure 1 highlights the relative importance of physical and non-physical forms of violence according to this survey.

Figure 1. The nature of aggression: Report on the Canadian Union of Public Employees' National Health and Safety Survey of Aggression Against Staff, 1994

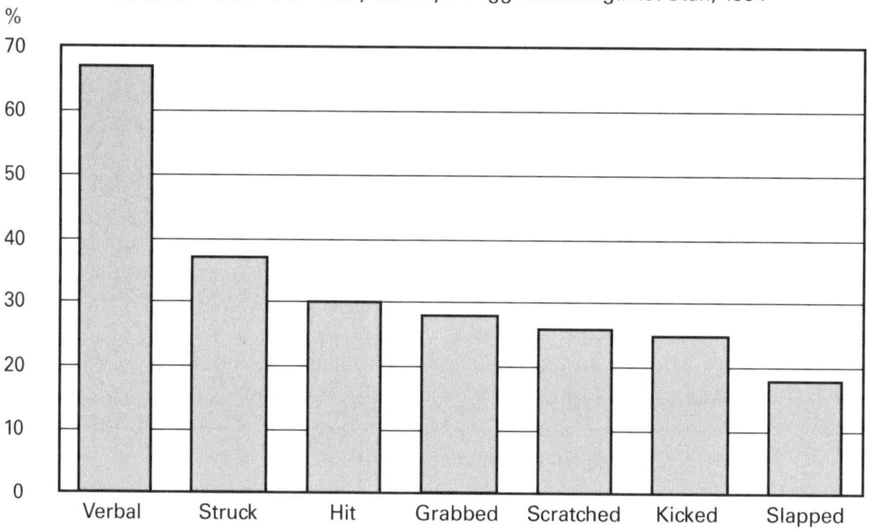

Source: Pizzino, 1994, p. 9. Reproduced with permission from the Health and Safety Department, Canadian Union of Public Employees.

Attention is also growing in respect of violence which is perpetrated through *repeated* behaviour, of a type which by itself may be relatively minor but which cumulatively can become a very serious form of violence such as **sexual harassment**, **bullying** or **mobbing**.

For example, although a single incident can suffice, **sexual harassment** often consists of repeated unwelcome, unreciprocated and imposed action which may have a devastating effect on the victim. Sexual harassment may include touching, remarks,

---

Sexual harassment

Sexual harassment means unwanted conduct of a sexual nature, or other conduct based on sex affecting the dignity of men and women at work. This can include unwelcome physical, verbal or non-verbal conduct. Thus, a range of behaviour may be considered to constitute sexual harassment.

It is unacceptable if such conduct is unwanted, unreasonable and offensive to the recipient; a person's rejection of, or submission to, such conduct on the part of the employers or workers (including superiors or colleagues) is used explicitly or implicitly as a basis for a decision which affects that person's access to vocational training or employment, continued employment, promotion, salary or any other employment decisions; and/or such conduct creates an intimidating, hostile or humiliating working environment for the recipient.

Source: European Commission's Code of Practice on measures to combat sexual harassment, Section 2 in *Official Journal*, L.49, 24 February 1997, Annex pp. 3-5.

---

looks, attitudes, jokes or the use of sexually oriented language, allusions to a person's private life, references to sexual orientation, innuendos with a sexual connotation, or remarks about dress or figure, or the persistent leering at a person or at part of his/her body.[26]

Workplace **bullying** constitutes offensive behaviour through vindictive, cruel, malicious or humiliating attempts to undermine an individual or groups of employees. These persistently negative attacks on their personal and professional performance are typically unpredictable, irrational and unfair.

Bullying

Bullying can occur in a number of different ways. Some are obvious and easy to identify. Others are subtle and difficult to explain. Bullying behaviour includes:

- Making life difficult for those who have the potential to do the bully's job better than the bully.
- Punishing others for being too competent by constant criticism or by removing their responsibilities, often giving them trivial tasks to do instead.
- Refusing to delegate because they feel they can't trust anyone else.
- Shouting at staff to get things done.
- Persistently picking on people in front of others or in private.
- Insisting that a way of doing things is always right.
- Keeping individuals in their place by blocking their promotion.
- If someone challenges a bully's authority, overloading them with work and reducing the deadlines, hoping that they will fail at what they do.
- Feeling envious of another's professional or social ability, so setting out to make them appear incompetent, or make their lives miserable, in the hope of getting them dismissed or making them resign.

Source: UNISON, 1996, citing BBC for Business.

In recent years, another form of systematic collective violence has been reported to be on the increase in countries such as Australia, Austria, Denmark, Germany, Sweden, the United Kingdom and the United States. It involves ganging-up on or **mobbing** a target employee and subjecting that person to psychological harassment. Mobbing includes behaviours such as making continuous negative remarks about a person or criticizing them constantly; isolating a person by leaving them without social contacts; gossiping or spreading false information about a person or ridiculing a person constantly. The impact upon a person of what might appear on the surface to be minor single actions of this type can be devastating. It has been estimated, for instance, that about 10-15 per cent of the total number of suicides in Sweden each year have this type of background.[27]

---

[26] See Aeberhard-Hodges, 1996, pp. 500-501.
[27] Leymann, 1990, p. 122.

Mobbing in a Norwegian factory

Leif worked in a large Norwegian factory. His job, as a repairman, was to keep the machine park running. He was a skilled worker, earning a high salary. He came originally from Denmark and his workmates often made fun of him as he spoke Norwegian with a Danish accent. This happened so often that his personal relations became seriously disturbed – he became isolated. On one occasion he became so irritated that he thumped the table with his fist and demanded an end to all further jokes about his accent. From that point, things became worse. His workmates intensified and widened the range of "jokes", one being to send him to machines which did not need repairing. In this way Leif gradually gained the reputation of being "The Mad Dane". At the beginning, many workers and foremen did not know that his sudden appearances were the results of "jokes". His social contact network broke down, and more and more workmates joined in the hunt. Wherever he appeared, jokes and taunts flew around. His feeling of aggression grew and this drew the attention of management. It was their impression that Leif was at fault and that, in general, he was a low-performance worker (which he gradually became). He was admonished. His anxiety increased and he developed psychosomatic problems and began to take sick leave. His employers reassigned him to less skilled work without discussing his problems; this Leif felt as unjust. He considered himself blameless. The situation gradually brought about serious psychosomatic disorders and longer periods of sick leave. Leif lost his job and could not find another, as his medical history was indicated in his job applications. There was nowhere in society where he could turn for help. He became totally unemployable – an outcast.

Source: Leymann, 1990, p. 119. Used by permission from Springer Publishing Company, Inc., New York, 10012.

The new profile of violence at work which emerges is one which gives equal emphasis to physical and psychological behaviour, and one which gives full recognition to the significance of minor acts of violence. It is also a profile which recognizes that violence at work is not limited to a specified workplace, like an office, factory or retail establishment. There is a risk of violence during commuting and in non-traditional workplaces such as homes, satellite centres, and mobile locations which are being used increasingly as a result of the spread of new information technologies.[28]

As the profile of violence at work is changing, so too is the definition of violence. A general definition of violence at work has yet to be agreed in the international arena. A substantial effort towards a common understanding in this area was, however, made at an Expert Meeting organized by the European Commission in Dublin in May 1995, where the following definition was proposed:

incidents where persons are abused, threatened or assaulted in circumstances related to their work, involving an explicit or implicit challenge to their safety, well-being and health.[29]

Abuse is used to indicate all behaviours which depart from reasonable conduct and involve the misuse of physical or psychological strength. Assault generally includes any attempt at physical injury or attack on a person, including actual physical

---

[28] On the spreading of telework, see ILO, *Telework*, 1990; Di Martino and Wirth, 1990, p. 529; Di Martino, 1996, p. 379; and Di Martino, *The high road to teleworking*, Geneva, ILO, forthcoming.

[29] Wynne et al., 1997, p. 1. Further discussion regarding the definition of violence at work is contained in Chs. 2 and 3 of this report.

harm. Threats encompass the menace of death, or the announcement of an intention to harm a person or damage their property. In real situations these behaviours often overlap, making any attempt to categorize different forms of violence very difficult. The emphasis on the impact of incidents on the safety, health, and well-being of a person, although important, appears primarily to be a reflection of the special concern of the experts who participated in the meeting.

FROM AWARENESS TO ACTION

With consensus emerging on a definition of violence at work, there would also seem to be widespread awareness that this form of violence is:

* **A major although still under-recognized problem.**
* **Not limited to individual instances of mass homicide, but extends to a much wider range of apparently minor but often devastating behaviours.**
* **An extremely costly burden for the worker, the enterprise and the community.**
* **Not just an episodic, individual problem but a structural, strategic problem rooted in wider social, economic, organizational and cultural factors.**
* **Detrimental to the functionality of the workplace, and any action taken against such violence is an integral part of the organizational development of a sound enterprise.**
* **A problem which has to be tackled, and tackled now.**

In responding to the problem of workplace violence, it is now realized to an increasing degree that violence cannot any longer be accepted as a normal part of any job, even where it would seem to be an occupational hazard, such as in law enforcement. As in the case of hazardous manufacturing and allied occupations, where risk management strategies are put in place to reduce the level of uncertainty and possibility of injury, so too should these strategies be adopted to minimize the possibility of assault, harassment and abuse to employees in the workplace.

There is also a growing recognition that in confronting violence it is important to think comprehensively. This means that instead of searching for a single solution to any problem and situation, the full range of causes which generate violence should be analysed and a variety of intervention strategies applied. These strategies should seek to implant a broad preventive approach to the problem, which addresses the organizational, managerial and interpersonal roots of violence at the workplace. They should also increase the security of workers and provide rehabilitation and psychological counselling, when necessary, to help victims to cope with the aftermath of violence.

THE ILO'S ENGAGEMENT

The concern expressed about violence at work, and the call for action voiced by public authorities, enterprises and workers, is now being transformed into specific initiatives. Guidelines have been issued by governments, trade unions, special study groups, workplace violence experts and employers' groups which address many aspects of the problem. A growing number of enterprises are also introducing violence prevention programmes which include an increasing participation by workers and their representatives in their development and implementation. Laws and regulations are becoming targeted with greater frequency and accuracy to deal with the problem of violence at work, and new collective agreements are being signed by the social partners in this area. The search for ways of ensuring a violence-free workplace is becoming a major policy issue and a concern for the ILO.

The primary goal of the ILO today is to promote opportunities for women and men to obtain decent and productive work, in conditions of freedom, equity, security and human dignity.[30]

This concern is part of the ILO's longstanding and continuing commitment to worker protection and dignity as well as to a safe and productive work environment – a workplace where cooperation, communication and the welfare of workers are keys to economic success. Previous ILO action in the areas of **stress, alcohol and drugs, and sexual harassment** has clearly shown that it is possible to combine these commitments with positive and successful outcomes.

The connections between **occupational stress and violence** have already been clearly demonstrated. A Finnish study on the effects of bullying on municipal employees, for example, indicated that 40 per cent of bullied workers felt much or very much stress, 49 per cent had been unusually tired and 30 per cent were nervous often or constantly.[31] These reactions are all typical indicators of stress. In turn, stress can itself incite or trigger violent behaviour. In the United States it has been shown that highly stressed workers tend to experience twice the rate of violence and harassment suffered by less-stressed employees.[32] A vicious circle is thus activated whereby the worker suffers increasing levels of both stress and violence.

The ILO has been long involved in the area of occupational stress. In 1984 a publication, *Stress in industry* highlighted the devastating effects of stress on the individual and the working environment. This was followed, in 1986, by the Report of the Ninth Session of the Joint ILO/WHO Committee on Occupational Health (1984) which was entirely devoted to stress.[33] The ILO's work led in 1992 to the publication of a volume of the *Conditions of Work Digest* dedicated to stress.[34] In 1996 and 1997 a series of five anti-stress manuals was produced to provide practical guidance on how the principles of risk audits and stress prevention can be translated into practice in specific sectors.[35] The work of the ILO in this area has shown that stress prevention makes much more economic and health sense than a series of reactive treatments for afflicted individual workers. It has also been established that a cycle of

---

[30] ILO, *Decent work*, Report of the Director-General, International Labour Conference, 87th Session, Geneva, 1999, p. 3.

[31] M. Vartia, "Bullying at workplaces", in *Research on violence, threats and bullying as health risks among health care personnel*, Proceedings from the Workshop for Nordic Researchers, Reykjavik, 14-16 August 1994, p. 29. For the connections between stress and bullying, see also: *Stress UK 97 – Workplace Bullying*, a project by A. Ellis, Ruskin College, Oxford, on web site: http://www.stress.org.uk/bullying.htm, retrieved on 21 October 1997.

[32] Northwestern National Life Insurance Company, 1993, p. 2.

[33] Levi, 1984; ILO, 1986.

[34] ILO, "Preventing stress at work", 1992.

[35] ILO, *Occupational stress and stress prevention in air traffic control*, CONDI/T/WP.6/1995; *Stress prevention in the offshore oil and gas exploration and production industry*, CONDI/T/WP.1/1996; *Bus drivers: Occupational stress and stress prevention*, CONDI/T/WP.2/1996; *Work-related stress in nursing: Controlling the risk to health*, CONDI/T/WP.4/1996; *Stress prevention for blue-collar workers in assembly-line production*, CONDI/T/WP.1/1997 (all published in Geneva, 1996-97).

stress auditing – changing the workplace to reduce the sources of stress; auditing again to confirm that these were the right modifications; and so on – is the best approach to stress education.

Similar principles have emerged from the work of the ILO in the area of **drug and alcohol abuse**, which also has links to violence at work.

Prevention through information, education and training programmes concerning alcohol and drugs

Information, education and training programmes concerning alcohol and drugs should be undertaken to promote safety and health in the workplace either by the employer, the employer in cooperation with workers and their representatives, or by workers' organizations alone. Such programmes should be directed at all workers, and should contain information on the physical and psychological effects of alcohol and drug use.

Source: ILO, *Management of alcohol- and drug-related issues in the workplace. An ILO code of practice*, Geneva, 1996, p. 19.

The ILO has been in the vanguard in addressing **sexual harassment**, particularly through the adoption of the Discrimination (Employment and Occupation) Convention, 1958 (No.111). Article 1 of the Convention provides a broad definition of the term discrimination to include "any distinction, exclusion or preference made on the basis of ...[inter alia]... sex, which has the effect of nullifying or impairing equality of opportunity or treatment in employment or occupation". In examining States' reports on Convention 111 over the years, the ILO Committee of Experts on the Application of Conventions and Recommendations has often noted with interest the advances made in the elimination of sexual harassment in employment. In its 1988 General Survey on the Convention, the Committee of Experts also listed a number of examples of sexual harassment in employment. These include insults; remarks; jokes; insinuations and inappropriate comments on a person's dress, physique, age, family situation; a condescending or paternalistic attitude undermining dignity; unwelcome invitations or requests that are implicit or explicit whether or not accompanied by threats, lascivious looks or other gestures associated with sexuality; unnecessary physical contact such as touching, caresses, pinching or assault. The Committee of Experts stressed that in order to be qualified as sexual harassment, an act of this type must also be justly perceived as a condition of employment or a precondition for employment; or influence decisions taken in this field or prejudice occupational performance; or humiliate, insult or intimidate the person suffering from such acts.[36] In its 1996 Special Survey on the Convention, the Committee of Experts again provided examples of sexual harassment in employment, stressing that it is the unwelcome nature of such behaviour and the direct or indirect impact it has on the working relationship that makes it an element of prohibited sexual discrimination under Article 1 of the Convention.[37]

---

[36] ILO, *Equality in employment and occupation*, General Survey by the Committee of Experts on the Application of Conventions and Recommendations, International Labour Conference, 75th Session, 1988, Report III (Part 4B), Geneva, 1988, paras. 45 and 46.

[37] ILO, *Equality in employment and occupation*, Special Survey by the Committee of Experts on the Application of Conventions and Recommendations, International Labour Conference, 83rd Session, 1996, Report III (Part 4B), Geneva, 1996, paras. 39 and 40.

The ILO has the distinction of being the first international body to adopt an instrument containing an express protection against sexual harassment. The Indigenous and Tribal Peoples Convention, 1989 (No. 169), states that governments shall adopt special measures to ensure "that workers belonging to these peoples enjoy equal opportunities and equal treatment in employment for men and women, and protection from sexual harassment" (Article 20(3)(d)).

The ILO's attention to the issue is also evident in a number of non-binding instruments: the 1985 International Labour Conference resolution on equal opportunity and equal treatment for men and women in employment;[38] the conclusions of the 1992 Tripartite Symposium on Equality of Opportunity and Treatment for Men and Women in Employment in Industrialized Countries, referring specifically to sexual harassment,[39] as well as the 1991 International Labour Conference resolution concerning ILO action for women workers, requesting the International Labour Office to develop guidelines, training and information materials on issues of specific and major importance to women workers, such as sexual harassment in the workplace.[40]

In 1992 an issue of the *Conditions of Work Digest* was devoted entirely to the subject of sexual harassment, and in 1999 the ILO published an annotated bibliography on the subject. Some of the main lessons emerging from the ILO action in this area are highlighted in the following box.[41]

Awareness of and action against sexual harassment

Awareness of the problem of sexual harassment at work in industrialized countries has come a long way in a relatively short period of time.

Sexual harassment at work was once regarded as a "personal" dispute between employees, to be resolved between them and of no concern to their employer. Now it is increasingly recognized that it is inappropriate behaviour which should be treated by the employer as a disciplinary offence.

Sexual harassment at work was once regarded by employers as something which happened in enterprises other than their own. Now it is increasingly recognized that it is a problem for every enterprise.

Sexual harassment at work was once regarded as harmless "flirting". Now it is increasingly recognized that whatever the innocent intent of the perpetrator, it can demean and damage the victim.

Sexual harassment at work was once regarded as an issue too sensitive for trade unions to handle because it involved their members being disciplined. Now it is increasingly recognized that it is an issue too sensitive for trade unions not to handle because it is their members who are being harassed.

Sexual harassment at work was once regarded as an area where the law should not be involved. Now it is increasingly recognized that it is inextricably linked with the right to be treated equally without regard to sex and with the right to a healthy working environment.

---

[38] ILO, *Official Bulletin* (Geneva), Vol. LXVIII, Series A, No. 2, 1985, pp. 85-95.

[39] ILO, 1990, paras. 24 and 25.

[40] ILO, *Official Bulletin* (Geneva), Vol. LXXIV, Series A, No. 2, 1991, pp. 81-83. A complete coverage of the ILO action in the area of sexual harassment is given in Aeberhard-Hodges, 1996.

[41] ILO, "Combating sexual harassment at work", 1992; ILO, *Annotated bibliography on sexual harassment*, Geneva, 1999.

Much still needs to be done to tackle the problem of sexual harassment at work. The priority now is to ensure that the problem is tackled. National governments, supranational institutions and international organizations such as the ILO have a vital role to play in promoting awareness, in setting standards and in disseminating good practice.

Sexual harassment is not an issue which has been dreamt up by academics or bureaucrats. It is women themselves who are demanding – ever increasingly – that they be allowed to pursue their working lives with dignity. That expectation will have to be met.

Source: M. Rubenstein, in ILO, "Combating sexual harassment at work", 1992, p. 19.

THE SCOPE OF THE REPORT

Building on this extensive and closely related experience, the ILO is now addressing the problem of violence at work with the production of this report. It is intended to constitute a stimulus for future action in this area. It is centred around the analysis of existing literature and information. While not claiming to be exhaustive in this regard, the authors have deliberately avoided the more "sensational" presentations of violence to concentrate on those data, experiences and publications which best help to explain and interpret the roots of violence at work, and to promote proactive initiatives in this field.

The report has a worldwide coverage. As has been shown earlier, violence in the workplace is to be found in both developing and industrialized nations. However, the information from developing countries about this violence is frequently limited, episodic and ill-defined. Different sensitivities in different contexts and cultures also contribute to variations in the reporting of violence at work, so that comparative data have to be used and interpreted with great caution. For these reasons the report concentrates principally on industrialized countries where violence at work is better documented and the field of investigation is more homogenous.

As already suggested, the underlying causes of violence at work are rooted in much wider social, cultural, economic and related areas. There is a vast literature available on the causes of violence at large. However, this material is so extensive and far reaching that, for the purpose of this report, it cannot be treated in detail. Instead, in Chapter 3 a review is made of the principal explanations of violence found in the literature as they relate to the specific issue of violence at work.

In order to avoid duplication of effort, only limited attention is paid in this report to issues already covered by extensive and specific ILO action, such as those already referred to of occupational stress, alcohol and drug abuse and sexual harassment, as well as others such as child labour [42] and migrant workers.[43] Certain technical issues,

---

[42] For an overview of the main issues concerning child labour see, ILO, 1996. Other recent publications include: V. Forastieri, *Children at work: Health and safety risks*, Geneva, ILO, 1997; A. Fyfe and M. Jankanish, *Trade unions and child labour: A guide to action*, Geneva, ILO, 1996; A. Bequele and W.E. Myers, *First things first in child labour: Eliminating work detrimental to children*, Geneva, ILO, 1995; A. Fyfe, *Child labour: A guide to project design*, Geneva, ILO, 1993. In June 1999, the International Labour Conference adopted the Worst Forms of Child Labour Convention (No. 182) and Recommendation (No. 190), by which ratifying member States must "take immediate and effective measures to secure the prohibition and elimination of the worst forms of child labour as a matter of urgency". These comprise: "(a) all forms of slavery or practices similar to slavery, such as the sale and trafficking of children, debt bondage and serfdom and forced or compulsory labour, including forced or compulsory recruitment of children for use in armed conflict; (b) the use, procuring or offering of a

(Continued on page 20)

including violence associated with terrorist attacks or military action, are also excluded from the scope of this report.[44]

The report is intended to provide a basis for understanding the nature of violence at work, and to suggest ways of preventing this violence in the future. It therefore highlights best practice and successful methods of prevention, illustrating the positive lessons to be drawn from such experience. The report is directed towards all those engaged in combating violence at work: policy-makers in government agencies, employers' and workers' organizations, health and safety professionals, consultants, trainers, management and workers' representatives.

The report is structured **in three parts:**

Part I is devoted to the **understanding of violence at work**. It covers the growing awareness and concern regarding this phenomenon; the catalyst for action; the changing profile of violence; and the commitment of the ILO in this area (Chapter 1). Part I also includes an analysis of data displaying patterns and trends of violence at work; areas and occupations most affected, vulnerable situations and groups; and the social and economic costs of violence for individuals, the enterprise and the community (Chapter 2). It concludes with an examination of the various explanations of the causes of violence at work (Chapter 3).

Part II examines **different types of response** to violence at work, and identifies the best solutions to the problem. It includes an analysis of legislative and regulatory interventions in this area; adaptation of existing legislation; emergence of specific legislation; growing attention to prevention strategies; and new collective agreements to combat workplace violence (Chapter 4). It also includes an analysis of policies and guidelines; their main messages about how to tackle violence at work effectively; guidance for specific occupations and for specific types of violence (Chapter 5). Finally, the growing international concern about violence at work and the initiatives undertaken in this area are considered (Chapter 6).

Part III considers the key lessons to be drawn from the preceding analysis, highlights the main messages to be delivered; and **suggests specific and practical action** based on successful experience.

---

child for prostitution, for the production of pornography or for pornographic performances; (c) the use, procuring or offering of a child for illicit activities, in particular for the production and trafficking of drugs as defined in the relevant international treaties; and (d) work which, by its nature or the circumstances in which it is carried out, is likely to harm the health, safety or morals of children.

[43] Recent ILO documents in this area include: Zegers de Beijl, 1997; ILO Governing Body, Committee on Employment and Social Policy, 1996, particularly Part III, Section D – *Persistent maltreatment of migrant workers*.

[44] The violence inflicted by terrorist groups at workplaces, or the threat they pose, can be enormous, as events like the Oklahoma bombing in the United States and a long series of Irish Republican Army (IRA) attacks in metropolitan areas of the United Kingdom demonstrate. The scope, causes and prevention of such attacks is a specialized area of concern which falls outside the immediate parameters of the present report, as does the subject of violence associated with military operations which impinge upon the workplace. The military, as an occupational group, can themselves be the victims of work-related violence, as well as inflicting such violence on others.

PATTERNS AND TRENDS

2

Through the media's lens

Media coverage has elevated workplace violence into a distinct category of crime, associated in the public mind with vengeance wreaked by disgruntled and often berserk employees or former employees on their superiors and co-workers. Unfortunately, stilted reporting of such dramatic incidents – driven by the media's need to attract attention and make stories meaningful to the individual while sparing them complicated explanations – often fail to communicate the full context or put incidents in proper perspective.

Undoubtedly the media have found a responsive chord in people's concerns about the unpredictability of so many aspects of life, and their inability to understand and control so much of what goes on around them. Journalists speculate that workplace violence reflects the stresses of an increasingly harsh business environment, proliferating layoffs, and disgruntled workers. Easy access to guns and abuse of drugs and alcohol are often seen as exacerbating factors for workplace violence, as for other forms of violence. These sometimes overheated concerns have to be tempered by consideration of actual statistics, which have accumulated gradually over the past decade and a half.[1]

The International Federation of Journalists

Each year the IFJ launches its annual list of journalists killed, and challenges media employers and governments to do more to protect and support journalists at risk. The IFJ report focuses on details of cases involving many journalists killed because of their investigative reporting.

However, killings are only the tip of the iceberg of violence against media. The IFJ also documents some horrific attacks on journalists as a specific warning to others not to investigate certain matters. There is a constant danger of serious assault for any reporter who insists on confronting censorship, corruption and media manipulation.[2]

TEMPERING CONCERN WITH CAUTION

Gathering the news can be a deadly occupation, as the announcements from the International Federation of Journalists demonstrate. Each year, countless journalists around the world put their personal safety at risk in order to provide an insatiable

---

[1] E.O. Bulatao and G.R. VandenBos, "Workplace violence: Its scope and the issues", chapter in VandenBos and Bulatao (eds.), 1996, pp. 3-4, reproduced with permission from the APA.

[2] A. White, "At least 50 journalists and media staff killed in 1996", in IFJ, 1996/1997, p. 1, reproduced with permission from the IFJ. See also Ch. 3 for recent data and information.

public with the latest information about a host of issues. The professional hazards are obviously greater in those nations unaccustomed to facing the scrutiny of a free press. Yet even in fully democratic states, such as Ireland or Canada, journalists can become victims of murderous attacks.

In 1996, the assassination of Veronica Guerin, an inquiring and persistent Irish investigative reporter, received worldwide attention in both the electronic and print media.[3] In 1998 the murder of Tara Singh Hayer shocked public opinion in Canada.

Tara Singh Hayer was shot to death in the garage of his suburban Vancouver home on the evening of 18 November 1998. Hayer, who published the *Indo-Canadian Times*, Canada's largest and oldest Punjabi weekly, was an outspoken critic of violent Sikh fundamentalists and had already been the target of an assassination attempt at his newspaper office in 1988. At the time, he was left partially paralysed.

Hayer's son, Sukhdev Hayer, said his father had arrived moments earlier at his Surrey, British Columbia home from his newspaper office, and had just transferred him from his vehicle to his wheelchair when he was shot. Hayer's son added that he went back to the newspaper office after the shooting to add a special insert that would let readers know of the killing. Hayer said it was important to continue work on the paper despite the murder because his father had fought for press freedom in Canada. 'He has fought for the freedom of human beings here. He always said if they were going to kill him for what he published – so be it,' said Hayer.

Source: Canadian Journalists for Free Expression (CJFE) – "Fifty-two journalists and writers killed in 1998: CJFE Annual Report", press release, 18 February 1999, retrieved at http://www.ccpj.ca/releases/1999/report98.html, on 5 May 1999.

These two murders were shocking events, involving prominent media figures, which demanded immediate condemnation and the closest media analysis of the circumstances surrounding the attack. Such analysis is, of course, also fully merited in other tragic cases like the shootings at Dunblane and Port Arthur. Our immediate information about these tragedies is very much dependent upon the work of the media – it is "through the media lens" that we obtain most of what we know about these and other major incidents of work-related violence.

Valuable though these media sources of information have proved to be, there is still a need to move beyond the lens of the media in order to seek an understanding of the patterns and trends in violence at work. As Bulatao and VandenBos caution, "sometimes overheated concerns [of the media] have to be tempered by consideration of actual statistics, which have accumulated gradually over the past decade and a

---

[3] See, for example, the following reports regarding the assassination and the work of Ms. Guerin: R. Peterman, "Memorial honours Guerin", *Irish Voice* (Sickerville, New Jersey), 5 May 1997 (Web site: http://www.irishvoice.com/paper/1997/0507/news7.htm. Retrieved 8 July 1997.); A. O'Connor, "Reporter was working on a series of major articles", *Irish Times* (Dublin) 27 June 1996 (Web site: http://www.irish-times.com/irish-times/paper/1996/0627/hom19.html. Retrieved 8 July 1997); M. Rosen, J. Klinke, E. Stein and L. Denworth, "Death of a Reporter", *People Online* (Time Warner's Pathfinder Network), 22 July 1996 (Web site: http://bigmouth.pathfinder.com/people/960722/features/guerin.html. Retrieved 8 July 1997). The British *Guardian's* review of the events of 1996 included the following description of Ms. Guerin's death on 27 June: "An award-winning crime journalist and scourge of Dublin's drugs underworld was shot dead in the Irish capital yesterday, apparently by contract killers. Veronica Guerin, who has exposed a number of Dublin's criminal godfathers in the *Sunday Independent*, was shot in her car on the Naas dual carriageway in County Dublin at around 1 pm. Two men on a motorbike, wearing white crash helmets, intercepted Ms. Guerin's car at traffic lights on a slip road in Clondalkin. One fired a handgun, killing her instantly. The shooting bore a chilling resemblance to the murder of one of Ms. Guerin's journalistic subjects, Martin Cahil, known as the General, who was shot dead by the IRA in August 1994. The deputy prime minister, Dick Spring, said no effort would be spared to bring her killers to justice. … Friends and colleagues said Ms. Guerin had been increasingly concerned about her safety following a warning shooting in February 1995." – D. Sharrock, "Dublin hitmen kill reporter", *The Guardian Year* (27 June 1996).

half ". Those statistics reveal that homicide makes up only a very small percentage of workplace violence. Before turning to consider these "actual statistics", more must be said about their general deficiencies and the perils associated with their interpretation.

DEFINITIONS AND SIMILAR MATTERS

There are at present few accurate, reliable and uniform statistics available regarding violence at work. This situation can be explained in part by the absence of a specific responsibility in most countries, at least until quite recently, for the gathering of this type of information. While statistical data has been compiled about occupational health and safety issues surrounding the workplace, and concerning crime and criminal justice issues associated with violence, the linkage between these areas has yet to become a common feature of most countries' statistical series.[4] There are some notable exceptions to this rule, as will be seen shortly. None the less, it is in general very difficult to draw firm conclusions about either short- or longer-term patterns and trends in workplace violence within or between countries.

Another significant challenge to any analysis of statistical data on this issue arises from a lack of agreement regarding the definitions of **violence**, and **work** or the **workplace**. The term **violence** is often used interchangeably with **aggression**, the former being more common in the area of criminology and criminal justice and the latter in the health arena. In a recent and authoritative review of the issues associated with the understanding and prevention of violence, the National Academy of Science in the United States defined violent or aggressive conduct as

behaviours by individuals that intentionally threaten, attempt or inflict physical harm on others or on oneself.[5]

This definition, while both succinct and compelling, is also narrow in the sense that it excludes violence which is directed at property and also violence which is exclusively psychological in nature, including emotional abuse and the infliction of fear and anxiety.[6] Behaviours of the latter type, as has been emphasized in Chapter 1, are associated with sexual harassment, bullying, and mobbing. They are also behaviours which fit into the broader operational definition of violence referred to earlier.[7]

Those statistical series which are maintained about crime and criminal justice usually adopt a definition of violence which is closely tied to a much narrower legal description of individual offences. Thus crimes of violence are typically categorized as homicide, rape, robbery, and simple and aggravated assault.[8] The legal

---

[4] On this point see Wynne et al., 1997, p. 5. As these authors emphasize, "the prevalence of workplace-related violence is difficult to estimate because of the general absence of either national level or occupational level data on this issue".

[5] Reiss and Roth (eds.), 1993, Vol. 1, p. 35.

[6] **Violence against property** is not considered in this report, even although it does represent a significant issue in the workplace. For sabotage see: Dibattista, 1996; Sprouse, 1992; Zabala, 1989; and Edwards and Scullion, 1982 and 1987. **Workplace crime** in a broad sense is excluded, to the extent that the term includes non-violent crimes like theft, fraud and embezzlement. The incidence and prevalence of non-violent crimes is significantly higher than violent crimes in the workplace, just as it is in the wider community. See in general Backman, 1994. **Workplace conflicts**, which can sometimes degenerate in violent behaviours, are also excluded from the scope of this report.

[7] See Ch. 1.

[8] See Jenkins, 1996, p. 1.

requirements of these various crimes can often differ from one jurisdiction to another, even within national boundaries.[9] These legal variations become still more marked between nations.[10]

The definition of **work** or the **workplace** is also fraught with problems. When official crime statistics do make a link with occupational data and provide information about the location at which incidents of criminal violence occur, they tend to adopt a quite constrained definition of these terms. Data may be provided about violent offences committed in offices, commercial premises like banks, and schools or other physical settings. This construction of the workplace does not allow for mobile or geographically diverse occupational activities such as those conducted by law enforcement officials,[11] taxi drivers or journalists, nor does it take account of occupational groups whose work takes them to people's homes, like meter readers, plumbers and postal officials, or those who use their own homes as their workplace. The latter category of employment is becoming far more prevalent as new technologies make many traditional workplaces redundant.[12]

It has been suggested that in order to capture information about violent behaviours occurring within this broader construct of the workplace, a convenient way to describe them is as "crimes of violence that occur in the workplace or while the victim is at work or on duty".[13] This proposal would still exclude some incidents related to psychological violence occurring at work or on duty, but which manifest themselves beyond these settings. For example, a worker who committed suicide following a sustained period of bullying at work or while on duty might fall outside the scope of this definition.

Definitional issues of this type are often the grist for complex and technical legal debate about whether or not a worker is entitled to compensation for injuries arising from or during the course of employment.[14] The intricacies of this debate do not need to be outlined here, but it is important to note the association between questions of definition, and questions of both civil and criminal legal liability and responsibility, when considering many statistics on violence at work. In the field of occupational health and safety, the recognition and expansion of the liability and responsibility for providing a violence-free workplace is now stimulating efforts in a number of jurisdictions to gather information about the incidence and prevalence of violent behaviours. The substantial gaps, which are at present commonplace, in the information on this subject are likely to be narrowed if not closed in the near future as national, regional and international bodies all focus major attention on the issue of violence at work.[15]

---

[9] See, for example, the variations between the requirements in Australia jurisdictions, and the dilemmas they have posed for the interpretation of crime trends, in Mukherjee, 1981.

[10] The general complexities of making international crime comparisons are discussed in Van Dijk et al., 1989.

[11] However, some official statistics may include information about crimes of violence committed against law enforcement officers in the course of their duties. Other vulnerable occupational groups like taxi divers and journalists are more likely to gather any such statistical data through their respective enterprises or trade union groups.

[12] See Ch. 1, note 28 above.

[13] Jenkins, 1996, p. 1.

[14] See, for example, Littler et al., 1994(b), Ch. 5; Industry Commission, 1995, Vol. 2, Appendix J.

[15] Some of these international activities, including those taking place at the regional level in the European Union and elsewhere, are discussed further in Ch. 6.

1996 INTERNATIONAL CRIME VICTIM SURVEY (ICVS)

One of the most important and significant sources of international information about violence at work comes from the ICVS, a comprehensive multinational comparative research exercise which has so far involved more than 50 countries.[16] The survey is coordinated by an International Working Group composed of representatives of the Ministry of Justice of the Netherlands, the United Nations Interregional Crime and Justice Research Institute (UNICRI) and the Home Office of the United Kingdom.

Due to its representative and wide geographical coverage, including both developed and developing countries in various parts of the world, the ICVS can be considered one of the major international comparative criminological projects. In the ICVS, random samples of the population aged 16 years and above are interviewed about their victimization experiences. The questionnaire includes questions on 13 types of crime against the household and at the personal level. It also seeks information on opinions and attitudes about reporting to the police and police performance, patterns of crime prevention, fear of crime and attitudes towards punishment. Therefore, the ICVS provides information on victimization experience, victimization risk, access to justice, fear of crime and victimization by criminal justice.

The results of the ICVS should be considered within the framework of the developmental profile of each participating country.[17] In table 1, participating countries have been divided into six groups according to geopolitical and developmental criteria.

Table 1.   International Crime Victim Survey – Participating countries in which data on violence at work were collected in 1996, by regions

Western Europe	New World	Countries in transition	Africa	Asia	Latin America
Austria	Canada	Albania	South Africa	India	Argentina
England	United States	Czech Republic	Uganda	Indonesia	Bolivia
and Wales		Georgia	Zimbabwe	Philippines	Brazil
Finland		Hungary			Costa Rica
Netherlands		Kyrgyzstan			
Northern Ireland		Latvia			
Scotland		Mongolia			
Sweden		Poland			
Switzerland		Romania			
		Russian Federation			
		The former Yugoslav Republic of Macedonia			
		Yugoslavia (Federal Republic)			

---

[16] The detailed information about the ICVS and its results, provided in this Chapter, have been generously supplied by the UNICRI, which is based in Rome. The authors of this report are particularly indebted to Dr. Anna Alvazzi del Frate at UNICRI, who undertook this special analysis of the 1996 ICVS data in response to a request for the latest survey findings available. The first survey in this series was carried out in 1989: see Van Dijk et al., 1990. The second survey took place between 1992 and 1994: see Van Dijk and Mayhew, 1992; Alvazzi del Frate et al., 1993; Zvekic and Alvazzi del Frate, 1995. The third survey was undertaken in more than 40 countries in 1996-97.

[17] In some countries, the survey was carried out at a national level, in others only in major cities. In Western Europe and the New World, data were collected using computer-assisted telephone interviewing; in others, by face-to-face interviewing. The survey was based on a population sample of, on average, between 1,000 and 2,000 respondents in each area surveyed, resulting in approximately 130,000 people from all over the world being interviewed.

Victimization at the workplace

The 1990 ICVS questionnaire included for the first time reference to victimization at the workplace.[18] Information was sought from victims of sexual incidents (women only), and from the victims of assault/threat (which is also defined as "non-sexual assault").[19] Since this is unique data, and the first occasion on which it has been published, a detailed account follows of the methodology used and the major findings.

Despite the use of standard methodology, the ICVS revealed that the cultural messages in different contexts or in the wording of a question might elicit different answers in different languages. The interpretation of the survey results on sexual incidents may thus be problematic and should be treated with caution. In fact, for this issue more than in other parts of the survey, special attention should be paid to the terminology used and, for example, the exact meaning attached to the words "incident", "assault" and "crime" should be carefully weighed. It has been argued that the wording of the question on sexual incidents might not be as clear as other questions referring to various victimization experiences, since it does not evoke a unique type of crime but quite a wide range of events. Victims were therefore asked to provide a description of what happened, and invited to describe the incident as rape, attempted rape, indecent assault or offensive behaviour. On average, half of the incidents were defined as "offensive behaviour", while approximately 5 per cent were described as rapes and 16 per cent as attempted rapes; 27 per cent of the victims described the incident as an indecent assault.

Different sensitivity to an issue in different contexts also contributed in some ways to distortions in reporting to the survey, either in the direction of over-reporting or under-reporting. In some of the most industrialized countries covered by the ICVS, it was noted that high sensitivity to, or awareness of, an issue corresponded to high rates of victimization reported to the survey.

Even though some incidents which had not been reported to the police may have been reported to the survey interviewers, many sexual incidents still remain unknown. Reporting to the survey may well be reduced because sexual incidents and assaults often happen within the family. In some cultural contexts the fact that the survey is carried out in the household may further reduce reporting. For example, in some developing countries face-to-face interviews were often carried out in the presence of other members of the family, which might have precluded the respondent from revealing victimization experiences suffered in the household and involving the partner or relatives or friends.[20]

In some cases, victimization of women that occurs at the workplace may also be kept concealed due to the difficulty women may face in obtaining employment out of

---

[18] No definition of the *workplace* was provided to survey respondents.

[19] The question on sexual incidents read as follows: "People sometimes grab, touch or assault others for sexual reasons in a really offensive way. This can happen either inside one's house or elsewhere, for instance in a pub, the street, at school, on public transport, in cinemas, on the beach or at one's workplace. Over the past five years has anyone done this to you?". Further specific issues addressed included rape, attempted rape, relationship with the offender. The question on non-sexual assault read: "Apart from the incidents just covered, have you over the past five years been personally attacked or threatened by someone in a way that really frightened you, either at home or elsewhere, such as in a pub, in the street, at school, on public transport, on the beach, or at your workplace?"

[20] The administration of the survey attempted to mitigate some problems of sensitivity to issues raised by the questionnaire. Both in the face-to-face and computer-assisted telephone interview (CATI) teams, male and female interviewers were included in order to try matching interviewer's and respondent's genders.

the household. If victimization suffered at the workplace is discovered, they may be forced by their family to abandon their job. It is also known that in most cases sexual abuse at work involves a power relationship, in which the male offender is usually hierarchically superior to the female victim. In these cases, most victims to not report what happened to the police or any other authority, being afraid of the consequences for their career, or future employment.

Prevalence of victimization

As table 2 below shows, the highest percentages of victimization at the workplace were observed for sexual incidents (irrespective of subtype). Victimization rates for both males and females were highest in industrialized countries, while rates of assault and sexual assault of women were very high in Latin America.

In general, victimization risk at the workplace was higher for women than for men, with the exception of non-sexual assault in countries in transition and Africa, which more frequently occurred to men than to women. In Western Europe, a form of "gender equality" was reached as regards male and female victims of non-sexual assault, with percentages levelled.

Lower victimization rates were observed not only in the regions where external employment for women is less frequent (Asia and Africa), but also in countries in transition, where low victimization rates of this type were reported throughout the region.

Table 2.   ICVS – Prevalence rates of victimization at the workplace, by type of incident, gender and region, 1996 (percentage)

	Assault		Sexual incidents
	Male	Female	Female
Western Europe	2.7	3.0	5.4
New World	2.5	4.6	7.5
Countries in transition	2.0	1.4	3.0
Asia	0.4	1.0	1.3
Africa	2.3	1.9	3.7
Latin America	1.9	3.6	5.2

Source: ICVS survey (see note 16 above).

Context of victimization

As can be seen in table 3, on average, 10 per cent of all the incidents involving women victims happened at the workplace. This was particularly the case with the least serious forms of sexual harassment (offensive behaviour) and non-sexual assaults. Furthermore, sexual incidents at the workplace included nearly 8 per cent of the cases of rape and approximately 10 per cent of attempted rapes and indecent assaults. Sexual harassment and violence against women at work thus include a substantial portion of very serious incidents. These findings suggest that the difficulties women face in obtaining access to the labour market are not limited to reduced opportunities, discrimination and disparity in wages, but extend to sexual abuse at the workplace itself.

Violence at work

An overall analysis of the context of the violent victimization of men also reveals that more than 13 per cent of incidents occurred at the workplace. Distribution of male victimization by place of occurrence shows that the workplace ranks before the respondent's home. It can also be seen that women victims of non-sexual assault, even though the percentage of incidents occurring at the workplace was similar to that of male victims, were twice as frequently victims of assault in their own home.

Table 3.   ICVS – Context of victimization by gender, type of incident and place of occurrence, 1996 (percentage of victims)

	In own home	Near own home	At the workplace	Elsewhere in the city	Elsewhere in the country	Abroad
Sexual incidents (women victims)						
Rape	37.4	24.3	7.5	19.6	8.4	2.8
Attempted rape	20.2	37.6	9.8	24.0	6.3	1.0
Indecent assault	8.3	31.7	9.4	36.8	9.6	3.6
Offensive behaviour	5.8	20.6	13.6	48.2	7.2	2.7
Non-sexual assault						
Men victims	11.8	29.2	13.2	38.5	5.2	1.5
Women victims	23.3	30.7	11.9	27.4	4.4	1.6

Source: ICVS survey.

Age of victims

Victimization at the workplace mostly affected the age categories between 25 and 49, although women victims were on average younger than men. Victims of sexual incidents often belonged to the youngest age categories: nearly half were younger than 29, and nearly a third were between 30 and 39 years of age.

Table 4 also shows that while male victims of non-sexual assaults were evenly distributed among the age groups between 25 and 49, more than one half of women victims of either type of crime fell into the age groups from 16 to 34 (more than 56 per cent of victims of non-sexual assault and 63 per cent of victims of sexual incidents).

Table 4.   ICVS – Victimization at the workplace, by gender, type of incident and age group, 1996 (percentage)

	16-19	20-24	25-29	30-34	35-39	40-44	45-49	50-54	55-59	60-64	65-70	70+	unknown
Non-sexual assault Male victims	3.6	9.1	15.0	1.2	13.1	12.7	10.8	8.2	5.1	1.9	1.5	2.5	0.3
Non-sexual assault Female victims	2.6	10.9	22.6	13.8	16.4	10.0	9.4	6.7	2.6	2.9	0.9	1.2	—
Sexual incidents Female victims	2.1	17.9	23.9	15.1	15.8	8.8	7.4	3.5	2.5	0.7	0.4	1.4	0.5

Source: ICVS survey.

Weapons used in committing crimes

Respondents who were victims of violent crime were asked whether weapons (and if so, which ones) were used in committing the crime (described as knives, guns or objects used as weapons). Due to the very small numbers involved, analysis of their response is made without distinction by geographic region. Table 5 shows that, in comparison with crimes occurring either in the victims' home or elsewhere, weapons were used least in crimes at the workplace and mostly against male victims of non-sexual assault, a quarter of whom were exposed to a weapon during the assault.

Between 10 and 15 per cent of women victims of non-sexual assault reported being threatened with a weapon at the workplace. Less than 5 per cent of women victims of attempted rape and indecent assault reported such an experience.

Table 5. ICVS – Incidents involving the use of weapons, by place of occurrence, gender and type of incident, 1996 (percentage)

	Non-sexual assault: Male victims	Non-sexual assault: Female victims	Rape: Female victims	Attempted rape: Female victims	Indecent assault: Female victims
In own home	27.0	29.0	17.9	14.8	11.1
Near own home	34.5	21.9	33.3	12.9	2.2
At the workplace	26.3	15.9	12.5	3.7	2.4
Elsewhere	34.5	21.2	36.0	15.7	1.4

Source: ICVS survey.

Table 6 reveals that in almost half of the cases in which a weapon was involved, a gun was used in committing non-sexual assaults against both male and female victims at the workplace. Guns were used much less frequently in incidents which occurred in locations other than the workplace.

Table 6. ICVS – Weapons used in non-sexual assault, by gender of victims, place of occurence and type of weapon, 1996 (percentage)

	Knife	Gun	Other weapon	Something used as a weapon	Do not know
Male victims					
In own home	31.0	20.7	12.1	32.8	3.4
Near own home	24.1	22.9	24.0	17.3	1.7
At the workplace	23.8	44.4	11.1	19.0	1.6
Elsewhere in the city	42.9	23.3	11.7	19.6	2.5
Elsewhere in the country	16.1	35.5	29.0	12.9	6.5
Female victims					
In own home	37.6	22.2	20.0	20.1	—
Near own home	29.9	28.7	19.5	19.5	2.3
At the workplace	28.0	48.0	—	24.0	—
Elsewhere in the city	40.8	31.0	5.6	22.5	—
Elsewhere in the country	33.3	25.0	16.7	25.0	—

Source: ICVS survey.

Reporting to the police or to other authorities

Table 7 makes it clear that non-sexual assaults which occurred at the workplace were more likely to be reported, by both male and female victims, than those which happened elsewhere. The relatively high rate of reporting to "other authorities" suggests that workplace victims often resort to the assistance of their employers, or possibly the disciplinary board of their firm, rather than to law enforcement officials.

Table 7.   ICVS – Non-sexual assaults reported to the police or to other authorities, by gender and place of occurence, 1996 (percentage)

	Reported to the police	Reported to other authorities	Not reported
Male victims			
In own home	29.6	6.9	63.5
Near own home	20.5	5.4	74.1
At the workplace	37.8	14.5	47.7
Elsewhere in the city	17.4	5.8	76.8
Elsewhere in the country	16.9	8.6	71.5
Abroad	17.9	14.8	67.3
Female victims			
In own home	35.0	10.9	54.1
Near own home	23.5	7.8	68.7
At the workplace	32.7	23.5	43.8
Elsewhere in the city	17.7	8.5	73.8
Elsewhere in the country	15.3	6.9	77.8
Abroad	14.3	—	85.7

Source: ICVS survey.

A UNIQUE BUT STILL LIMITED VISION

It is difficult to overemphasize the unique quality of the information which has been gleaned from the ICVS regarding violence at work. This is the first occasion on which survey-based data of this type has been gathered utilizing a methodology that allows comparisons to be made between these countries and regions in regard to the rates of victimization at the workplace, and the portrayal of other important variables associated with this violence. The data presented here must be seen as a key starting-point for any discussion of international patterns of workplace violence and, as future surveys are conducted, for the analysis of trends.

Most of the survey findings tend to speak for themselves, although to many observers it may come as a surprise to discover how prevalent *violent victimization* is at workplaces in many countries, and in particular *sexual victimization* against women.[21] The survey did not explore the relationship between the victim and the offender – an issue which may well be considered in future versions of this research. From existing

---

[21] In most categories of violence, men are far more likely than women to be both the victims and perpetrators. Exceptions to this situation occur in the setting of the family, where women and children are most frequently the victims of violence and men the perpetrators. See, for example, the report of the National Committee on Violence, 1990, Ch. 5, "Risk of violence in Australia", pp. 33-34 (hereafter referred to as the Australian NCV Report).

knowledge of the patterns of violent offending, it is reasonable to presume that males were most typically responsible for most of the victimization of women in the workplace.[22]

The survey findings provide an intriguing insight into the dimension of the "dark figure", or non-reported aspects of violence at work. Overwhelmingly, this form of violence does not currently find its way in most countries into the official records of the police, employers or other authorities.[23] This lack of reporting may be influenced by a number of factors, some of which have already been mentioned. Thus many employees, and in particular women, may feel constrained to remain silent about their victimization because of fear of reprisals being taken against them, including the possibility of losing their job. Unequal power relationships between employers and employees can undoubtedly influence reporting behaviours, and increase the risks of exploitation.

Reporting behaviours may also be influenced by different cultural sensitivities to violence and the context in which it occurs. As has been suggested in Chapter 1, an enhanced awareness that sexual harassment, bullying and mobbing are completely unacceptable behaviours has resulted in higher rates of reporting of such incidents by victims. In some countries included in the ICVS, this awareness may still be low, perhaps affecting the reporting of incidents of this type to survey interviewers as well as to any other source.

Low levels of reporting violent incidents to the police or other authorities can also be explained by a lack of trust in those bodies, or a belief that there is little they could do to provide any real redress. Criminologists are already familiar with such reporting behaviours among crime victims, many of whom may also view an incident as being too trivial to warrant bringing to the attention of the police. A similar view may exist on the part of a victim of workplace violence.

The search for new information at the international level about violence at work will continue in planned extension of the ICVS, and through the possible development of an International Commercial Crime Survey (ICCS). A small ICCS was conducted in 1994, involving a survey of crimes against business in eight countries. The survey showed a high rate of crime victimization among retail businesses, with more than one quarter reporting their premises had been burgled during the previous year. The financial costs of these crimes were substantial. While crimes of violence like robberies and assaults were less frequent, they too were costly both in monetary terms and in the fear, anxiety and physical trauma they caused to employees and employers.[24]

WORKPLACE VIOLENCE: REGIONAL AND NATIONAL DATA

Our attention will now turn to selected regional and national data relating to patterns and trends in violence at work. It is neither the intention nor purpose of this report to provide an exhaustive account of the nature and extent of such violence in each country and region of the world. Indeed, such an account would for most practical

---

[22] UNICRI reports that a revision to the ICVS questionnaire has been made in 1997 to include the category "colleague or boss" as part of the question on sexual incidents in order to obtain information about the offenders.

[23] See in general Liss and McCaskell, 1994, p. 1244.

[24] This information was also provided by UNICRI.

purposes be quite meaningless, since in many jurisdictions the data about this issue are of very limited quality and quantity. As a recent review of this data for the European Commission stated:

> The prevalence of workplace-related violence is difficult to estimate because of the general absence of either national level or occupational level data on this issue. Specific barriers exist in relation to acquiring this information. These include:
>
> * In many countries, incidents involving violence at work fall outside the scope of health and safety requirements, e.g. reporting requirements for accidents at work.
> * Where data is collected, it is often only collected on the fatal outcomes of violence. This data tends to focus on incidents involving extreme violence, e.g. physical assaults which involve the use of weapons.
> * Employers do not generally have in place appropriate mechanisms and procedures to either record or deal effectively with the problem of violence to their employees.
> * There are several problems with procedures used to record incidents of violence in workplaces. In many cases, records are collected on accident forms, thereby making it difficult to assess the true number of incidents in which violence is involved. Also, reporting procedures do not record the emotional or psychological conditions caused by threats of violence or exposure to threatening behaviour.
> * Certain categories of violence, e.g. threats of violence, fights between employees and vandalism may not be reported outside of the organization where the incident occurs.[25]

Within these limitations, what follows is an attempt to provide some impressions of the more significant patterns and trends in workplace violence which emerge from the published data under five main headings – scale and severity; homicide; assaults; occupations at special risk; and costs and consequences.

Scale and severity: Europe

While specific trend data are in very short supply, the scale and severity of workplace violence would appear to be both recognized and documented with greatest detail in Europe and North America. In Europe, for example, a major union-sponsored workshop on the topic of tackling violence at work concluded that:

> Today, throughout Europe, millions of workers whose jobs bring them into contact with the public are at risk – whether they handle cash or valuables, provide services (of all kinds), exercise authority, or work with violent or disturbed people. This means that violence is a major health and safety issue in sectors such as: banking; sports and leisure industries; national and local government employment; postal services; office cleaning; or public utilities.[26]

In reaching this conclusion, the workshop organizers pointed to a number of statistics, including:

* An increase of 73 per cent in the number of reported robberies of financial institutions in the Nordic countries between 1988 and 1992. A survey conducted in 1992 involving 512 financial institutions in these countries revealed 5,000 incidents "of violence and threatening situations" associated with the workplace.[27]
* A survey by the British Health and Safety Executive, in which 30 per cent of shop staff interviewed said they were verbally abused or threatened more than once a week.[28]

---

[25] Wynne et al., 1997, p. 5.

[26] FIET (International Federation of Commercial, Clerical, Professional and Technical Employees), 1994, p. 21.

[27] ibid., pp. 23-25.

[28] ibid., pp. 27-28.

- A report from an Italian union describing violence at the workplace involving property cleaning companies – an industry employing approximately 450,000 people, 80 per cent of whom were women. Widespread sexual harassment was experienced by these women, some of whom spoke of threats and blackmail that ranged from a reduction in the number of hours of work to job transfers or redundancies if they did not submit to the advances of a supervisor, employer or even the staff of the company awarding a cleaning contract.[29]

More recent data for the European Union are available from the European Foundation for the Improvement of Living and Working Conditions.[30] Their Second European Survey on Working Conditions, carried out in 1996, was based on 15,800 interviews with workers throughout the EU.[31] Their findings indicate that 4 per cent of workers (6 million) were subjected to physical violence, 2 per cent (3 million workers) to sexual harassment, and 8 per cent (12 million workers) to intimidation and bullying, as shown in table 8.

There were considerable differences between the various member States, which may be due to under-reporting in some countries and to greater awareness in others.

Sexual harassment

Sexual harassment affected 2 per cent of workers. As illustrated in figure 2, the highest exposure was found in catering services (hotels and restaurants) with 6 per cent; among workers aged under 24 (5 per cent); among female workers (4 per cent); and among employees with precarious status (3 per cent of employees with fixed-term contracts and temporary agency contracts). The cumulative effects of different conditions of exposure to risk can consequently make certain groups of workers highly vulnerable to sexual harassment.

Table 8. Violence at work in the European Union, 1996 (percentage)

	Belgium	Denmark	Germany (West)	Greece	Italy	Spain	France	Ireland	Luxembourg	Netherlands	Portugal	United Kingdom	Germany (East)	Finland	Sweden	Austria	European Union
Subjected to:																	
Physical violence	1	3	4	2	0	2	3	6	3	3	8	7	3	3	5	4	4
Unwanted sexual attention	1	2	3	2	1	1	2	2	1	1	1	4	0	2	2	4	2
Intimidation	4	6	8	5	4	5	9	8	7	7	5	16	6	9	10	7	8

Source: European Foundation for the Improvement of Living and Working Conditions, 1997, p. 312.
Note: Answers to yes/no questions.

---

[29] ibid., pp. 31-33.

[30] Data kindly provided by Mr. Pascal Paoli, Project Manager, European Foundation for the Improvement of Living and Working Conditions, 1997.

[31] A Third European Survey is underway, but data were not yet available at the time this new edition was going to press.

Violence at work

Figure 2.   Sexual harassment in the European Union, 1996

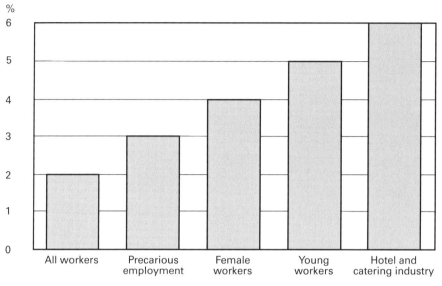

%

Source: European Foundation for the Improvement of Living and Working Conditions, 1997

Physical violence

Four per cent of all workers were subjected to physical violence. The highest incidence was in services (public administration with 6 per cent, and the trade and retail industry with 5 per cent).

Figure 3.   Bullying in the European Union, 1996

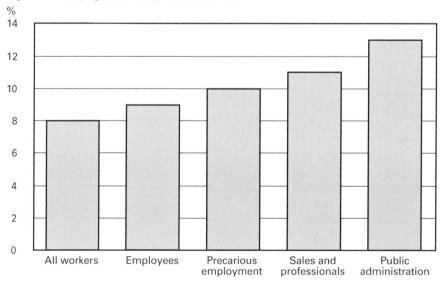

%

Source: European Foundation for the Improvement of Living and Working Conditions, 1997.

Intimidation and bullying

Intimidation and bullying was found among 8 per cent of workers (see figure 3), with the highest exposure rates in services (13 per cent in public administration, and 10 per cent in banking and other services). Service and sales workers and professionals (11 per cent) are the most affected categories.

Employees (9 per cent) are more prone to bullying than the self-employed and, among them, employees in precarious employment are most affected (10 per cent of workers on fixed-term contracts and temporary agency contracts).

Female workers (9 per cent) are more concerned than male workers (7 per cent), while 12 per cent of young workers under 24 are exposed to bullying.

Health effects of violence at work

Violence at work clearly leads to an increase in health complaints, particularly with regard to stress, which was experienced by 40 per cent of workers exposed to physical violence, 47 per cent of workers exposed to bullying and 46 per cent of workers exposed to sexual harassment (see figure 4). This compares with an average exposure to stress among the workforce of 28 per cent.

Figure 4.   Exposure to stress in the European Union, 1996

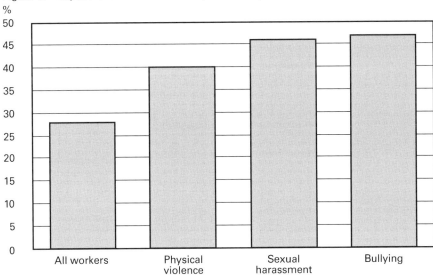

Source: European Foundation for the Improvement of Living and Working Conditions, 1997

Effects on absences from work

Health-related absences increased with violence at work. As shown in figure 5, 35 per cent of workers exposed to physical violence were absent from work over the last 12 months, as well as 34 per cent of those exposed to bullying and 31 per cent of workers exposed to sexual harassment, compared to an average of 23 per cent among workers in general.

Figure 5.   Absences over the last 12 months in the European Union, 1996

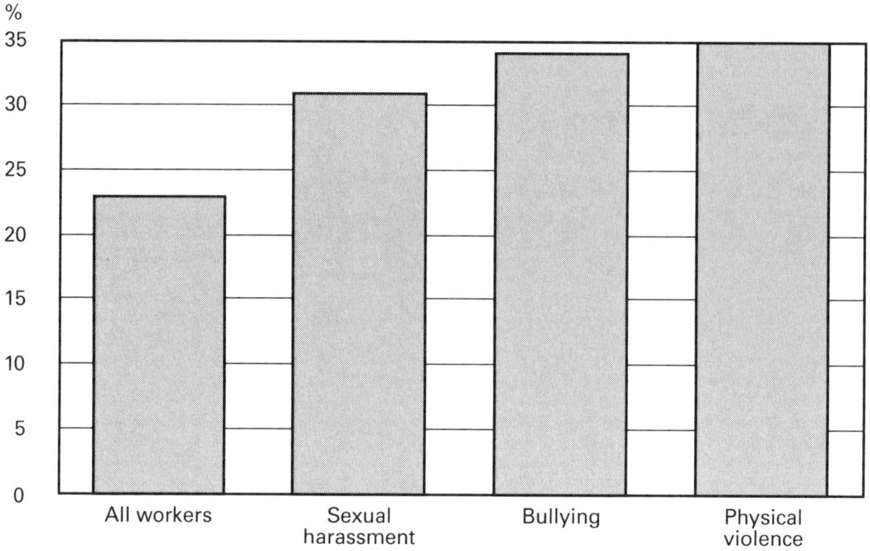

%

```
35

30

25

20

15

10

5

0
        All workers        Sexual            Bullying          Physical
                          harassment                           violence
```

Source: European Foundation for the Improvement of Living and Working Conditions, 1997.

Scale and severity: North America

In North America, and in particular in the United States, much more detailed data are available about many aspects of violence at work. Much of this information is gathered and reported upon by the authoritative United States National Institute for Occupational Safety and Health (NIOSH)[32]. A recent and comprehensive overview by NIOSH of the risk factors and prevention strategies related to violence at work contains many valuable insights including reasons for looking separately at this aspect of violence in the United States.[33]

These reasons include the fact that:

*   Violence is a significant contributor to death and injury at the workplace; data indicate that, after motor vehicle accidents, homicide is the second leading cause of occupational injury death.

*   Workplace homicides differ in their circumstances from those committed elsewhere; for example, in 1993, 75 per cent of all workplace homicides were robbery related (compared with 9 per cent in the general population) and in the majority of such crimes the victim and offender were not known to one another (compared with 47 per cent of all murder victims who were related to or acquainted with their assailant).

*   Workplace violence is clustered in particular occupational settings rather than randomly distributed across workplaces. Rates of both fatal and non-fatal violence are highest in the retail trade and service industries.

---

[32] The passage in 1970 by the United States Congress of the *Occupational Safety and Health Act* is said to have been the stimulus for much of the data gathering in this area by NIOSH and other official bodies. See VandenBos and Bulatao, 1996, p. 4.

[33] See Jenkins, 1996, p. 2.

- Violence at work risks are associated with specific workplace factors including dealing with the public, the exchange of money and the delivery of services and goods.

In the current absence of any significant comparative research with regard to workplace violence, it is difficult to assess the general relevance of these observations to the situation prevailing beyond the confines of the United States. A tentative assessment, based on the cross-national information obtained in the course of the compilation of the present report, suggests that they are broadly relevant although, as will be seen shortly, much of the American concern and information is concentrated upon homicide – a form of violence which is still rare in almost all workplaces, including those in the United States.

Homicide

In the United States two national surveillance systems now trace workplace homicide – the NIOSH-maintained National Traumatic Occupational Fatalities (NTOF) surveillance system, and the Bureau of Labor Statistics (BLS) National Census of Fatal Occupational Injuries.[34] The NTOF data show that during a 13-year period from 1980 to 1992, almost 10,000 workplace homicides occurred in the United States. Table 9 shows the annual number and rates of these homicides.

Table 9.   Workplace homicides in the United States, 1980-92[1]

Year	Number	Rate [2]
1980	929	0.96
1981	944	0.94
1982	859	0.86
1983	721	0.72
1984	660	0.63
1985	751	0.70
1986	672	0.61
1987	649	0.58
1988	699	0.61
1989	696	0.59
1990	725	0.61
1991	875	0.75
1992	757	0.64
Total	9937	0.70

[1] Data not available for New York City and Connecticut for 1992. [2] Per 100,000 workers.

Source: Jenkins, 1996, p. 3. Tables 9 to 12 and figures 6 and 7 are reproduced with permission from the National Institute for Occupational Safety and Health, Cincinnati, Ohio.

The overwhelming majority (80 per cent) of workplace homicides during this period occurred among male workers, although homicide was the leading cause of

---

[34] For a more detailed description of these surveillance systems and their respective strengths and limitations, see VandenBos and Bulatao, pp. 4-8.

occupational death among female workers.[35] The largest number of workplace homicides occurred among workers aged 25 to 34, but the rate of workplace homicide increased with age.[36]

Table 10 shows the incidence of these workplace homicides according to the industry involved. It will be seen that the highest rates of homicide occurred in retail trades, public administration and transportation/communication/public utilities. However, when detailed occupational data were analysed, they showed that the highest homicide rates occurred among taxicab drivers/chauffeurs, sheriffs and bailiffs, police and detectives, gas station/garage workers and security guards (see table 11).

Table 10. Workplace homicides by industry, United States, 1980-92[1]

Industry	Number	% of total	Rate[2]
Retail trade	3 774	38.0	1.60
Public administration	889	8.9	1.30
Transportation/communication/ public utilities	917	9.2	0.94
Agriculture/forestry/fishing	222	2.2	0.50
Mining	45	0.5	0.40
Services	1 713	17.2	0.38
Construction	335	3.4	0.37
Finance/insurance/real estate	327	3.3	0.35
Wholesale trade	155	1.6	0.27
Manufacturing	650	6.5	0.24
Not classified	910	9.1	—

[1] Data for New York City and Connecticut were not available for 1992. [2] Per 100,000 workers.

Source: Jenkins, 1996, p. 4.

In table 12, the circumstances of workplace homicides are shown for the period 1992-94. Firearms were used in 76 per cent of these homicides; in American homicides overall during 1993, 71 per cent were committed with firearms. An important conclusion to be drawn from table 12 is that:

The circumstances of workplace homicides differ substantially from those portrayed by the media and from homicides in the general population. For the most part, workplace homicides are not the result of disgruntled workers who take out their frustrations on co-workers or supervisors, or of intimate partners and other relatives who kill loved ones in the course of a dispute; rather, they are mostly robbery-related crimes.[37]

The American data regarding workplace homicides have been presented in some detail in this report since they represent by far the most comprehensive information available for any country in the world about this most serious of all workplace crimes.

---

[35] Jenkins, 1996, p. 3. As Jenkins suggests, differences in the leading causes of occupational injury and death by gender can be attributed, in part, to variations in employment patterns. Women are likely to be less exposed than men to hazards such as heavy machinery, work in elevated areas and driving heavy trucks. Similar variations exist between hazards likely to be encountered by workers in industries such as construction, mining and fishing contrasted with those employed in the retail, financial or services sector of the economy.

[36] Jenkins, 1996, pp. 3 and 9.

[37] Jenkins, 1996, p. 10.

Table 11.   Workplace homicides in high-risk[1] occupations, United States, 1983-89 and 1990-92[2]

	1983-1989		1990-1992	
	Number	Rate[3]	Number	Rate[3]
Taxicab driver/chauffeur	197	15.1	140	22.7
Sheriff/bailiff	73	10.9	36	10.7
Police and detective – public service	267	9.0	86	6.1
Hotel clerk	29	5.1	6	2.0
Gas station/garage worker	83	4.5	37	5.9
Security guard	160	3.6	115	5.5
Stock handler/bagger	189	3.1	95	3.5
Supervisor/proprietor, sales	662	2.8	372	3.3
Supervisor, police and detective	12	2.2	0	[4]
Barber	14	2.2	4	[4]
Bartender	49	2.1	20	2.3
Correctional institution officer	19	1.5	3	[4]
Salesperson, motor vehicle and boat	21	1.1	17	2.0
Salesperson, other commodities	98	1.0	73	1.7
Sales counter clerk	13	1.2	18	3.1
Firefighter	18	1.4	8	1.3
Logging occupation	4	[4]	6	2.3
Butcher/meatcutter	11	0.6	12	1.5

[1] High-risk occupations have workplace homicide rates that are twice the average rate during one or both time periods. [2] Data for New York City and Connecticut were not available for 1992. [3] Rates are per 100,000 workers. [4] Rate was not calculated because of instability of rates based on small numbers.

Source: Jenkins, 1996, p. 5.

Table 12.   Circumstances of workplace homicides, United States, 1992-94

Circumstance	Homicides (% of total)[1]		
	1992 (N = 1 004)	1993 (N = 1 063)	1994 (N = 1 071)
Robbery and other crime	82	75	73
Business dispute/work associate	9	10	9
Co-worker/former co-worker	4	6	5
Customer/Client	5	4	4
Police in line of duty	6	6	7
Security guard in line of duty	[2]	5	7
Personal dispute/acquaintance	4	4	4

[1] Percentages total more than 100 because of rounding (and multiple circumstances). [2] This category was not included in 1992.

Source: Jenkins, 1996, p. 9.

It must be strongly emphasized, however, that almost certainly these data do not portray specific patterns and trends which would be replicated in other countries if comparative data of this type were available. The overall homicide rate in the United States is, for example, high in comparison with many other industrialized countries in the world, (see table 15 in Chapter 3) and, as observed, firearms account for a very substantial proportion of all of these felonious deaths in the country. In other developed nations, including those in Europe, rates of homicide of all types are not only in general much lower, but the involvement of firearms is also far less frequent.

It is also very important to place the risk of becoming the victim of a workplace homicide in some broader perspective, by examining other lethal hazards at the workplace. Figure 6 below shows the leading causes of occupational injury deaths in the United States between 1980 and 1992. It will be seen that the greatest risk of death came from motor vehicle accidents – a situation which would probably be found to be mirrored in the occupational fatality data of other industrialized countries.

Figure 6.   Leading causes of occupational injury deaths, United States, 1980-1992

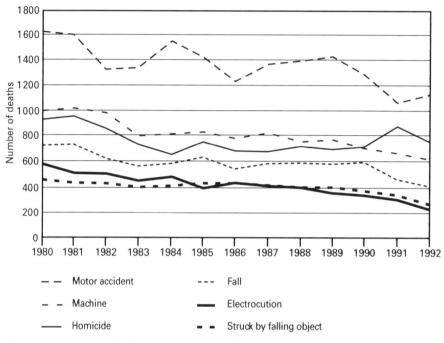

— — Motor accident   - - - Fall

- - Machine   ▬▬ Electrocution

—— Homicide   ■ ■ Struck by falling object

Note: Data were not available for New York City and Connecticut for 1992.

Source: Jenkins, 1996, p. 4.

Assaults

The ICVS data have already demonstrated that the risk of becoming a victim of assault at the workplace is far greater than that of becoming the victim of a homicide. Beyond the ICVS, comprehensive information about the nature and dimensions of non-fatal violence occurring in the workplace is hard to obtain in most jurisdictions. Even in the United States, such data are sparse, coming either from criminal justice or public health bodies, but estimates have been made of the magnitude of the problem from three primary sources.

The first of these, the Bureau of Labor Statistics (BLS) Annual Survey of Occupational Injuries and Illnesses, involving the surveying of about 250,000 private establishments, found that about 22,000 workplace assaults occurred in 1992. These assaults, which were much more narrowly defined than the type of incident reported in the ICVS, accounted for 1 per cent of all days off work.[38] The assaults were distributed almost evenly between men and women, and the majority were reported in the service and retail trade industries.[39] The source of the injury reported is shown in figure 7.

Figure 7.   Violent acts resulting in days away from work, by source of injury, United States, 1992

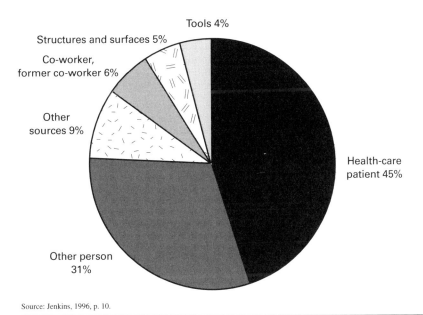

Source: Jenkins, 1996, p. 10.

A second source of estimation is the frequently cited survey conducted by the Northwestern National Life Insurance Company, which indicated that 2.2 million workers had been assaulted, 16.1 million harassed and 6.3 million threatened at the workplace in the United States between July 1992 and July 1993. Commentators have questioned the reliability of this estimate because of perceived faults in the survey's methodology.[40]

A third estimate of the number of non-fatal assaults occurring in American workplaces comes from the American National Crime Victimization Survey (NCVS) – a massive, annual and nationwide, household-based study of more than 100,000 individuals aged 12 or older. According to 1992-1996 National Crime Victimization Survey (NCVS) "during each year, US residents experienced more than 2 million violent victimizations while they were working or on duty. The most common type of workplace violent crime was simple assault with an estimated average of 1.4 million

---

[38] These assaults recorded in the BLS survey were ones which inflicted injuries. See in general Jenkins, 1996, pp. 10-11; BLS, 1994.

[39] See Jenkins, 1996, p. 11.

[40] Northwestern National Life, 1993. Constant references are made in the literature on workplace violence to the striking results obtained in this survey. However, the methodology of the survey has been criticized, the estimates of the assaults being based on only 3 per cent (18 cases) of a sample of 600 workers, and the respondents being unrepresentative of the workforce – see Castillo, 1995, pp. 226-227.

victimizations occurring each year. While at work US residents also suffered 395,000 aggravated assaults, 50,000 rapes and sexual assaults, (and) 83,000 robberies."[41]

Data on the scale available in the United States on this subject are not replicated elsewhere. However, from the information that can be obtained from other national and regional sources, patterns and trends similar to those already reported from the ICVS and the American data do emerge. Thus work-related violence is shown to be an issue which is of particular concern to **women**. In Sweden, for example, as figure 8 indicates, work-related violent incidents decreased or stayed about the same for men but increased for women during the period 1985-1992.

Figure 8.   Registered work injuries caused by violence and threat, by gender, Sweden, 1985-94

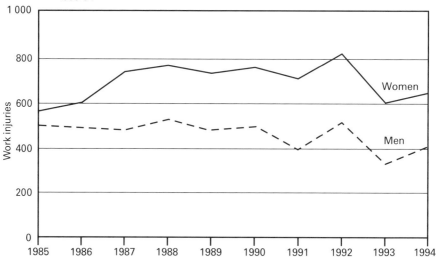

Source: Reproduced with permission from H. Nordin, *Fakta om våld och hot i arbetet*, Solna, Occupational Injury Information System (ISA), Swedish National Board of Occupational Safety and Health, 1995, p. 4.

The global impact of violence on women, both inside and outside the workplace, is dramatic.[42] More than 12,000 Canadian women were interviewed in 1993 regarding their experience with physical or sexual attacks. Of the respondents, 51 per cent indicated that they had experienced such attacks, 18 per cent of which resulted in physical injury.[43] In a sample of 1,500 Swiss women in a relationship, 20 per cent reported being physically assaulted. Out of 619 husbands with at least one child residing in Bangkok, in 1994, 20 per cent acknowledged physically abusing their wife at least once. From a sample of around 1,000 women in Midlands, Zimbabwe, in 1996, 32 per cent reported physical abuse by a family or household member.[44]

---

[41] See Backman, 1994.

[42] *Workplace Violence, 1992-96: National Crime Victimization Survey,* Washington, DC, Bureau of Justice Statistics, United States Department of Justice, Special Report, June 1998.

[43] Data from the 1993 Statistics Canada Survey (*Canada First National Survey on Violence Against Women*), based on telephone interviews with 12,300 women, as reported in the *Globe and Mail* (Montreal), 19 November 1993. See also H. Johnson, *Dangerous domains – Violence against women in Canada*, Scarborough, Ontario, Nelson Canada, 1996.

[44] WHO, *Violence Against women fact sheets*, retrieved on 30 June 1999 at: http://www.who.int/frh-whd/VAW/infopack/English/VAW_infopack.htm.

Why is so much violence perpetrated against women, particularly in the workplace? Women are concentrated in many of the high-risk occupations, particularly as teachers, social workers, nurses and other health-care workers, as well as bank and shop workers.[45] The continued segregation of women in low-paid and low status jobs, while men predominate in better-paid, higher status jobs and supervisory positions also contributes to this problem.[46] On the other hand, the majority of cases of aggression or violence are experienced by men. It has been argued that, in general, men are more likely to meet aggression with aggression, while women are better at defusing, coping with and avoiding aggressive incidents, and indeed are best at some of the most vulnerable jobs.[47]

Another common finding would seem to be the vulnerability of **younger workers** to violent victimization at the workplace. This finding appears to confirm the importance of experience in dealing with violent situations. Previous experience enables employees to react more wisely and behave with more self-confidence than inexperienced staff. This may in turn reduce aggression and the likelihood of violence. In the United Kingdom, for example, staff aged 18 to 30 working on the London Underground have a higher probability of becoming victims of assault than older staff, as indicated in figure 9.

Figure 9.   Age profile of London Underground Ltd. employees and staff assaulted, January 1993 to August 1996

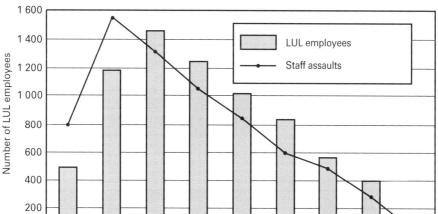

Source: London Transport Occupational Health. *Report to Staff Assaults Working Group. Quantitative Analysis of Staff Assaults* – Trident Consultants Ltd., J.2909, London, March 1997, figure 5.45. By courtesy of Mr. C. Lipscomb, Business Manager, London Transport Occupational Health and Mr. S. Harris, Business Manager, London Transport Working Group, London Underground Ltd. Information provided 2 April 1997.

---

[45] Aromaa, 1993, p. 145. See also chapters in VandenBos and Bulatao, 1996: J.J. Hurrell et al., "Job stress, gender and workplace violence: Analysis of assault experiences of state employees"; and M.L. Lanza, "Violence against nurses in hospitals", pp. 163-170 and pp. 189-198 respectively.

[46] Lim, 1996, p. 17.

[47] D. Lamplugh, 1994, p. J:13:9:5 to J:13:9:6.

Violence at work

When different types of psychological violence are considered, data comparison and quantification across countries and regions becomes still more problematic. The boundaries between sexual harassment, bullying and mobbing can be very uncertain, but there are a number of studies which require mention under each of these headings of violence.

Sexual harassment

Sexual harassment is a significant workplace problem, as the ICVS data have demonstrated so forcibly and recently. These data confirm findings from a number of earlier studies. In the Netherlands, the results of a government study published in 1986 indicated that 58 per cent of the women questioned had experienced sexual harassment at work. In Norway, a 1988 survey found 41 per cent of the women responding had been subjected many times to sexual harassment. In the United Kingdom, a 1987 survey found 73 per cent of respondents reporting some form of harassment had happened in their workplace.[48] In Germany, as noted earlier, a 1991 federal study found that 93 per cent of women questioned had been sexually harassed at the workplace during the course of their occupational life.[49] In Spain, estimates of women's exposure to sexual harassment vary from 40 to 84 per cent of the workforce.[50] In Italy, the first official survey on the extent of rape, attempted rape, sexual harassment and sexual blackmail, carried out in 1997-98 on a sample of more than 20,000 women, confirms the magnitude of these forms of violence (see table 13).

Table 13. Violence against women at the workplace, by age and education, Italy, 1997-98 (percentage)[1]

By age

Age group	At least one type of violence	Blackmail to obtain a job	Blackmail to advance in their career or retain their position	Sexual harassment	Rape or attempted rape
14-24	5.0	2.1	1.3	3.5	0.5
25-34	8.8	4.3	3.0	4.1	0.4
35-44	8.6	3.3	2.3	4.6	0.6
45-54	6.5	2.0	1.6	3.7	0.4
55-59	5.3	2.0	1.3	2.1	0.9
Total	7.4	3.0	2.1	3.9	0.5

By education

Education	At least one type of violence	Blackmail to obtain a job	Blackmail to advance in their career or retain their position	Sexual harassment	Rape or attempted rape
Degree	6.0	3.1	2.4	2.5	0.4
High school diploma	8.2	3.4	2.5	4.3	0.4
Intermediate	8.1	3.6	2.3	4.2	0.5
Elementary	5.2	1.1	1.1	3.4	0.9
Total	7.4	3.0	2.1	3.9	0.5

[1] Percentage of women in the sample who, in the course of their life, were subjected to rape, attempted rape, sexual harassment and blackmail to obtain a job or to advance in their career.

Source: ISTAT (National Institute of Statistics) special tabulation for the ILO from the 1997-98 Survey on Citizens' Security, section on sexual violence, by M.G. Muratore, 1 July 1999, Rome.

---

[48] ILO, "Combating sexual harassment at work", 1992, pp. 286-289.

[49] Beermann and Meschkutat, 1995, p. 21.

[50] CERES – Circular Información General – No. 11/93, May 1993, p. 2.

Bullying

Several surveys in Finland have shown that approximately 10 per cent of the workers interviewed have experienced some form of bullying.[51] Research carried out in the United Kingdom found that 53 per cent of employees had been bullied at work, and that 78 per cent had witnessed bullying at work.[52] Consequently, bullying at work has moved up the management agenda. Two-thirds of the employers in a 1999 survey in the United Kingdom covering 157 organizations employing 687,000 employees confirmed that this is the case.[53] However, bullying still appears largely unreported. The same survey indicates that the number of formal bullying complaints handled by employers is relatively low. In contrast, the perception of the importance of bullying is that it seems to be on the increase. Interim results from a survey on bullying in further and higher education in Wales clearly indicate that workplace experience of bullying is ranked higher than sex discrimination and sexual and racial harassment, as shown in figure 10.

Figure 10. Respondents' experience of workplace bullying, further and higher education, Wales, 1998

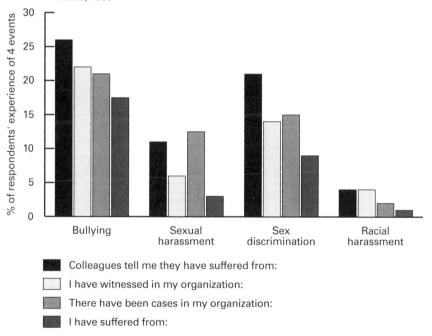

[51] M. Vartia, "Bullying at workplaces", in Bast-Pettersen et al. (eds.), 1995.

[52] Data from a 1994 survey from Staffordshire University, as cited in *Hazards* (Sheffield), No. 48, Autumn 1994, p. 2.

[53] "Bullying at work: A survey of 157 employers", in *IRS Employment Review*, April 1999, No. 677 – Employee Health Bulletin, 8 April 1999, p. 4. See also Lyn Quine, "Workplace bullying in NHS community trusts: Staff questionnaire survey", in *British Medical Journal*, No. 7178, 23 January 1999, pp. 228-233.

Mobbing

Mobbing would appear to affect 1 per cent of the working population in Norway.[54] Similar data are reported for Germany,[55] while in Sweden the percentage is 3.5 per cent. More than 150,000 of approximately 4.5 million workers in Sweden would appear to have experienced one or more mobbing events.[56] Even higher rates of mobbing are reported from Austria, with figures cited of more than 4 per cent in private industry and nearly 8 per cent in public services (hospitals).[57]

Occupations at special risk

Reference has already been made in this chapter, and in Chapter 1, to occupations which give rise to a much higher risk of experiencing violence at the workplace. In fact no occupation can be said to be entirely immune from some form of violence, but it is widely acknowledged that workers performing certain tasks are at special risk, as the following box indicates:

Who is at risk?

Workers in the following types of job are probably most at risk:

handling money or valuables	cashiers delivery staff transport workers bank and post office staff commissionaires security staff shop assistants
providing care, advice or training	nurses ambulance staff social workers teachers housing office staff
carrying out inspection or enforcement duties	traffic wardens ticket inspectors park keepers
working with mentally disturbed, drunk or potentially violent people	prison officers landlords mental health workers
working alone	home visitors taxi drivers domestic repair workers

Source: Health and Safety Executive, 1991, p. 2. Crown copyright is reproduced with the permission of the Controller of Her Majesty's Stationery Office.

---

[54] Leymann, 1990, p. 122.

[55] Nowosad, 1995.

[56] Leymann, 1993, p. 84.

[57] Beermann and Meschkutat, 1995, p. 15.

The level of exposure to violence when performing one of these tasks can vary greatly depending on the specific occupation. Some occupations, such as those in the health care sector, appear to be at high risk, as shown in figure 11.

Figure 11.   Number of work accidents involving violence or threats in Sweden, by occupational sector, 1994

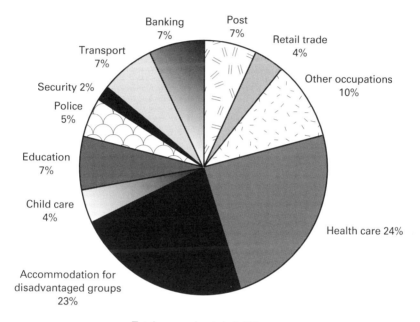

Total: approximately 2,400 cases

Source: Reproduced with permission from H. Nordin, 1995, p. 3. See acknowledgement to figure 8 above.

Certain occupations seem increasingly exposed to exceptional risk, as has been seen already in the case of the American workplace homicide data. In the United States, the extent of such exposure for certain occupations, such as taxi drivers, is up to 15 times higher than the average exposure, as shown in table 11 above. More will be said in Chapter 3 about the situational factors that can also play a significant part in explaining the particular vulnerability of certain occupations to workplace violence.

Costs and consequences

Like a stone thrown into water, violence at work not only has an immediate impact on the victim, but also expands in progressively larger ripples, affecting other people directly or indirectly involved, as well as the enterprise concerned and the community. This effect explains why the cost of violence at work has often been underestimated.

It is only in recent times that experts have started quantifying the multiple and massive costs of such violence. In the United States, crime victimization occurring in the workplace has been estimated to cost approximately 1.8 million lost working days each year.[58] In Germany, the total cost of mobbing has been estimated at 2.5 billion marks per year.[59] Within these global figures the impact and cost of violence can be considered at a number of different levels.

Individual costs

On an individual level, the cost of personal suffering and pain resulting from violence at work is hard to quantify. Suffering and humiliation are not self-contained events. They usually lead to lack of motivation, loss of confidence and reduced self-esteem, depression and anger, anxiety and irritability. As noted earlier, a 1993 Finnish study on psychological harassment at work indicated that 59 per cent of victims viewed the situation as "unjust", 47 per cent had thought of leaving their job, and 37 per cent suffered from depression.[60] All of these indicators are typical of stress, and stress is a very costly matter. If the causes of violence are not eliminated, or the effects of violence are not contained by adequate intervention, these symptoms are likely to develop into physical illness, psychological disorders, tobacco and alcohol abuse, and so on; they can culminate in occupational accidents, invalidity and even suicide.[61]

These negative consequences not only affect the person who is the focus of such violence, but often extend to people in proximity to the act, and even to people far removed or physically absent from the place where violence occurs. The effects of violence can thus pervade the entire workplace, the family of the victim and the community in which they live.[62]

Organizational costs

At the level of the workplace, violence causes immediate – and often long-term – disruption to interpersonal relationships, the organization of work and the overall working environment. Employers bear the direct cost of lost work and improved security measures. There can also be indirect costs of reduced efficiency and productivity, loss in product quality, loss in company image, and a reduction in the number of clients. Table 14 presents some aspects of the negative impact of workplace violence, which all adversely affect the performance of enterprises.

The labelling of an enterprise as "violent" is one of the most deleterious effects of workplace violence. The following figures on these costs of violence speak for themselves.
- In Germany, the direct cost of mobbing in an enterprise of 1,000 workers has been calculated at 200,000 DM per year, plus indirect costs of 100,000 DM per year.[63]

---

[58] National Crime Victimization Survey, 1987-1992, quoted in *Crime Data Brief* (Washington, DC, US Department of Justice), July 1994, p. 1.

[59] Nowosad, 1995, p. 10.

[60] Vartia, 1993, p. 21.

[61] ILO, "Preventing stress at work", 1992.

[62] For a moving and graphic account of the traumatic impact of the Port Arthur shootings upon the entire community see the Doyle Report (Joint Parliamentary Group, 1997).

[63] Nowosad, 1995, pp. 4 and 5.

Table 14.   The impact of violence at the workplace, United States, 1996

Impact	Per cent of respondents
Decreased morale	9
Increased stress	22
Increased fear	18
Lower productivity	10
Increased absenteeism	3
Decreased worker trust	11
Increased staff turnover	3
Other	19

Source: Society for Human Resource Management, *Workplace Violence Survey 1996* (Alexandria, Virginia, SHRM, 1996). Reproduced with permission.

- In the United States, a study made by the National Safe Workplace Institute estimated that the total costs to employers for workplace violence amounted to more than US$4 billion in 1992.[64]
- In Canada, the British Columbia Workers' Compensation Board has reported that wage-loss claims by hospital workers due to acts of violence or force have increased by 88 per cent since 1985.[65]
- In New Zealand the cost of labour market income loss forgone due to work days assumed to be lost through family violence has been calculated to be at least NZ$1.2 billion in 1993/94.[66]

Community costs

The cost of violence at work also affects the community as a whole. Health care and long-term rehabilitation costs for the reintegration of the victims of violence at work; unemployment and retraining costs for those who lost their job because of such violence; disability and invalidity costs for those whose working capacities are impaired by violence at work; are all part of the price paid.

An assessment of the total magnitude of the costs to the community of workplace violence also requires consideration of the indirect impact of this violence on the partners and relatives of the victim and, in a broader perspective, of its disruptive effect as a multiplier to the fear and anxiety about crime and violence in any society.

---

[64] J. Kinney, "Breaking point: The workplace violence epidemic and what to do about it", cited in Littler et al., 1994(b), p. 7.

[65] Pizzino, 1994, p. 6.

[66] Suively, 1995, p. ii.

EXPLANATIONS

3

Single cause, single solution?

It is tempting (or convenient) for many to regard violence as arising from a single cause, and consequently to perceive a reduction in violence as certain to arise from a single solution. For example, there are those who think that the removal of televised violence represents the answer to violent behaviour. There are others who perceive more rigorous controls on firearms as the way to eliminate violence.

The most vocal commentators on violence often reflect ideological predispositions or institutional interests. As convenient and as reassuring as it may be to crusade on behalf of a panacea, a proper understanding of violence (and ultimately, of the means for its control) requires an understanding of the variety and complexity of contributing factors.[1]

Looking for ticking bombs

Violent crime has penetrated and gripped our society. The ticking clock of crime moves swiftly throughout the day, and a pervasive fear of violence in the workplace has become the most recent threat to the way decent people live...

It has been called an epidemic by those who study disgruntled employees and angry spouses and the violence they perpetrate on innocent employees...

Violent crime is no longer restricted to urban centres and ghettos. The offices, factories, school playgrounds, post offices, fast-food restaurants, hospitals, shopping malls, hotels, grocery stores, banks, convenience stores, and in fact, nearly everywhere people are employed and business is carried out have become the latest sites for disgruntled, unhappy, desperate, often psychiatrically impaired people to vent their rage.[2]

COMPLEX CAUSES, COMPLEX SOLUTIONS

There is a strong and natural desire among most citizens to seek simple explanations and solutions to the violence which may be gripping their society and threatening "the way decent people live". As has been observed, it is often the media who provide

---

[1] Reproduced with permission from the Australian Institute of Criminology, from National Committee on Violence, 1990, p. 60.

[2] Reproduced with permission from The McGraw-Hill Companies, from M. Mantell and S. Albrecht, *Ticking bomb: Defusing violence in the workplace* (Burr Ridge, Illinois, Irwin Professional Publishing), 1994, pp. ix-x.

such explanations and convey lasting impressions of the type of people responsible for "an epidemic" of violence in the workplace. Those impressions are often dominated by images of "disgruntled employees" and "angry spouses", "unhappy, desperate, often psychiatrically impaired people", venting their anger on colleagues at the workplace. Those media images, of course, also spread with amazing speed around the globe and affect public and official perceptions of violence far beyond their place of origin.

The analysis made of the nature and scope of workplace violence in Chapter 2 suggests that there are cases where these media-created perceptions are both inaccurate and misleading. Despite this, they are still perceptions that can influence policy, as well as the way governments and other bodies think about and respond to the problems of violence in general, and workplace violence in particular. Thus a principal strategy to deal with the disgruntled, angry and possibly mentally ill people who may explode into violence at the workplace is to either deny these "ticking time-bombs" access to work sites, or to try and identify or defuse their rage before it detonates.

Much of the current workplace violence prevention literature reflects such an approach, with the development of pre-employment tests to screen out and exclude those who might be violent; of profiles to identify those who might become violent in the existing workforce; and of measures to deal with violence when it occurs.[3] This approach is also characterized typically by an emphasis on the need for "target hardening" through the use of a range of security measures to restrict entry to and movement within the workplace.[4]

Measures of this type, like those mentioned earlier restricting access to firearms in the wake of the tragedies at Dunblane and Port Arthur, may well assist in reducing the incidence of violence at the workplace, and in the wider community. To this extent they are measures which deserve approbation, but this praise must be restrained by the realization that they are still measures addressing limited symptoms of an extremely complex and diverse problem which defies either an easy explanation or solution.

A recognition and an understanding of the variety and complexity of the factors which contribute to violence must be a vital precursor of any effective violence prevention or control programme. In this chapter it is sought to provide such understanding, first through a brief review of a number of factors that have been identified as the most significant in explaining violence in general, and second by considering how these factors may interact to produce violence at work.

FACTORS LEADING TO VIOLENCE

A vast literature exists in regard to violence and its causes. That literature has been reviewed in depth, and the principal findings distilled in an accessible and authoritative way, by two recent national inquiries into violence – one in Australia and the

---

[3] A bibliography containing reference to much of this prevention literature will be found in Mantell and Albrecht, 1994, pp. 264-5. The issue of prevention strategies is taken up in some detail in Part II of this report.

[4] See D.F. Bush and P.G. O'Shea, "Workplace violence: Comparative use of prevention practices and policies", in VandenBos and Bulatao, 1996, pp. 283-298.

other in the United States.[5] The points which follow are adapted from these sources unless otherwise indicated.

Violence, or aggression, as it is also termed, is deeply ingrained in the behavioural repertoire of humans. It is a behaviour which seems to have served originally as an adaptive mechanism necessary for the survival of the species. To this extent aggression forms a part of the human genetic heritage.

Violence does not occur randomly across the human species, nor does it occur evenly throughout any given society. As was noted in Chapter 2, some nations experience more violence than others. Table 15 below illustrates this point by displaying the homicide rates of a number of countries. It will be seen that wide variations exist in these rates.

Table 15.   National homicide rates per 100,000 inhabitants, 1994

Country/area name	Homicide rate, 1994	Total homicide cases reported by police, 1994	Total population 1994 (estimate)
Bahamas	82.85	227	274 000
Colombia	78.59	27 130	34 520 000
Kuwait	58.02	940	1 620 000
Jamaica	29.77	743	2 496 000
Estonia	25.68	385	1 499 000
Nicaragua	25.63	1 128	4 401 000
Bolivia	23.31	1 687	7 237 000
Russian Federation	23.18	34 302	147 997 000
Northern Ireland	20.90	341	1 631 822
Ecuador	18.47	2 073	11 221 000
Latvia	16.17	412	2 548 000
Zimbabwe	15.96	1 779	11 150 000
Zambia	15.83	1 456	9 196 000
Kazakhstan	15.65	2 664	17 027 000
Lithuania	15.05	560	3 721 000
Georgia	14.44	788	5 458 000
Saint Vincent and the Grenadines	14.41	16	111 000
Bermuda	12.70	8	63 000

[5] The Australian inquiry was commissioned by the Prime Minister and other heads of government of the Australian states in the country following two mass shootings in 1988 in Melbourne. The National Committee on Violence (NCV), comprised of experts in the field, was established to conduct the inquiry. It was given broad terms of reference to consider the state of violence in the nation; the causes of this violence; and ways of preventing or controlling it. The NCV was chaired by Professor Duncan Chappell, the then Director of the Australian Institute of Criminology, and one of the authors of this book. The NCV conveyed its findings to Australian and state governments in February 1990 in a report entitled *Violence: Directions for Australia* (NCV, 1990). This report, which was tabled and debated in each of the Australian parliaments, has subsequently been the catalyst for the implementation of many violence prevention strategies in Australia, as well as being widely cited as a key reference source in the literature on violence around the world.

The United States National Academy of Science – National Research Council study was convened to examine the available literature and research regarding the causes of violence and its prevention. A Panel on the Understanding and Causes of Violent Behaviour was set up in response to the expressed interest of three federal agencies. The National Science Foundation's Program on Law and Social Sciences sought a review of current knowledge on the basic causes of violent behaviour, and recommendations about priorities in funding research in the future. The National Institute of Justice sought advice on how to prevent and control violent crimes committed by individuals and small groups, such as adolescent gangs, and the Centre for Disease Control's Injury Control Division sought advice that would assist them in setting priorities in preventing injuries and deaths from violent behaviour. The results of this study are conveyed in the four volumes of Reiss and Roth (eds.), 1993.

Violence at work

Country/area name	Homicide rate, 1994	Total homicide cases reported by police, 1994	Total population 1994 (estimate)
Panama	12.50	323	2 583 000
Kyrgyzstan	12.27	564	4 596 000
Sweden	11.96	1 050	8 780 000
Bulgaria	11.23	948	8 443 000
Finland	10.46	533	5 095 000
Republic of Korea	10.15	4 514	44 453 000
Belarus	9.94	1 029	10 355 000
Costa Rica	9.70	298	3 071 000
Ukraine	9.65	5 008	51 910 000
Republic of Moldova	9.52	414	4 350 000
Philippines	9.45	6 338	67 038 000
United States	8.95	23 330	260 651 000
Azerbaijan	8.93	667	7 472 000
Croatia	8.15	367	4 504 000
India	7.90	72 543	918 570 000
Romania	7.62	1 732	22 736 000
Israel	7.23	389	5 383 000
Western Samoa	6.10	10	164 000
Jordan	5.73	298	5 198 000
Slovenia	5.72	111	1 942 000
Italy	5.32	3 040	57 193 000
Denmark	5.05	263	5 205 000
Australia	4.88	875	17 931 000
Hungary	4.65	477	10 261 000
Chile	4.47	626	13 994 000
Slovakia	3.83	205	5 347 000
The former Yugoslav Republic of Macedonia	3.73	80	2 142 000
Marshall Islands	3.70	2	54 000
Austria	3.52	283	8 031 000
Sudan	3.46	1 002	28 947 000
Belgium	3.40	343	10 080 000
Malta	3.02	11	364 000
Turkey	2.93	1 794	61 183 000
Greece	2.86	298	10 426 000
Qatar	2.22	12	540 000
Scotland	2.20	113	5 132 400
Canada	2.04	596	29 248 000
Morocco	1.78	472	26 590 000
Singapore	1.74	51	2 930 000
Cyprus	1.63	12	734 000
Hong Kong, China	1.62	98	6 061 000
Egypt	1.51	871	57 851 000
England and Wales	1.41	726	51 439 203
Japan	1.40	1 746	124 793 000
Syrian Arab Republic	1.26	174	13 844 000
Madagascar	0.44	63	14 303 000

Numbers are rate by 100,000 recorded population of each country/area provided in UN Crime Survey.
Source: UNICRI, 1997, using data drawn from the *Fifth United Nations Survey of Crime Trends and Operation of Criminal Justice Systems*, unpublished report, Vienna, 1995.

Criminologists regard these homicide figures as among the most accurate and reliable of any official crime statistics.[6] Similar confidence does not exist in regard to many other categories of crime data. However, nations experiencing high levels of homicide are also likely to have high rates of non-lethal violence, including violence at work. The reverse is not necessarily true as has been noted in regard to the current situation in the United States: "workplace violence may, indeed, reflect societal violence in general. But even if societal violence appears to be stable or abating at the moment, the data on workplace violence are not adequate at this time to allow us to draw the same conclusion about it."[7]

Even within countries, rates of violent crime can differ significantly over time and according to region; rural and urban setting; the season of the year; and other variables. In Australia, for example, there have been significant changes in homicide rates over the course of the nation's history.[8] Current Australian homicide rates have remained relatively stable for several decades, and now equate with those which prevailed in the country at the turn of the last century.[9]

Violence can take many forms both in a workplace and in society at large. An argument between two employees in an enterprise that erupts into physical violence is far removed from an armed robbery of a financial institution which results in the shooting of a teller. A fight in a bar between two customers in which a manager intervenes and is injured involves very different circumstances from the predatory rape of a female employee as she travels home from her workplace. Any individual act of violence will clearly have a complex explanation.

Bearing in mind that the risk of violence depends on the interaction of a range of potential factors, the following have been identified as the most significant, listed in descending order of relative importance.

Violence risk factors

Child development and the influence of the family
- Families constitute the training ground for aggression. It is within the family that aggressive behaviours are first learned; to the extent that if families fail to instil non-violent values in their children, those children will be more likely to develop a repertoire of violent behaviours as they negotiate life in society at large.
- There are correlations between aggression in children and certain characteristics in their parents, notably maternal rejection and parental use of physical punishment and threat.
- Abusive parents themselves tend to have been abused or neglected as children, but only one-third to one-fifth of abused or neglected individuals will maltreat their own children.

Cultural factors
Norms of behaviour
- In general, the orientation of a culture, or the shared beliefs within a subculture help define the limits of tolerable behaviour. To the extent that a

---

[6] See in general Dobrin et al., 1996.
[7] See VandenBos and Bulatao, 1996, p. 16. See also Alvazzi del Frate et al., 1993.
[8] National Committee on Violence, 1990, pp. 17-20.
[9] See ibid., pp. 17-18; Mukherjee, 1981.

society values violence, attaches prestige to violent conduct, or defines violence as normal or legitimate or functional behaviour, the values of individuals within that society will develop accordingly.
- The use of violence to achieve ends perceived as legitimate is a principle deeply embedded in any culture. Violence on the sporting field, in the home and in school is tolerated by many people.

Economic inequality
- Violence is more common in those societies characterized by widespread poverty and inequality. Worldwide, those countries with high income inequality have the highest homicide rates.
- In most societies, both victims of violence and violent offenders are drawn from the most disadvantaged socio-economic groups.

Cultural disintegration
- The loosening of social prohibitions against violence may flow from feelings of alienation on the part of marginal members of society. This is particularly the case with a number of young people and with a large segment of indigenous populations.

Setting
- The physical characteristics of a location and the kind of activity occurring there can communicate that violence is more or less acceptable. A dilapidated environment has the potential to invite violence; a clean, modern setting can inhibit aggressive behaviour.

Gender
- Attitudes of gender inequality are deeply embedded in many cultures and rape, domestic assault and sexual harassment can all be viewed as a violent expression of the cultural norm.

Personality factors
- The best predictor of future aggression is past aggressive behaviour – aggressive children tend to grow into aggressive adults.
- Two personality traits often associated with violent behaviour are lack of empathy or regard for the feelings of others, and impulsiveness, or the inability to defer gratification.
- Hostile impulses in people with unusually strong internal controls – those referred to as the over-controlled personality – can result in extreme violence.

Substance abuse
- The suggestion that "drugs cause violence" is an oversimplification. The effect of a drug on an individual's behaviour is the product of a range of drug and non-drug factors which include the pharmacological properties of the substance in question, the individual's neurological foundation, personality and temperament, his or her expectations of the drug's effects, and the social setting in which the individual is located.
- Drug use and violent behaviour may result from a common cause – the inability to control one's impulses. Beyond this, drug use may compound the impairment of impulse control in an otherwise aggressive person.
- Alcohol – a close association exists between alcohol and violence, but the relationship is complex. It is probably less a result of alcohol's pharmacological properties, but rather more a product of co-existing psychological, social and cultural factors.
- Illicit drugs – except in the case of PCP (angel dust), and to a lesser extent amphetamines, violence is rarely associated with the pharmacological effects of illicit drugs. Of course, violence is frequently associated with the trafficking and distribution of these substances.

Biological factors
- Violent behaviour does not appear to be an inherited characteristic.
- Adverse perinatal experiences may indirectly result in violent behaviour.
- Autonomic nervous system dysfunction may lead to psychopathic behaviour.
- Hormones, particularly testosterone, may play a part in violent behaviour.
- Men are at least ten times more likely than women to be charged with violent offences, which indicates a real sex-based difference in behaviour, whether due to actual gender or to behavioural expectations arising from gender.
- Violence tends to be perpetrated most commonly by those aged between 15 and 30.

Mental illness
- Some forms of mental illness, notably paranoid schizophrenia, may occasionally result in violent acts, although prediction of violence in the mentally ill is regarded as extremely difficult.

Media influences
- Television viewing may be associated with subsequent aggression in some viewers. Research indicates that the relationship is bi-directional, that is, violence viewing gives rise to aggression and aggression engenders violence viewing.
- Video and film viewing may have the same effects as television viewing.

Peers and schooling
- The company of delinquent or aggressive peers may influence individuals to become aggressive.

Source: Adapted from National Committee on Violence, 1990, pp. 61-63.

In terms of long-term strategies to tackle the general problem of violence in any society, this list indicates that the most significant positive outcomes are likely to be achieved through a concentration on child development programmes linked to the family. It is within the family that aggressive behaviours are first learned. To the extent that families can instil non-violent values in their children, those children are more likely to negotiate life in society at large without resorting to a repertoire of violent behaviours.

From the perspective of preventing violence in the workplace, long-term strategies like these are obviously of great significance, just as are measures to deal with the range of cultural factors associated with violence. To the extent that a society values violence, attributes prestige to violent conduct, or defines violence as normal or legitimate or functional behaviour, the values of individuals within that society, and within that society's workplaces, will develop accordingly. Changing these values is clearly a formidable challenge to any society, but that challenge has been taken up in many parts of the world through broad-based programmes designed to reduce economic inequality; address problems of youth education and the marginalization of indigenous groups; and achieve gender equality.[10]

---

[10] The Australian NCV Report provides an example of an attempt to spell out a comprehensive national strategy to prevent or control violence. The strategy encompasses recommendations affecting public sector agencies like health and welfare, education, employment and training, housing, transportation, sport and recreation, aboriginal affairs and criminal justice. It also extends to private enterprise including specific industries like the media and the liquor trade; to non-government bodies like religious organizations and sporting authorities; and to professional and other groups including trade unions.

It will take time for many of the benefits of programmes in these various areas to have a widespread or macro-level impact, and to spread their influence to the workplace. Meanwhile, there are many ways in which positive micro-level change can be achieved through targeted programmes and actions within a particular society, and the workplaces of that society. Before considering these programmes and activities, however, it is necessary to examine more closely certain risk factors identified as being associated with violence, to see how they may interact to produce violence at work.

INDIVIDUAL BEHAVIOUR AND WORKPLACE VIOLENCE

"Workplace violence can be viewed as individual behaviour, with particular psychological roots and occurring in a specific situational context. Some writers have discussed workplace violence from this perspective. Most reports of this type specifically addressing workplace violence usually have been case-studies or accounts of personal experiences in workplace violence prevention, rather than systematic research on the interaction between personality and situational causes. Nonetheless, these reports provide useful leads."[11]

Research-based literature explaining the causes of workplace violence is very limited in its scope and disciplinary perspective, as this quotation from a recent American Psychological Association publication implies. Most of this literature focuses upon risk factors associated with individual aggressive and self-destructive behaviour, rather than upon what may be broadly termed social issues, and the link between the two. A useful framework which classifies these risk factors under these two broad heads is shown in the box below.

Classification of risk factors

1. **Individual**
    1.1 Psychosocial
        1.1.1 developmental factors
        1.1.2 mental illness
        1.1.3 individual histories of violence and criminal justice system involvement

    1.2 Biological
        1.2.1 genetics
        1.2.2 neurobiology and brain injury
        1.2.3 alcohol and other drugs

2. **Social**
    2.1 Macro-social
        2.1.1 socio-economic inequality
        2.1.2 access to firearms, alcohol and other drugs
        2.1.3 media influences
        2.1.4 other aspects of culture

    2.2 Micro-social
        2.2.1 gender and family violence
        2.2.2 situational factors

Source: Reproduced with permission from the Australian Institute of Criminology, from McDonald and Brown, 1997.

---

[11] VandenBos and Bulatao, 1996, p. 16.

A recent summary of the British literature on workplace violence reflecting this "individual behaviour" approach concluded that the most common features seemed to be:

- **Feeling aggrieved.** A sense of being treated unfairly, whether real or imagined, could lead to violence.
- **Being forced to wait, causing irritation and frustration.** An anger eliciting stimulus, perhaps from another person, could spark violence.
- **Perceived intrusions into private life.** Loss of self-esteem from reprimands, downsizing, layoffs and such like experiences could precipitate aggression.
- **Prejudice.** Whether racial or sexual, this could provoke violence against members of another group.
- **Staff attitudes.** Violence could occur if one staff member was seen as a threat to another.
- **Uncomfortable physical conditions.** These could contribute to the display of aggression.
- **Mental instability.** This may lead to aggressive behaviour.[12]

Significant efforts have been devoted by those seeking to explain violence in this way to predict also when an individual might behave in an aggressive manner. There is no doubt that certain identifiable factors do increase the likelihood that certain individuals and population groups will behave in such a way. These factors are to be found in both the long-term life experience of the people concerned, and in immediate, situational factors.

The fact remains that, when seeking to predict whether aggressive behaviour will occur, a distinction must be made between predicting at the level of the general population, or at that of the individual. The available evidence does permit statements to be made, with some degree of accuracy and reliability, about the heightened risk of violence at work being committed by population groups who display the following key characteristics:

- a history of violent behaviour;
- being male;
- being a young adult;
- experience of difficulties in childhood, including inadequate parenting, troubled relationships within the family and low levels of school achievement;
- problems of psychotropic substance abuse, especially problematic alcohol use;
- severe mental illness, the symptoms of which are not being adequately identified or controlled through therapeutic regimes; and/or
- being in situations conducive to self-directed or interpersonal violence, including having access to firearms.[13]

Each of these factors can interact with one another. They are also cumulative in effect – the more of these factors that a population group possesses, the higher the risk that the group may engage in violent behaviour. The dilemma remains, however,

---

[12] Hoad, 1996, pp. 64-86.
[13] Adapted from McDonald and Brown, 1997, p. 2.

of predicting with sufficient accuracy and reliability that a particular individual within that group may become violent. It is not possible in the current state of knowledge to predict with complete certainty that a specific person will behave in an aggressive way. Thus there is always the possibility, if prediction techniques are applied based on a list of key characteristics like those referred to above, that some individuals may be falsely identified as being at risk of committing acts of violence, and others of not being at risk.

These so-called "false positive" and "false negative" aspects of the prediction equation mean that these techniques, if considered for use in the context of the workplace, should only be applied with extreme caution and care. Enterprises and workers alike have a vested interest in ensuring that individuals who do represent a credible threat to the safety and well-being of the workplace are denied entry, or are provided with assistance to minimize the likelihood that they will behave aggressively, either towards themselves or others. There is, however, a clear potential for these predictive tools to be used in a prejudicial or discriminatory fashion, in order to exclude from the workplace undesirable persons, or even groups, who are judged to fit a loosely defined category or profile.

The case of Joseph T. Wesbecker

On the morning of 14 September 1989, Joseph T. Wesbecker, an emotionally disturbed employee on long-term disability leave from the Standard Gravure Company in Louisville, Kentucky, entered the plant in downtown Louisville and killed eight co-workers and injured 12 others with a semi-automatic "assault" rifle, before taking his own life with a pistol.

The facts surrounding Wesbecker's life and the events leading up to the tragedy were examined to determine the degree of "fit" to a model for the prediction of violent behaviour proposed by Monahan.*

Monahan, a leading authority in the field of dangerous and violent behaviour, has suggested that the following questions may assist in making a meaningful clinical assessment about a person's potential for violence:
- What events precipitated raising the issue of the person's potential for violence, and in what context did these events take place?
- What are the person's relevant demographic characteristics?: [A suggested profile given is of a non-white male in his late teens or early twenties, occupying a low socio-economic class, with a history of alcohol or drug abuse, a relatively low IQ, relatively less formal education, and a tendency to move or change jobs frequently].
- What is a person's history of violent behaviour?
- What is the base rate of violent behaviour among people of this person's background?
- What are the sources of stress in the person's current environment?
- What cognitive and affective factors indicate that a person may be predisposed to cope with stress in a violent manner?
- What cognitive and affective factors indicate that a person may be predisposed to cope with stress in a non-violent manner?
- How similar are the contexts in which the person has used a violent coping mechanism in the past to the contexts in which the person will likely function in the future?
- In particular, who are the likely victims of the person's violent behaviour, and how available are they?
- What means does the person possess to commit violence?

Although several of the predictors identified by Monahan demonstrated validity, several others did not.

Dr. Lee A. Coleman, the physician who treated Wesbecker for more than two years, met with Wesbecker just three days before the shootings. In hospital records obtained by the coroner's office, Coleman noted that Wesbecker exhibited "tangential thought" and "increased levels of agitation and anger... I encouraged the patient to go into the hospital for stabilization but he refused".

Furthermore, Wesbecker did not fit the demographic profile of a violent person.
- He had not previously engaged in violent behaviour at work.
- He did not have a police record of domestic violence, although he had been sued for harassment on two occasions by his first wife. He was found not guilty in both cases.
- He had shown a predisposition to cope with stress in a non-violent manner through at least two years of voluntary outpatient treatment; three occasions of voluntary hospitalization; filing grievances both through his union and with the county Human Relations Commission; and by discussing work problems with a labour attorney.

Wesbecker – although he was fatherless (his father was killed when he was about a year old) – grew up with his mother and grandmother and had lived in Louisville his entire life. He was married, had children, had no criminal record, did not abuse drugs or alcohol, had several friends, held his job at Standard Gravure for 17 years, and was financially secure.

However, certain of Wesbecker's thoughts and behaviours did conform closely to elements of Monahan's model:
- There were sources of considerable stress in Wesbecker's work environment. His divorce and lawsuits concerning his first marriage also indicated significant stress in his personal life.
- Although he demonstrated a willingness to manage stress in non-violent ways, both cognitive and affective factors indicated a potential to react to stress in a violent manner: psychiatric reports of anger, bringing a revolver to work, plans to kill company executives, and a bizarre scheme to blow up the plant with explosives attached to model aeroplanes.

The Wesbecker case underscores both the difficulty in predicting violence and the challenges that occupational mental health professionals face in minimizing acts of violence in the workplace.

Source: Adapted from: Kuzmits, 1990, pp. 1014-1020, with permission.

* Monahan, 1986, pp. 559-568, with permission.

The case of Joseph T. Wesbecker, described above, illustrates the lack of precision which still exists in the prediction of workplace violence, even when assisted by the application of a detailed clinical assessment tool. The present status of violence prediction efforts has been summarized in the following terms:

Violence can be predicted, meaning that within a given population we can assign different probabilities of violence to populations members based on the characteristics of these members. Nevertheless, there are significant concerns with validity, reliability and accuracy of predictions.[14]

---

[14] J. Chaiken et al., "Predicting violent behaviour and classifying violent offenders", in Reiss and Roth, 1993, Vol. 4, pp. 279-280.

INTERACTIVE MODEL AND EXPLANATION

It is suggested that a far more promising approach to an understanding of workplace violence is to be found in an interactive analysis of both individual and social risk factors, with particular attention being given to the situational context in which certain types of work tasks are performed. Analysis of this type is limited principally to a single study that also has attached to it a most valuable framework in which to consider violence at work. The study, conducted for the United Kingdom Health and Safety Executive by the London-based Tavistock Institute of Human Relations,[15] recognized that a number of factors could cause or contribute to a risk of violence at work:

> The problem may lie in the assailant, in that there may be something about him which makes him strike out at the employee. The employee may be partly to blame because of incompetence or because of an unsympathetic attitude, or the way the organization works may sometimes lead to misunderstanding or frustration.[16]

The Tavistock researchers then brought together in a framework or model the various factors they found to be relevant in explaining how an interaction between an assailant (perpetrator) and an employee (victim) produced a violent outcome in the workplace. This model, modified substantially, is displayed in figure 12.[17]

It should be emphasized that while the basic Tavistock model has been maintained, it has to a significant degree been expanded here in order to incorporate some of the issues explored earlier in this Chapter, and in Chapter 2, including the risk factors associated with the prediction of violence and the types of work task or situation recognized as having an increased vulnerability to aggressive acts. The model shown here also adds detail to the **outcome** or consequences of a violent interaction, linking the impact of the aggression back to the workplace, and to the victim and perpetrator.

The model requires more detailed elaboration under each of the principal headings shown.

PERPETRATORS

The assailant or perpetrator of the violence is likely to fall into three principal categories – a client of the particular enterprise; a colleague or fellow worker; or a stranger. The latter category will include those who intend committing a crime at the workplace, such as a bank robbery or armed hold-up of a retail establishment.

The nature and outcome of the interaction between these categories of perpetrator and victim will almost certainly differ according to the type of work being performed and the work environment itself. More will be said about this shortly. However, in most circumstances the key characteristics of the perpetrator that are most likely to be associated with a heightened risk of violence are those which were

---

[15] Poyner and Warne, 1988.

[16] ibid., 1988, p. 2. Bowie has also stressed the importance of this interactive approach in his analysis of ways of coping with workplace violence. See Bowie, 1996.

[17] See Poyner and Warne, 1988, pp. 2-7. A revised version of the model has also appeared in HSE: "Review of workplace-related violence", prepared by the Tavistock Institute for the Health and Safety Executive, *Contract Research Report*, No. 143/1997, London, 1997.

Figure 12.   Workplace violence: An interactive model

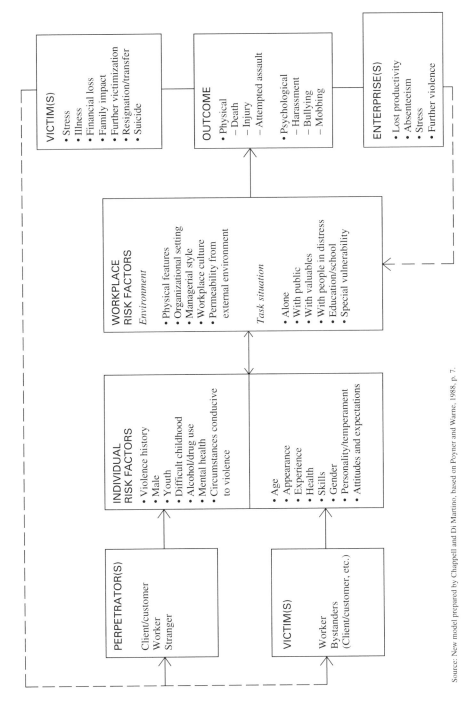

Source: New model prepared by Chappell and Di Martino, based on Poyner and Warne, 1988, p. 7.

mentioned earlier[18] – a history of violence; being male; being young; having a troubled childhood; substance abuse; certain forms of mental illness; and being in a situation conducive to violence.[19] The Tavistock study identified five characteristics, most of which overlap substantially with this list – personality; temporary conditions; negative/uncertain expectations; immaturity; and people with dogs.[20]

VICTIMS

There are many attributes of a victim of workplace violence, who is in most cases likely to be an employee, which could be associated with the risk of violence.[21] These include appearance, health, age and experience, gender, personality and temperament, attitudes and expectations.

Appearance and first impressions are important in any job, as they can set the tone of the interaction and establish the role characteristics for an encounter. In occupations involving direct contact with members of the public, for instance, the wearing of a uniform may encourage or discourage violence. Uniforms are often worn in occupations where employees are expected to act with authority or have the respect of members of the public. Uniforms also identify staff and distinguish them from the public. It is likely that in many circumstances uniforms will discourage violence, but there are situations in which the presence of uniformed staff is resented, and which can provoke abusive or violent behaviour. In the United Kingdom, for example, an increasing number of cases of aggression against ambulance staff has been reported because of general public hostility towards people wearing a uniform like those of police officers. For this reason, ambulance staff are now beginning to wear green boiler suits rather than blue uniforms, to distinguish them from law enforcement officials.

The health of workers can also influence how they interact with clients and the public at large. Stress from a heavy workload, or mild forms of mental illness, may lead to misunderstandings or misleading behaviour which precipitate aggressive responses. The age and experience of workers is another factor that can either increase or diminish the possibility of aggression. Previous experience of handling similar difficult situations, which is obviously associated with age, should enable workers to react more wisely than inexperienced staff.

As has been made clear earlier, a person's gender can influence aggressive behaviour in a number of ways. Men are more likely than women to respond in an ag-

---

[18] See box on "Violence risk factors", above.

[19] See McDonald and Brown, 1997, p. 2.

[20] See Poyner and Warne, 1988, p. 3. In the case of **personality**, the Tavistock researchers emphasized that some jobs involved contact with clients who may react more aggressively or violently, while **temporary conditions** referred to members of the public who were under the influence of alcohol or drugs, or who were suffering from some illness or stress which made their behaviour unpredictable or less controlled. **Negative/uncertain expectations** included people who anticipated an interaction which was to be difficult or frustrating, or who were uncertain about what to expect, and as a consequence were in a stressed and belligerent mood. **Immaturity** related to children or young people whose behaviour was less controlled than adults, and who in groups could be easily led or influenced to engage in aggressive behaviour. **People with dogs** reflected the phenomenon, perhaps exacerbated in Britain, of dogs biting postal workers and refuse collectors.

[21] The Tavistock study equated employees with victims. There are likely to be some situations, however, where workplace violence affects non-employees. An armed robbery during business hours of a financial institution, for example, could well result in the victimization of any customers present, as well as the staff of the enterprise.

gressive way to many workplace situations, while women are also at much greater risk of certain types of victimization at work than men.

The personality and attitude of workers is also relevant in considering risks of victimization. Some staff members are often better than others in handling difficult situations – a quality which is usually associated with an individual's less tangible personality characteristics and style of behaviour. The attitude of workers, and their job expectations, can also be factors influencing aggressive behaviours. For example, staff members who are working in an enterprise which is about to be shut down, or which is experiencing massive layoffs, are less likely to be tolerant in their encounters with clients. Similarly, uncertain role definitions associated with a particular job can influence how a violent or potentially violent incident is handled. Schoolteachers expect to deal with unruly children, but bus drivers may not; police officers anticipate encounters with disturbed or dangerous people, but firemen and other emergency service providers may not.

Overall, the ways in which victims react to aggressive behaviour appear to be important in determining whether that aggression diminishes or escalates. It seems to be important that the victim is not seen by the aggressor to behave in some unfair or unreasonable way. Anxious or angry behaviour by the victim may also trigger violence, while controlled behaviour may help defuse tensions.

ENVIRONMENT

Both the perpetrator and the victim interact at the workplace. The working environment, including its physical and organizational settings or structure and its managerial style and culture, can influence the risks of violence resulting from this interaction.

The physical design features of a workplace can be a factor in either defusing or acting as a potential trigger for violence. Australian research has shown, for example, that the levels of violent and destructive behaviour in or near licensed premises (pubs, clubs, bars and such like establishments) are influenced by a range of situational factors including the physical design and comfort of the premises. Overcrowded, poorly ventilated, dirty and noisy premises experience higher rates of violence than do those which exhibit good physical design features.[22]

The organizational setting appears to be equally if not more important in this respect. Poor organization may, for instance, lead to an excessive workload for a specific group of workers (while others may be relatively inactive), slow down their performance, create unjustified delays and queuing, develop negative attitudes among such workers and induce aggressive behaviour among the customers. The same effects may be induced by labyrinthine bureaucratic procedures, putting both employees and customers under serious stress.

In a broader context, the type of interpersonal relationship, the managerial style, the level at which responsibilities are decentralized, and the general culture of the workplace, must also be taken into consideration. A "participatory" working environment, for instance, where dialogue and communication are extensively exercised, may help defuse the risks of violence. In contrast, a "closed" authoritarian working environment where people work in isolation, with mutual suspicion and defensive attitudes towards external people, may increase the risk of violence.

---

[22] See Homel et al., 1992, pp. 679-697; Homel and Clark, 1994, pp. 1-46.

Along the same lines, the decentralization of services and responsibilities at a local level may help employees to become more aware of local issues and better respond to the needs of the customers, as well as to forecast difficult situations which might degenerate into violence. This would be quite difficult to achieve within a centralized, depersonalized organization where relationships are highly formalized. A company culture based on racial tolerance, equal opportunities and cooperation can also contribute to the establishment of a working climate where violence has little play. In contrast, if discrimination and segregation are explicitly or implicitly part of the culture of the company, this can be reflected in all behaviours and relationships, both internally and with the outside world.

The interrelationship between the external environment and the working environment also appears significant in terms of predicting violence. Although the "permeability" of the working environment to the external environment is far from automatic, it is evident, for instance, that a bank or shop located in a very dangerous area will be more likely to be subject to robberies; that bus routes will have different levels of risks of violence depending on which part of the city they serve; and that the level of frustration and aggression of the public in an office may vary according to the level of frustration and aggression in their living environment.

Any prediction of the possibility of violent incidents occurring at the workplace will thus depend upon a thorough analysis of the characteristics of the working environment, the external environment, and those of the perpetrator and victim in the particular situation. Each situation is a unique mixture and thus requires a unique analysis. That is why the prediction of specific acts of violence occurring is extremely difficult. Nonetheless, it seems possible and useful to identify, in much greater detail than has previously been attempted, a number of working situations which appear to be both highly relevant to an understanding of this type of aggression, and to the development of strategies for its prevention or control.[23]

SITUATIONS AT RISK

The data discussed in Chapter 2, and in particular those relating to workplace homicide, indicate that the magnitude of exposure to violence at work depends not only on a person's occupation, but also upon the circumstances or situations under which that person is performing their specific task or duty. As already mentioned, these "situations at risk" include those associated with working alone; working with the public; working with valuables; working with people in distress; working in education; and working in conditions of special vulnerability. Each of these situations requires separate analysis and discussion.

Working alone
The number of people working alone is increasing. As automation spreads in factories and offices, often accompanied by processes of rationalization of production and reorganization of the workplace, solitary work becomes more frequent. This trend extends outside the traditional workplace into the growing practice of subcontracting, outplacement, teleworking, networking and "new" self-employment. The push towards increased mobility and the development of interactive communication tech-

---

[23] Grainger, 1996, p. 17; Toohey, 1993.

nologies also favour one-person operations. Working alone full-time is only part of the picture. A much greater number of people work alone part of the time. In a survey among public employees in Canada, for example, nearly 84 per cent of respondents indicated that they *often* worked alone.[24]

Solitary work does not automatically imply a higher risk of violence. It is generally understood, however, that working alone may increase the vulnerability of the workers concerned. This vulnerability level will depend on the type of situation in which the lone work is being carried out. For the lone worker, a short cut down a back street may be perfectly reasonable in broad daylight, but might be asking for trouble on a dark night. Mail delivery may be a dangerous activity in a crime-infested area, while being completely safe in a crime-free district.

People can find themselves working alone in a wide variety of situations:

- **Working alone in small shops, petrol stations and kiosks**
  Such workers are often seen as an "easy" target by aggressors, and are therefore particularly exposed to violence. In the United States, petrol station workers rank fourth among the occupations most exposed to homicide.[25]
- **Working alone outside normal hours**
  Cleaners, maintenance or repair staff appear at special risk. For example, the cleaning sector, characterized by a large number of small enterprises and by precarious and unskilled work, is a typical case where women workers are frequently abused or harassed. These women are often migrant workers and, as such, particularly exposed to harassment and abuse both by superiors in the cleaning company and by someone in the client company.[26]
- **Journalists, especially investigative reporters, often work alone and appear to be exposed to violence in a great number of situations**
  The work of journalists may include investigations on criminal activities, on political corruption or on abuses among the army or the police, as well as field reporting from areas where wars, conflicts or unrest are taking place. In other cases, the very fact of asserting their ideas and their independence can put journalists at risk. At least 118 journalists were in prison in 25 countries at the end of 1998; in the same year, 24 journalists in 17 countries died because of violent incidents while on duty.[27]
- **Of lone workers, taxi drivers in many places are at the greatest risk of violence**
  Night-time is the highest-risk driving period for taxi drivers and, as in other types of violence, customer intoxication appears to play a role in precipitating violence. A 1993 Australian study of taxi drivers revealed that 81 per cent had experienced abuse, 17 per cent threats and 10 per cent physical attacks.[28]

---

[24] Pizzino, 1994, p. 15.

[25] See Chapter 2, table 11 above.

[26] International Confederation of Free Trade Unions (ICFTU), 1995, p. 2.

[27] *CPJ (Committee to Protect Journalists) Online*, "Attacks on the Press in 1998" (Web site: http:/www.cpj.org/news/1999/attacks98.html). Retrieved on 23 June 1999. See also Chapter 2 above.

[28] C. Mayhew, "Occupational violence: A case study of the taxi industry", in Mayhew and Peterson, 1999, Ch. 10.

Working in contact with the public

A wide variety of occupations and numerous working situations involve contact with the public. While in most circumstances this type of work can be generally agreeable, there are cases where exposure to the public can create a higher risk of violence.

Table 16, which is based on responses from 100 union representatives in the United Kingdom covering a total of 90,000 workers, provides an overall – though subjective – impression of the magnitude of violent incidents across a number of commercial and service sectors where workers came into contact with the public during the course of their work.

Table 16. Types of violent incidents experienced at work, by industry, United Kingdom, 1994, (percentage of workplaces)

Industry	Assaults	Threats	Verbal abuse	Sexual harassment[1]	Racial harassment[1]
Banking/finance	—	33	67	100	100
Civil service	40	100	100	—	—
Education	60	60	100	33	n/a
Health service	100	67	83	33	n/a
Local government	81	81	94	10	33
Passenger transport (buses)	73	55	73	17	50
Passenger transport (rail)	63	38	75	100	100
Postal services	50	100	100	—	n/a
Probation	100	100	100	100	50
Retail	45	50	56	14	—
Manufacturing	17	17	17	18	20
Other	50	33	33	20	—
All	54	54	65	27	41

[1] Figures given for workplaces where a breakdown of the workforce is given for women/black workers.

Source: With permission from Labour Research Department, *Bargaining Report* (London), No. 139, May 1994, p. 8.

The reasons for such violence are multiple, as has been suggested earlier in this chapter. In very large organizations, dealing with a large number of the general public, workers are likely to meet some individuals with a history of violence, dangerous mental illness or who are intoxicated. This "random" aggression is very difficult to predict and can lead to very serious incidents.

In other cases, violent behaviour may be provoked by or result from a perceived or poor quality of service. Violence may also be triggered by dismissive and uncaring behaviour by the worker providing the service, or be a more general attack on the organization itself, based on a general non-fulfilment of the wishes and expectations of the customer, which has nothing to do directly with the actual conflict at a particular moment.

- **Bus, train and subway workers appear at special risk**

  These workers are often the easiest target of blame for any inadequacy regarding the standard of transport. Disputes over the cost of fares, hooliganism and traffic accidents increase the risk of aggression against transport workers, while aggression against passengers and vandalism to property complete the picture. In Japan, for example, violence against railway station personnel and train personnel is reported to be increasing. In the six-month period from April to September 1994 a record number of 120 assaults (40 per cent more than the year before) were sustained by station staff and crew from passengers on Japan Rail East lines in the Great Tokyo area.[29] The numbers of assaults on bus crews in London as a percentage of passengers has also risen.[30] In Paris in 1997, stress "was becoming the first cause of occupational disease among RATP bus drivers. Over 600 of them (i.e. 5.8 per cent of a total of 9,936) had been put on 'temporary incapacity', in other words, off their buses for several months, for medical reasons. Half of that number had been rested from driving for 'psychological' reasons related to stress, insecurity and psychological difficulties."[31]

- **Flight attendants are also at risk**
  Sexual harassment appears to be substantial in the airline industry. A study conducted in Australia, for example, revealed that more than one-half of a sample of cabin attendants interviewed claimed to have been so harassed.[32] Non-sexual harassment is also common. Some air passengers are acutely aware of time, and aggression is not unusual under conditions of time anxiety. Alcohol abuse and the prohibition of smoking on board have often exacerbated the situation. Reports from Japan Airlines showed a steep increase of abuses and attacks on cabin crews, which almost tripled in 1996.[33] Air rage, as this form of violence is commonly known, is becoming a growing concern for airlines and their crews – a survey from the German airline pilots association, Cockpit, shows that in the 12 months to June 1998, there had been 1,252 cases of "unruly" passengers on German airlines. The spokesman for the association estimated that the number of cases is actually between 80,000 and 100,000, given the extremely low proportion of cases that are ever reported.[34]

- **For shop workers in the retail sector violence is a growing problem**
  Shopworkers can be exposed to violence from customers due to poor retail service or inferior products. Violence may also originate from customers who have grown impatient at checkouts, or who try to pay with illegal credit cards or to exceed their cash limit. Drunken customers wanting to buy alcohol can also pose a problem to shopworkers. The risks to staff are increased by late-night opening hours.[35] As noted earlier, the latest British Retail Consortium (BRC) survey of losses in the retail industry shows that more than 11,000 staff were subjected to

---

[29] *Mainichi Daily News*, 2 November 1994.

[30] Gibson, 1995, p. 8.

[31] *Libération*, 27 October 1998, p. 16.

[32] Swanton, 1989, p. 3.

[33] S. Young, "Crass causing bumpy flights", in *The Japan Times*, 6 August 1996, p. 3.

[34] J. Lovigno, "Air rage growing – Pilots say nicotine patches and less alcohol might help", in *Sightings* (Web site http://www.sightings.com/ufo/airrage.htm), retrieved on 6 July 1999. See also *Business Traveler Online* (New York), Special Reports: "Plane crazy", December 1999 (Web site http://www.btonline.com/cgi-bin/frontend.cgi?showlink~usbtonline~report~100014~.htm.), retrieved on 6 July 1999.

[35] *Tackling Violence at Work*, Background Report for the ETUC Health and Safety Forum, London, February 1993, p. 8.

physical violence in 1996, more than 98,000 threatened and another 242,000 subjected to verbal abuse. While the number of violent incidents represented a drop of 4 per cent on the previous year, threats and verbal abuse had increased by 9 per cent and 15 per cent, respectively.[36]

- **Workers providing social service are also exposed to high levels of violence at work**
  In this case, violence may be the final product of desperation and extreme marginalization of members of the public searching for a response to their pressing basic needs. Desperation does not automatically involve violence; however, it can pave the way for attitudes of revolt against what is felt to be unjust treatment, and eventually lead to abuse against the workers providing the service. In Canada, for example, 61 per cent of the social service and institutional workers in the province of Alberta reported having been verbally threatened, 42 per cent physically threatened and 30 per cent physically assaulted, according to a 1994 survey.[37]

- **Hotel, catering and restaurant staff are another "easy" target**
  The relationship with the customer is often considered a "personal" one, and any lack of commitment to the service, or insensitivity to the client's needs, may be perceived as a personal offence and lead to aggressive behaviour. Bar staff appear particularly exposed to assault by members of the public. A recent survey on the extent of violence in southern England's pubs revealed that 24 per cent of licensees felt "highly" at risk, and nearly another quarter felt themselves to be at risk "quite a lot". In 1995, 1,080 incidents were reported, of which around 600 involved weapons.[38]

Working with valuables and cash handling

Whenever valuables are, or seem to be, within "easy reach" there is a risk that crime, and increasingly violent crime, may be committed. Workers in many sectors are exposed to such a risk. At special risk are workers in shops, post offices and financial institutions, and particularly those who handle cash.

- **Thefts and robberies from shops are on the increase**
  Low numbers of staff, a lack of training and poor security measures compound the problem caused by such incidents. Small shops can be particularly vulnerable, especially at opening and closing times.[39] In 1991 alone, 1,530 hold-ups were carried out in shops and businesses in the Netherlands.[40]

- **Violence is reported to be a major problem in the postal service**
  A 1992 survey of postal workers from across Europe found that assaults and animal attacks accounted for nearly 17 per cent of all injuries – more than for falls, road traffic or lifting and handling accidents.[41] Within the postal services, delivery staff and letter carriers appear particularly exposed to crime. In the

---

[36] British Retail Consortium (BRC), *Retail Crime Costs – 1994/1995 Survey*, London, January 1996, p. 17.

[37] Pizzino, 1994, p. 6.

[38] Incomes Data Services Ltd., 1997, p. 17.

[39] ETUC, 1993, p. 8.

[40] Evers and van der Velden, 1993, p. 18.

[41] Postal, Telegraph and Telephone International, 1992, pp. 2 and 16.

United States, for example, according to the Postal Inspection Service, robberies of carriers increased almost fourfold (from 30 to 103) from 1990 to 1993.[42]

- **The number of criminal attacks on financial institutions seems to have risen sharply during recent years**

  In Denmark, Finland, Norway and Sweden the number of such robberies has almost doubled in the three years from 1989 to 1991, as noted earlier.[43] In London, bank raids and building society robberies in 1991 were double the figure for the previous year. Staff were facing increasingly violent attacks with nine out of ten robberies involving a weapon or a threat of violence.[44] There are signs, however, that the actual pattern of workplace violence is changing. The heightened security adopted by many banks and building societies in recent years has made them safer places in which to work. This is seen in figures from the British Bankers' Association, which reveal a decline in the number of bank raids. These fell from a peak of 847 in 1992 to 279 in 1995 and, although the total increased to 316 in 1996, this was still less than half of the 1993 level.[45]

- **For some workers, such as police officers and people employed in the private security industry, exposure to violence may be almost routine**

  Although these workers usually receive special training to cope with violence at work, the extent of such violence and the pace of its growth are such that coping becomes more and more difficult. This is particularly the case for police officers, frequently at the sharp end of violence-prone operations such as anti-drug operations, undercover work and anti-hostage/terrorist operations.

- In the private security business, the cash-in-transit sector is possibly the most susceptible to violence. In Western Europe, in 1993, approximately 50,000 employees working in 9,000 armoured vehicles were employed by nearly 200 specialized transportation firms in this sector.[46]

Working with people in distress

Violence is so common among workers in contact with people in distress that it is often considered an inevitable part of the job. Frustration and anger arising out of illness and pain, old-age problems, psychiatric disorders, alcohol and substance abuse can affect behaviour and make people verbally or physically violent. Increasing poverty and marginalization in the community in which the aggressor lives; inadequacies in the environment where care activities are performed, or in the way these are organized; insufficient training and interpersonal skills of staff providing services to this population; and a general climate of stress and insecurity at the workplace, can all contribute substantially to an increase in the level of violence.

---

[42] National Association of Letter Carriers (NALC), 1994, p. 11.

[43] ETUC, 1993, p. 5.

[44] Banking, Insurance and Finance Union, 1992, p. 1.

[45] Incomes Data Services Ltd., 1997, p. 3.

[46] ETUC, 1993, p. 8.

Health care workers are at the forefront of this situation:

- **Health care workers operating in emergency care units are at special risk**
  Fifty-six per cent of staff working in the emergency care unit of a major hospital in Barcelona (Spain) reported being exposed to verbal aggression by patients or their relatives.[47]
- **Psychiatric hospital staff are considered at high risk of violence**
  In psychiatric hospitals the majority of patients are usually not violent, and violent episodes are in most cases non-traumatic; however, some episodes of violence can be extremely severe.[48] In Sweden, psychiatric nurses are five times more likely to experience violence, and three times more likely to experience sexual harassment by patients, compared to nurses in other disciplines.[49]
- **Violence is also common in old-age care units**
  A study carried out in eight old-age nursing wards in Sweden in 1993 showed that 75 per cent of the medical staff reported having been exposed to threats, 93 per cent to minor physical violence and 53 per cent to severe physical violence during the previous 12 months.[50] A survey in 1992 conducted in seven aged care facilities in the city of Adelaide in South Australia found that 91 per cent of all staff and 96 per cent of all personal care attendants in these nursing homes or hostels stated that they had experienced aggressive behaviour from a resident.[51]
- **In drug abuse rehabilitation centres, violence can be the norm**
  In one of such centres in Manila (Philippines) violence and provocation occurred so often that they were described as "part of the way of life of the centre".[52]

Some idea of the overall spread and importance of violence towards health-care workers around the world is given in table 17.

Working in an environment increasingly "open" to violence

Working environments which traditionally have been quite immune from violence are becoming progressively affected. This worrying trend seems to reflect a general growth in community violence and unrest, and the collapse of a number of societal values.

Violence in school is part of this trend. Teachers have been exposed to the risk of violence for a long time. However, the level of risk to which they are now exposed in a number of countries is most disturbing.

- An alarming escalation of violence is taking place in several countries. In Canada, violent situations in schools occurred infrequently, and they tended to involve young people not attending school.[53] This situation is changing. An extensive 1993 survey of the Saskatchewan Teachers' Association showed that

---

[47] Nogareda Cuixart, 1990, p. 11.

[48] B. Bonnesen, "Violence and threats in psychiatric hospitals", in Bast-Pettersen et al., 1995, p. 21.

[49] Arnetz et al., 1994.

[50] A.-M. Bergström, "Threats and violence against health-care personnel", in Bast-Pettersen et al., 1995, p. 17.

[51] Beck et al., 1992, pp. 21-23.

[52] Interview with Dr. Acampada, National Center for Mental Health, Manila, 1995 (material provided by ILO Manila Office).

[53] King and Peart, 1992, p. 87. For a review of the contemporary situation in Australian schools, see House of Representatives Standing Committee on Employment, Education and Training, 1994.

Table 17. Violence towards health-care personnel, as shown in the literature around the world, 1981-94

Author/Year	Violence reported	Time period	Personnel category	Study size	Workplace studied
Lion et al., 1981	203 assaults	12 months	nursing staff	800	psychiatric state hospital
Adler et al., 1983	639 staff injured	72 months	all staff	–	private psychiatric hospital
Conn and Lion, 1983	62 incidents of physical violence	18 months	all staff	–	university hospital
Tardiff, 1983	384 assaultive patients	2 months	nursing staff	–	2 psychiatric hospitals
Ionno, 1983	87 assaults	6 months	all staff	–	private psychiatric hospital
Lanza, 1988b	67 assaults	$3^{1}/_{2}$ months	nursing staff	–	veterans' hospital
Carmel and Hunter, 1989	135 injuries = 16 injuries/100 staff	12 months	inpatient staff	–	forensic state hospital
Reid et al., 1989	197 assaults/ beds	12 months	staff, patients	–	27 psychiatric wards 29 non-psychiatric wards
Mahoney, 1991	36 per cent of nurses assaulted	12 months	registered nurses	1 209	149 emergency departments
Pane et al., 1991	686 police responses 7 incident reports	12 months	all staff	–	emergency department university hospital
Binder and McNeil, 1994	510 assaults	34 months	medical and nursing staff	203	short-term psychiatric unit
Graydon et al., 1994	199 nurses (reporting abuse)	last 5 days	nursing staff	603	3 hospitals
Yassi, 1994	242 injury reports (physical abuse)	24 months	all staff	–	teaching hospital

(–) indicates unavailable information

Source: J.E. Arnetz, *Violence towards health care personnel: Prevalence, risk factors, prevention and relation to quality of care*, doctoral dissertation, Stockholm, Karolinska Institutet, Departement of Public Health Science, Division of Psychosocial Factors and Health, 1998, p. 6.

66 per cent of teachers report having suffered abuse – either verbal insults, profane gestures, physical assaults or destruction of personal property – at the hands of students, parents, fellow teachers, administrators or others during their career. Sixty-five per cent of incidents reported for 1993 were verbal abuse or rude or obscene gestures; 18 per cent were physical abuse; and 17 per cent were damage to property. Seventy-eight per cent of teachers said they think school violence is growing. Seventy-one per cent said "the media contributes to the atmosphere which spawns abuse against teachers". Sixty per cent said teacher abuse is increasing in their school.[54] Attacks on teachers by students are reported in Japanese schools, with parents taking the initiative, in some schools, of monitoring classes on a daily basis.[55] In France, harassment in schools affects large numbers of staff – 15.3 per cent stated that they had been faced with hostile acts "each week or every day", while 61 per cent had suffered these "occasionally"

[54] Saskatchewan Teachers' Association, 1994, p. 3.
[55] *Mainichi Daily News,* 6 March 1995.

and only 14.4 per cent had "never" been harassed at work. The main harassers were pupils (36 per cent), management (21 per cent), colleagues (17 per cent) and parents of pupils (15 per cent).[56]

- **Schools in metropolitan areas, particularly in deprived areas, appear at special risk**
  In Detroit, Michigan, United States, attacks on public school teachers and other school employees jumped 900 per cent in the period from 1985 to 1990.[57]
- **Also in rural areas, often considered violence free, violence in school is on the increase**
  In Central America, women teachers, especially those working in marginal areas with a high delinquency rate, or in remote areas, are reported as to be vulnerable to social and sexual violence. They are also exposed to violence when commuting at night to attend training courses.[58]

Working in conditions of special vulnerability

Increasing numbers of workers are becoming involved in precarious and occasional jobs. Such workers are the majority of the employees in a growing number of enterprises, and some are likely to become exposed to violence because of their marginal status. In table 18 the findings from six large-scale studies on the distribution of occupational violence across some groups of precarious workers in Australia are presented. In most of these studies, more than one occupational group was surveyed (exceptions were young casual workers in the fast food industry and taxi drivers). All studies were based on face-to-face interviewing of randomly selected workers, and utilized a detailed questionnaire.

While the level of violence appears high for all occupations included in the table, and dramatic for occupations such as young casual workers in the fast food industry and taxi drivers, it is difficult to make generalizations about differences in levels of risk for precariously employed workers and regular employees doing the same jobs. The empirical data were limited, but there is a suggestion that occupational violence is higher in some cases (e.g. clothing outworkers, primarily because of their limited control over their job tasks; or among outsourced building workers, where competition was so high that competing deadlines increased levels of verbal abuse). However, in other cases (childcare), employees suffered higher levels of violence. In some of the smaller groups studied, the findings did not clearly indicate differences. The primary determinant of occupational violence seems to be the industrial sector of employment and the level of customer/worker contact, although power to control the labour process is likely to be an important mediating factor (and control is lower among precarious workers).

- **Immigrant workers and people of different ethnic origin experience a disproportionate share of violent incidents**
  In the United States, Blacks, Asians, Pacific Islanders and Hispanics incur a disproportionate share of workplace homicides, compared with their share of

---

[56] J.-Mario Horenstein et al., *Les pratiques du harcèlement en milieu éducatif*, Paris, Mutuelle Générale de l'Education Nationale, 1998, pp. 60-79.

[57] D. Nemeth, in *American Teacher* (Washington, DC, American Federation of Teachers), October 1992, p. 7.

[58] Martine, 1994, p. 64.

Table 18.   Occupational violence incidents experienced by 1,438 workers in selected occupational groups (percentage of each sample), Australia, 1993-98

Sectors/occupations	Year done	Total No. interviewed	Abuse	Threats	Physical attack	Held up or snatch and grab
Fast food industry						
Young casual workers	1998	304	48.4	7.6	1.0	2.3
Clothing industry	1997/98	200				
Factory-based workers			4.0	1.0	1.0	
Outworkers			49.0	23.0	7.0	
Building industry[1]	1997	331				
Contractors			8.0 (17.3)	2.7 (8.0)	2.7 (2.7)	
Cabinetmakers			13.3 (16.0)	6.7 (2.7)	1.3 (2.7)	
Demolishers			35.7 (23.5)	7.1 (5.9)	7.1 (–)	
Small businesses	1996/97	248				
(less than 5 employees)						
Garage (owners/managers)			9.7	4.2	–	
Café (owners/managers)			45.7	15.7	1.4	
Newsagency (owners/managers)			62.9	11.4	1.4	
Printing shop (owners/managers)			37.1	2.9	2.9	
Subcontracting, multisectoral[1]	1995	255				
Childcare			50.0 (15.0)	13.0 (2.5)	11.0 (–)	
Hospitality			57.0 (53.0)	46.0 (30.0)	11.0 (7.0)	
Transport			47.0 (13.0)	6.0 (13.0)	– (13.0)	
Building			15.0 (56.0)	– (17.0)	– (–)	
Taxi drivers	1993	100	81.0	17.0	10.0	

[1] The first figure shown in each line for the industry sectors in this study are for employees in the industry; the number in brackets is the comparable percentage for outsourced workers in the same industry sub-group.

Source: Adapted from C. Mayhew and M. Quinlan, *The relationship between precarious employment and patterns of occupational violence: Survey evidence from thirteen occupations*, paper presented at the "Health Hazards and Challenges in the New Working Life" conference, Stockholm, 11-13 January 1999.

total workplace fatalities and their employment share. Immigrants to the United States also have a high risk of homicides at work. This group comprises 25 per cent of the workplace homicide victims, and approximately 9 per cent of all workers.[59] Among Filipino workers overseas, 3,500 cases of maltreatment, physical abuse, rape, sexual abuse and sexual harassment were reported in 1994. More than 1,000 of such workers had to be repatriated because of this maltreatment.[60] For clandestine immigrants the risk is even higher. For these workers, abuse and maltreatment can be the rule rather than the exception, although given the nature of their employment relationships, evidence on the extent of violence at work for such workers is extremely difficult to obtain.

[59] Windau and Toscano, 1994, p. 1.
[60] ILO Manila Office, 1995.

- **Workers in export processing enterprises operating in free trade zones also experience exploitative conditions and exposure to violence**
  In such enterprises, an especially vulnerable workforce – largely composed of unskilled young people and women on precarious jobs – is often used in production processes dominated by a highly intensive workplace, poor working conditions and long working hours. Physical aggression and sexual harassment are part of this environment.[61]

- **Workers in rural areas and miners, particularly in developing countries, experience high levels of violence**
  The extent of such violence and its implications are beyond the scope of this report. Against a background of extremely deteriorated working and living conditions, of political and social exploitation, violence is often of the worst type – the poor against the poorer. Reports about rival groups of workers confronting each other over possessions, labour replacement in case of strikes, as well as on personal or tribal grounds, are frequent and alarming. In 1999, for example:

  A top South African mine union leader was beaten to death after angry miners attacked union officials during a meeting at one of the country's biggest gold mines, police and union officials said on Thursday. Selby Mayise, a regional chairman for the National Union of Mineworkers (NUM), was addressing nearly two thousand miners at the West Driefontein mine on Wednesday when the attack occurred. Irate over changes to their pension fund, the miners surged forward and attacked the union leaders, pelting them with stones and bricks. Mayise died from his wounds. Four other union officials were hospitalized and released on Thursday.[62]

  The following excerpts from *Mining Journal* (London) also refer to the situation in South Africa, but cases of violence related to mining activities are reported from other countries as well:

  The industrial unrest that broke out in December escalated into the current quarter and involved coercive behaviour including physical violence among employees. While there were only minor work stoppages, uncooperative employee attitudes prevailed. The Christmas break and the new public holidays also disrupted operations. These factors combined to cause a shortfall in underground production relative to targets and the previous quarter, *28 April 1995, p. 5*.
  Underground production was affected by the uneven and unsatisfactory manner in which employees returned to work following the violent unrest in the previous quarter. Replacements for those employees who resigned voluntarily as a result of the violence, particularly machine operators, were only in place halfway through the quarter. These problems were compounded by the Easter break, new public holidays and worker attitudes, *28 July 1995, p. 8*.
  Eleven miners were killed on 20 July during inter-tribal clashes at the East Driefontein gold mine in South Africa, and 29 others were seriously hurt. Mine spokesman Gavin Hepburn said that it was too early to determine the cause of the violence, and added that management and unions began talks on 21 July to try and resolve the problem. The South African police service has begun an investigation into the incident and has started patrolling the area to keep the feuding groups apart, *26 July 1996, p. 62*.

- **The most vulnerable group of all, children, are working by the millions, both in industrialized and developing countries, often exposed to physical and mental abuse**
  This may take several forms, but perhaps the worst kind involves separation from parents, isolation sometimes amounting to virtual imprisonment and physi-

---

[61] ILO, 1995, p. 33. Pérez and Valera, 1995, p. 31.
[62] *CNN interactive*, "Mob kills South African mine union leader", 13 May 1999, retrieved on 13 May 1999.

cal cruelty. This is the case for children who are traded, sold or employed as domestic servants. Such child workers may be subjected to harsh practices, including beating, starvation and sexual exploitation.

According to a 1990 survey in the United Republic of Tanzania, 5 per cent of housegirls had experienced physical abuse from their employing family and 76 per cent had been exposed to constant insults and abusive language.[63] Far from being an exception, violence against child domestic workers appears to be becoming increasingly widespread.

Abuse of domestic workers

Several studies show that, in Latin America, many men who grow up in homes with domestic workers have their first sexual encounter with a domestic worker. In Lima, Peru, one study estimated the proportion at 60 per cent. Whether there is an assumption that sexual availability is an unspoken part of a domestic worker's contract varies from culture to culture. In the view of one international NGO, the media's stereotypic portrayal of domestic workers as promiscuous is an important factor in their widespread sexual abuse in Latin America. In Fiji, 8 out of 10 domestic workers reported that their employers sexually abuse them. In Bangladesh, girl domestic workers may be returned home or married off at puberty. A study of 71 domestics in Bangladesh found that 25 per cent of the girls interviewed (average age: 11) considered that they had been sexually abused, and seven had been raped. Often families reject these 'spoiled girls' because 'their behaviour' has brought dishonour to the family. In these instances, domestic work typically becomes a precursor for prostitution, as the young girls have few other options available.

In one small-scale study in Calcutta, India, the majority of interviewees said they had experienced physical or psychological brutality. In the Philippines, co-worker violence is also reported, including sexual harassment from male-co-workers. Quantifying the brutality endured by child domestics is difficult, as few will be bold enough to say anything about it except to a trusted confidante. Cases in which domestic workers suffer gross abuse and violence are occasionally reported in the press. NGO newsletters document a steady stream of individual cases of severe abuse perpetrated against both girl and boy domestic workers.

In South Asia, violence often takes the form of attack by a hot iron. In Sri Lanka, lawyers have spoken openly about the extreme violence used against child domestic workers, and in the Juvenile Court in Colombo cases have revealed brutality by employers towards their child domestic workers including branding, dousing in boiling water, rubbing chilli powder on the mouth, beatings and stabbings. Deaths caused by starvation, burning and forcing excessive intake of salt have also been reported.

Source: UNICEF, "Child Domestic Work", in *Innocenti Digest*, Florence, May 1999, p. 8.

Children working on the street are at very special risk. This includes not only exposure to a hazardous social environment, but also being an easy target for all forms of violence. When involved in marginal or illegal activities, and thus coming into contact with the world of crime, violence against children is dramatic.[64]

---

[63] Sheikh-Hashim, 1990.
[64] Black, 1993, pp. 7, 15 and 22.

Abuse of street children

Children who live and work on Bulgaria's streets support themselves by begging, performing odd jobs for shopkeepers, gathering waste materials for recycling, prostitution, and theft. Many of the children are addicted to glue or liquid bronze which they inhale from plastic bags. As a result, street children are viewed by police and private citizens as criminals. Their Roma identity further reinforces this image; Roma are often perceived by the Bulgarian public to be a criminal element of society. For these reasons, street children are often subject to violence and abuse at the hands of both skinheads and police. Police often harass and abuse the children because they perceive them to be criminals, and skinhead gangs attack and beat the children because of their Roma identity.

Source: Human Rights Watch, "Children of Bulgaria – Police violence and arbitrary confinement", report prepared for the United Nations Committee on the Rights of the Child, New York, 1996.

Children are also the victims, in war zones, of forced labour and forced recruitment in military or paramilitary groups. The most appalling forms of violence and violations of basic human rights became the norm in this kind of situation.

Abuse of children in war zones

Children are stolen from their families during military raids by government forces on villages in war zones. They are then taken by soldiers to their homes in western and northern Sudan, where they are threatened with beatings and forced into unpaid labour – essentially, child slavery. One not unusual case among many which Human Rights Watch/Africa has documented is the case of a Dinka girl who was captured in a government raid on her village in Bahr el Ghazal when she was six. She then spent six years with a family in northern Sudan, where she was beaten, forced to go hungry, branded, and made to work long hours without pay doing housework and herding animals. Her identity was even denied her, as she was given a new name. Consequently, she did not recognize her older brother when he finally tracked her down. It took two more years of litigation to officially "free" her from her "master".

Source: World Vision International, "Sudan – Cry, the divided country", *Policy Papers*, issue No. 1, Monrovia, California, Sept. 1996, p. 3.

OUTCOME

The final issue to be considered within the framework of the interactive model is the outcome or consequences of any violence which occurs at the workplace. At the most extreme levels of violence, as in the case of the shootings at Dunblane and Port Arthur, this outcome can amount to death and destruction of a form normally only seen and to be coped with on a battlefield, or in a war zone.

For the survivors of such violence, including those workers responding to provide emergency care and assistance as well as witnessing the events, the personal trauma and distress involved can be both extreme and long lasting. As mentioned earlier, in the case of the Port Arthur shootings, an official inquiry reported that some 500 visitors were within the historic site at the time of the massacre, in addition to more than 30 members of the staff of the national park. A large number of police, local fire units, ambulances and other official emergency groups also became involved. The inquiry observed that the incident was a very heavy drain on the health and well-being of many individuals, including the park staff who were employed by a government statutory authority.

Port Arthur Inquiry: Long-term consequences

The inquiry has particularly investigated the problems associated with the staff members of the Authority who have been so adversely affected by the shootings. These staff included those who were affected by the event, but have been able to return to work, those who have decided that they can no longer return to the site and therefore have resigned, or have been placed in rehabilitation jobs generally in the Hobart area, and a small, but desperately affected group, who have not been able to return to their previous duties and, indeed, may never do so because of health reasons. The inquiry is concerned that some of this group may never be able to again lead a full and active life within society.

It must also be fully understood that such devastating disabilities that affect this group individually, also have tragic and ongoing adverse affects on their family members and friends. Submissions have shown that whole families have been affected, including areas of:

- marriage breakdowns;
- financial hardships;
- suicidal tendencies of those affected and by children of the victims of this crime;
- inability to become involved in social activity;
- terror of noise, and so on...

There is no doubt that some victims and their family members will be burdened by the shooting for many years. Accordingly, special funds must be made available to provide ongoing assistance with medical and health service provision. Where families have had to be relocated away from Port Arthur, again some assistance should be available to help with the sale of existing homes, purchase or leasing of new residences, and the legal costs involved in such transactions.

A further area to be considered is that where the husband and/or wife of a victim is forced to take up full-time care activity of that victim and family. The loss of a regular wage or salary cannot be compared with a Carer's Assistance payment, and some financial assistance is necessary, at least in the interim period, to address the difference in quantum.

There is a real need for these staff members who, as yet, have not been able to return to work at the Historic Site, to be assured of their positions. During the past 12 months, many changes have occurred in the operational structure of the Site, and there is a feeling that the jobs of those who will eventually return have been lost. Such thoughts of lost job security is adding stress to already affected people.[65]

This account of the aftermath of the Port Arthur shootings on the personal and working lives of the park staff shows how widespread and devastating the consequences of such a tragedy can be. It is now well recognized, and reflected in the "best practice" case examples discussed later in this report, that timely and professional

---

[65] Joint Parliamentary Group, 1997, pp. 55-57.

counselling and other forms of assistance can do much to alleviate the post-traumatic stress and other problems frequently experienced by survivors of violence. It is important to note that the impact of almost any incident of violence in the workplace can affect not only the immediate victim(s), but also the surrounding workplace. There is, in essence, a feedback loop produced by such violence, which can be reflected in lost productivity, absenteeism and other negative consequences for the enterprise as a whole. That feedback loop may even extend to the perpetrator. Where that person is a fellow worker, and the victim has to resume normal duties at the workplace, the risk of further violence occurring may be exacerbated if remedial action is not taken. This type of situation is not uncommon, as earlier references in the report to the circumstances surrounding sexual harassment, bullying and mobbing behaviours at the workplace have shown.

TOWARDS FINDING RESPONSES

The need for remedial action applies not only to workplace violence involving fellow workers, but to all forms of this extremely perplexing, pervasive and pressing problem. The various forms that this remedial action either can or should take is the subject matter for discussion in Part II of this report.

Part II: Responding to violence at work

LEGISLATIVE AND REGULATORY INTERVENTIONS

4

Legal responsibility: The Cullen Report

The principal legal basis for the [employers'] responsibility for the protection of staff against violence which they encounter in the course of their work lies in section 2 of the Health and Safety at Work Act, 1974, under which every employer has "to ensure, so far as is reasonably practicable, the health, safety and welfare at work of all his employees". This duty is not confined to the physical working environment, but covers also the provision of information, training and supervision. Subsection (3) of section 2 supports the main provision by imposing a duty to prepare and issue a statement of policy, and the organization and arrangements for carrying it out...

It is important that there should be no misunderstanding as to the persons on whom the legal responsibility for safety, and hence the responsibility for seeing that action is taken, lies. An employer may delegate the performance of various functions to others, but he cannot delegate his responsibility under the Health and Safety at Work Act.

In Scotland the employer in regard to schools is the local authority, except in the case of self-governing schools, where the employer is the board of management: and in the case of independent schools, where it is the proprietor. In England and Wales the position in regard to legal responsibility is different.[1]

Compensation rights: The Doyle Report

In many of the cases the amount [of compensation] has been minimal and has not been sufficient to meet the costs involved in medical, health and legal costs associated with the recipient. Therefore, there is a need for the Authority and the Government to be aware of the personal difficulties of many of those affected by the tragedy, and to be prepared to address any special cases that may arise in the future.

Other sources of compensation are available through the Criminal Injuries Compensation Legislation and also through the Attorney-General's Discretionary Fund. This information should be made available to those who may be able to seek assistance through such funds.

There should be no doubt in anyone's mind that the Port Arthur tragedy and its ongoing effects on the health and lives of families will be comparable to [the situation for] veterans of the Vietnam War, where stress and trauma-related issues are still causing misery and family discomfort after some 30 years.

---

[1] Cullen, 1996, p. 135.

> The Commissioner has been made aware that prior to the April incident, the site did not conform to the requirements of the Workers' Rehabilitation and Compensation Act, because it did not have a Rehabilitation Policy in place. It is understood that this issue is being addressed by the Authority.
>
> It may be that the State's Workers' Compensation Legislation may need to be considered so that such legislation is not proven deficient in addressing such an event as the Port Arthur tragedy.[2]

LEGAL RESPONSIBILITIES AND RIGHTS

An important part of the terms of reference of the official inquiries into both the Dunblane and Port Arthur shootings involved consideration of the various legal responsibilities and rights of those involved.[3] As can be gathered from the two brief excerpts taken from the reports of these two inquiries, these responsibilities and rights can arise under a range of quite complex and diverse statutory and regulatory provisions. They are provisions which touch upon difficult questions of criminal as well as civil law; on health and safety at work legislation; on workers rehabilitation and compensation statutes and policies; and on environmental and labour law.

The reports which have emerged from the Dunblane and Port Arthur inquiries each contain, within the constraints of their individual terms of reference, an appraisal of the strengths and weaknesses of the legal regimes established in these two jurisdictions relating to violence at work.[4] They are regimes which, like their counterparts in most parts of the world, have until now responded to this form of violence within the broader band of protective legislation and regulation surrounding the workplace at large. At present only two countries – Sweden and the Netherlands – have enacted specific and comprehensive statutory measures regarding violence at work.

These Swedish and Dutch measures reflect a growing consensus that the magnitude of the problem of violence at work is such that it now demands a much more concerted and focused legal response. The general nature and scope of this quite recent legal development is traced in this chapter, drawing upon examples taken principally from the statute books and regulations of a number of industrialized nations who have been leaders in the field.

LEGAL AND REGULATORY EXPANSION

Criminal law

The criminal law has long been used as a principal bulwark against the commission of acts of violence in all locations, including the workplace. Those who have failed to be deterred by the threat of punishment for traditional crimes of violence like homicide, rape, robbery and assault have, if caught and convicted, been subjected to personal sanctions by the criminal justice systems involved. In most cases these systems

---

[2] Joint Parliamentary Group, 1997, p. 58.

[3] Although quite widely framed, the Cullen Report's findings and recommendations dealt principally with firearm regulation, and the safety and security of schools, rather than traversing broader issues regarding the causes and prevention of violence. The Report also makes no mention of measures which should be taken to assist the survivors of this tragedy – an issue which formed the main thrust of the terms of reference and the recommendations of the Doyle Report on Port Arthur.

[4] Both are common law jurisdictions, although the Scottish legal system has also been influenced by the civil law.

have regarded crimes of violence as meriting some of the most severe sanctions available, ranging in many jurisdictions from the death penalty for murder, to lengthy terms of imprisonment for rape and robbery.[5] Harsher punishment has also commonly been prescribed for offences involving violence directed at certain workers while acting in the course of their duty, such as police, corrections officials or judicial officers.[6]

In recent years a significant change has taken place in community attitudes towards violence occurring in the context of the family, and sexual assault. Linked closely to the movements to advance women's rights and those of children, behaviour which has in the past gone largely unreported and unpunished in many countries has now become a matter of widespread attention and action under criminal law and criminal justice.[7]

These developments have also had an influence and impact at the workplace, providing a fresh impetus to apply the protection of assault laws to sexual and non-sexual violence occurring in the context of employment, as well as bolstering efforts to combat such violence in the wider community. In addition, they have prompted some jurisdictions to broaden their criminal law regarding violence to encompass harassment and allied activity.[8]

In the United Kingdom, for instance, recent legislation has made it a criminal offence to pursue a course of conduct which amounts to harassment of a person. Although not directed specifically at violence at work, the legislation is of sufficient breadth to cover harassment at this and many other locations.[9] In France legislation was enacted along similar lines in 1992, although the French provision on abuse of authority and sexual matters in employment relations does make specific mention of sexual harassment in the workplace as a penal offence, punishable under both the Labour and Penal Code with imprisonment and fines.[10]

Civil and common law

Both the civil and common law systems provide important bases for legal action and avenues of redress for victims of workplace violence. Here too the scope of protection is broadening progressively. In Paraguay, for instance, new provisions in the

---

[5] In Scotland, where the Dunblane massacre occurred, and in Tasmania, which was the location of the Port Arthur shootings, the death penalty was abolished many years ago, and the maximum penalty for murder is life imprisonment.

[6] Penalties have also tended to be more severe, both in criminal statutes and in the sentences imposed by the courts, where an offender is armed at the time of committing a violent crime.

[7] For example, Article 19 of the UN Convention on the Rights of the Child provides that:

"1. States Parties shall take all appropriate legislative, administrative, social and educational measures to protect the child **from all forms of physical or mental violence, injury or abuse, neglect or negligent treatment, maltreatment or exploitation, including sexual abuse, while in the care of parent(s), legal guardian(s) or any other person who has the care of the child.**

2. Such protective measures should, as appropriate, include effective procedures for the establishment of social programmes to provide necessary support for the child and for those who have the care of the child, as well as for other forms of prevention and for identification, reporting, referral, investigation, treatment, and follow-up of instances of child maltreatment described heretofore, and, as appropriate, for judicial involvement."

The Convention was adopted by the UN General Assembly on 20 November 1989.

[8] For an excellent and comprehensive account of the development of contemporary legal provisions concerned with sexual harassment in employment, see Aeberhard-Hodges, 1996, pp. 499-533.

[9] Protection from Harassment Act, No. 40, 21 March 1997.

[10] Act No. 92-1179 of 2 November 1992 amending the Labour Code and the Code of Criminal Procedure.

United Kingdom: Protection from harassment legislation, 1997

Harassment: It is an offence for a person to pursue a course of conduct – involving conduct on at least two occasions – which he or she knows or ought to know amounts to harassment of another person. It is not necessary to show an *intention* on the part of the harasser to cause the victim to feel harassed: the prosecution has only to prove that the conduct occurred in circumstances where a reasonable person would have realized that this would be the effect. "Harassment" expressly includes "alarming the person or causing the person distress", and "conduct" includes speech.

It is a defence for the harasser to show that the course of conduct was pursued for the purpose of preventing or detecting crime; it was pursued under statutory authority; or, in the particular circumstances, the pursuit of the conduct was "reasonable".

A person guilty of the offence of harassment is liable on summary conviction to a term of imprisonment not exceeding six months, or a fine, or both. The court has the power to make a restraining order immediately after convicting a person of the offence.

Civil remedy: An actual or apprehended commission of the offence of harassment can be the subject of a claim in civil proceedings by the person who is or may be the victim of the course of conduct in question. An order restraining the harassment and/or damages can be sought.

Offence of putting people in fear of violence: A "higher-level" offence has been created – punishable by up to five years in prison, or an unlimited fine, or both – where a person pursues a course of conduct which he or she knows or ought to know causes another person to fear, on at least two occasions, that violence will be used against him or her. Once again, a convicting court has the power to make a restraining order (but in the case of this offence, the Act does not provide for the possibility of civil action by the victim).

The above measures apply to England and Wales only, but the legislation contains separate provisions appropriate to the law in Scotland.

Source: Based on an analysis of the Protection from Harassment Bill, in *Industrial Relations Law Bulletin* (London), No. 560, January 1997, p. 4.

Labour Code include sexual harassment among violent behaviours which can lead to justified termination of employment.[11]

- In the United States, at least 15 state jurisdictions recognize the tort of negligent hiring that holds an employer to a duty of reasonable care in selecting employees, thus precluding the hiring of persons who may present dangers to other workers and the public. Employers may be found negligent, for example, for failing to conduct a proper background investigation, such as checking references and contacting former employers, which would have shown that a job applicant had a propensity for violence.[12]

---

[11] Law No. 496/95, art. 81, inc. w and art. 84, inc. d, in *Gaceta Oficial* (Asunción).

[12] Some recent and somewhat disturbing examples of failures to check the background of employees come from the following media report: "❐A routine police inquiry disclosed that a private guarding company was employing an individual using a false name. It turned out that not only had he escaped from prison, but was a convicted murderer. The company had employed the man without any background checks. ❐ Police investigating a theft suspected a private security guard, and conducted a

(Continued on page 87)

American courts have in certain circumstances recognized as a valid cause for action an employer's negligent training of its employees that results in injury to a third person. An employer may also be liable in the case of retaining an employee who has demonstrated a propensity for violent behaviour. In other decisions American courts have recognized liability for an employer who should have taken reasonable care in supervising an employee who threatens others with violent behaviour. The courts have also held employers responsible for the murder of employees by outside perpetrators, where security measures at the workplace were found to be inadequate.[13]

- In the United Kingdom, the TUC urges affiliates as follows:

Unions need to take a lead in workplaces on violence, not only expressing the fears and concerns of working people, but also pressing employers to accept that it is their legal responsibility to prevent violence in exactly the same way as they would address any other threat to health and safety.[14]

- In Australia, a recent case (Burazin v Blacktown City Guardian Pty. Ltd.) proposed enlargement of the scope of the employment contract which would include an implicit obligation on the employer to ensure that the contract:

will not, without reasonable cause, conduct itself in a manner likely to damage or destroy the relationship of confidence and trust between the parties as employer and employee. (Burazin v Blacktown City Guardian Pty. Ltd. 142 ALR 154).

Further argumenting, the judge indicated that:

As the very purpose of the implied term is to protect the employee from oppression, harassment and loss of job satisfaction, it is difficult to see why it should not be regarded as a term designed "to provide peace of mind or freedom from distress." (Burazin v Blacktown City Guardian Pty. Ltd. 142 ALR 154).

This case is seen as offering important new opportunities in the use of civil remedies against all types of violence at work.[15]

As employers in general attempt to prevent workplace violence and meet obligations to provide a safe workplace, they often seek to identify and "weed out" potential problem employees. Various methods may be employed, such as questionnaires and interviews, conducting background checks, polygraph tests, alcohol and drug tests, psychological or personality tests and honesty tests. In doing so, however, consideration must also be given to privacy rights, which can limit the method chosen or the

---

full check on all 26 employees at his company. Eleven were found to have previous convictions for a total of 74 crimes, including rape, threats to kill, illegally possessing guns, burglary and assault. The firm's directors were not aware of their staff's criminal backgrounds. ❐ The managing director of one company gave a reference to support an employee's application for a shotgun certificate. The director said he had known the man for a year, he had a "sociable nature and a good and even temperament", and was "an honest and very reliable person who can be trusted". Police inquiries showed he had 15 convictions for dishonesty and violence, and one for the manslaughter of his wife while attempting to carry out an illegal abortion. ❐ A man with previous convictions for theft, deception and stealing cars was released from prison after serving time for driving while disqualified. He then set up his own security company, installing intruder alarms, security lighting and CCTV. ❐ A private security guard working at a court was found stealing money from a judge's handbag in his own Chambers", in *The Guardian*, 16 July 1997.

[13] Littler et al., 1994(b), p. 11.

[14] TUC, *Violent times*, London, 1999, p. 7.

[15] Oonagh Barron, *Bullies, media and the law*, paper presented at the *Bullying at Work 1998 Research Update Conference*, at Staffordshire University, United Kingdom, 1 July 1998, Carlton, Victoria, Australia, Job Watch Inc., 1998 (October).

way it is implemented. Employers who do not exercise due care in finding out about a person who may have a history of violence could be liable for negligent hiring or failure to provide a safe workplace. On the other hand, employers face restrictions on seeking information which could be considered an invasion of a person's privacy or be discriminatory. Thus in many situations it will be necessary to balance the duty to protect employees from a violent individual, and to provide a safe working place, with an individual's right to privacy.

Psychological tests and other background checks to exclude "unstable" or unfit employees may lead to disability discrimination under the Americans with Disabilities Act or the Rehabilitation Act of 1973. Employers may be considered liable for racial discrimination under Title VII or equivalent state laws when their screening practices have a disparate impact on a protected class. In addition, inquiries into arrest records during background screening have been held to violate Title VII of the Civil Rights Act because of their negative impact on minorities.[16]

Caught between violence and ADA compliance

Companies face a Catch-22 when an employee with a psychiatric disorder poses a risk of violence: they must comply with the Americans with Disabilities Act (ADA) while also maintaining a safe workplace, according to *Fair Employment Practices*, published by Bureau of National Affairs, Washington, DC.

The dilemma: employers may be considered liable for discrimination if they dismiss workers who have mental disabilities. Under the ADA, employers cannot discriminate against such employees unless they pose a "direct threat" to someone's health and safety that cannot be solved with a reasonable accommodation. But if the company does not dismiss the worker, because the actual or threatened misconduct does not amount to a direct threat, co-workers or other injured parties may charge the employer with negligence.

Strong policies against workplace violence are one safeguard, says *Fair Employment Practices*. For example, employees who violate such policies may not be fit for duty, even if the violation is due to a disability. That's the tack taken by Wells-Fargo. The bank's workplace violence policy calls for the immediate dismissal of employees who engage in bodily harm, physical intimidation or threats of violence.

Employers also can protect themselves and their workers by asking a professional to evaluate an employee who exhibits disruptive behaviour. If a suit is later brought under the ADA, a court will see that the employer made an effort to comply with the law and protect its workers, says the newsletter.

Source: Reprinted by permission of the publisher, from *HR Focus* (New York, American Management Association), March 1996, p. 19. Web site http://www.amanet.org. All rights reserved.

Employment injury legislation

This type of legislation, including social security or workers' compensation, is generally the exclusive remedy for work-related injury and disease occurring during, or arising from employment. Whether or not injury from workplace violence is covered by specific employment injury schemes will depend on the interpretation of their particular legislative provisions. In most situations, incidents of workplace violence involving assault and bodily harm are likely to be covered, although there may be

---

[16] National Clearinghouse for Legal Services, 1994.

exceptions, as in the case of a quarrel between employees that is purely personal, or if the injured employee is the original aggressor.

An important and general issue for victims of violence is whether mental stress (even in the absence of physical injury) is compensable. Since violent incidents at the workplace can produce stress reactions or have other psychological consequences, compensation for lost days of work or special counselling can be a significant issue for workers who are the victims of such violence or who witness violent incidents. Thus, until recently all Australian workers' compensation jurisdictions, for example, recognized stress related to workplace violence as a form of compensable injury. However, the state of Victoria has now legislated to severely restrict payment of compensation for stress-related conditions. Coverage for workplace violence in that state is therefore problematic.[17]

Companies in the United States are facing – and losing – an increasing number of compensation claims from employees suffering from job-related stress. Employees who have not traditionally filed such claims, such as white-collar workers, women and younger employees, are expected to do so in greater numbers.[18] A study by the California Workers' Compensation Institute (CWCI), citing Californian data, showed a 700 per cent increase in workers' compensation claims for mental stress between 1979 and 1988.[19] Even in countries such as Canada, where the compensation stakes for many workers are not as high as those in the United States because of the extent of that nation's social security coverage, stress-related compensation claims are becoming more frequent and the subject of growing discussion and concern.[20]

Rights to compensation in Quebec

The Occupational Accidents and Diseases Act aims to provide compensation for occupational injuries and their consequences for beneficiaries. A wide definition is used because some kinds of injury are not covered by the Act. In fact, indemnities are payable for psychological injuries if they are termed as occupational injuries, accidents or diseases or relapses/recurrences, or injuries covered by article 31 of the Act if it is deemed to be work-related.

Therefore, in the first instance the existence of an injury has to be proved. When blows are exchanged or weapons used between workers, that is clearly physical violence, but psychological violence is more discreet. The symptoms are apparent enough, but psychological violence leaves no visible scars, so it is more difficult to prove. The worker can thus suffer stress, anxiety, distress, hypertension, depression, temperamental troubles, post-traumatic shock and even psychosis, without allowing one to identify an occupational injury. However, compensation is in proportion to the proof of injury, which requires clear and strong evidence. The worker's perception is not enough: he/she has to prove a strong causal link between the psychological damage done and the harassment.

Speech by Maître Marie-Christine Dufour, during a forum given by the Continuing Training Board of the Quebec Bar, 21 Feb. 1997, Île Charron.

Source: Lucie Desjardins: "Violence en milieu de travail : Les victimes sont rarement indemnisées", in *Le Journal du Barreau* (Québec), Vol. 29, No. 6 – 1 April 1997 (Web site: http://www.barreau. qc.ca/journal/vol29/no6/).

---

[17] See Toohey, 1993, p. 14 (unpublished paper). In other countries the trend is towards a growing recognition of compensation for occupational stress.

[18] La Van et al., 1990, pp. 61-64.

[19] Barth, 1990, p. 358.

[20] Lippe, 1990, pp. 398-399.

Health and safety legislation

In most countries, a duty of care is placed on employers for supervising and taking appropriate measures to protect workers and to prevent accidents, health hazards and dangerous situations. Although not addressed to workplace violence in particular, this type of legislation is, in a growing number of countries, considered to impose on employers an obligation to provide a violence-free workplace.

In the United Kingdom, as the Cullen Report has emphasized, employers have a legal duty under Section 2(1) of the Health and Safety at Work Act 1974 to ensure, so far as is reasonably practicable, the health, safety and welfare at work of their employees. This duty can be extended to protecting employees from violence. Further, the Management of Health and Safety at Work Regulations 1992 require employers to undertake a "suitable and efficient" assessment of the risks to which employees are exposed while they are at work.[21] If they have five or more employees, employers must record the significant findings of that assessment. The risk assessment must also identify the extent and nature of the risk; the factors that contribute to the risk; the causes; and the changes necessary to eliminate or control the risk.

In New Zealand, the Health and Safety in Employment Act 1992 has been used as the basis for developing a guide for employers and employees on dealing with violence at work.[22] Under that law, employers have a legal duty to take all practicable steps to identify all hazards in the place of work; to determine their significance; and to eliminate, isolate or minimize the likelihood that the hazard will be a source of harm.[23] In many workplaces the potential for violence is a significant hazard and thus the duty on employers extends to protecting employees from violent behaviour from whatever source, just as for any other hazard in the place of work.

In the United States, the Federal Occupational Safety and Health Act[24] and counterpart state laws generally require employers to provide their employees with a place of employment which is "free from recognized hazards that are causing or are likely to cause death or serious physical harm to ... employees".[25] Within the general requirement, employers have an obligation to do everything that is reasonably necessary to protect the life, safety and health of employees, including furnishing safety devices and safeguards, and the adoption of practices, means, methods, operations and processes reasonably adequate to create a safe and healthful workplace. OSHA guidelines can play a significant role in this respect. The guidelines are not in the form of a standard or regulation, and thus failure to implement the guidelines is not in itself a violation of the Occupational Safety and Health Act 1970. Since the guidelines are issued by the Occupational Safety and Health Administration (OSHA), an official body, and they "identify" the hazards of workplace violence, they differ from the guidelines to be described in Chapter 5, which emanate from non-official bodies. The OSHA guidelines can become legally relevant in specific cases and have a direct

---

[21] See in general Incomes Data Services, 1997, pp. 12-14.

[22] Department of Labour, Occupational Safety and Health Service, Government of New Zealand, *Guidelines for employers and employees on dealing with violence at work*, Wellington, 1995.

[23] Health and Safety in Employment Act 1992. Act No. 96 dated 27 October 1992 (Statutes of New Zealand, 1992) as amended up to Act No. 56, dated 26 February 1993 (Statutes of New Zealand, 1993).

[24] Occupational Safety and Health Act, dated 29 December 1970, Public Law 91-596, 91st Congress S. 2193.

[25] 29 USC, Section 654 (a) (1).

bearing on court decisions. The guidelines are both detailed and comprehensive, dealing with the establishment of violence prevention programmes; management commitment to and employee involvement in such programmes; workplace risk analysis; hazard prevention and control; training and education; record-keeping and evaluation; and specific programme elements for different types of operation and facilities.

The role of OSHA guidelines

Proponents of OSHA's involvement in the regulation of workplace violence envision that the agency can establish by rule a ... new legal regime applicable to a field of law in need of reform.* Administrative agency theorists have noted that agencies might be preferable even to courts as promoters of tort law reform, since theoretically, agencies can promulgate regulations that are both comprehensive and detailed.**

OSHA's *Draft Guidelines for Workplace Prevention Programs for Health Care Workers in Institutional and Community Settings*, (see the box on "Published guidelines on violence" in Chapter 5) released June 21, 1995, provide a glimpse at the type of guidance that OSHA should be able to offer to all employers. The guidelines detail preventive measures that have been taken to reduce a perpetrator's ability to commit violence in the workplace. The OSHA draft guidelines were put together on the basis that "more useful ways of identifying [violent workplace] settings or the hazards in them may be available from individuals and organizations who have expertise in preventing and mitigating violent assaults in various health care settings."

The guidelines are "not a new standard or regulation". Instead "failure to implement the guidelines is not in itself a violation of the General Duty Clause of the OSHA Act, but employers can be cited if there is a recognized hazard of workplace violence in their establishments and they do nothing to prevent or abate it".***

* Richard Pierce, "Alternative compensation schemes and tort theory: Institutional aspects of tort reform", in *California Law Review*, Vol. 73, 1985, pp. 917 and 937.

** See idem, p. 937; see also Guido Calabresi, *A common law for the age of Statutes 44-45 (1982)*. But see idem, p. 53 (arguing that in spite of the theoretical potential, agencies have been a "dismal disappointment" in legal reform).

*** *OSHA issues draft copy of guidelines to protect health care sector workers*, 25 O.S.H. Rep. (BNA) No. 5, p. 187 (5 July 1995) (quoting OSHA Administrator, Joseph A. Dear).

Source: Robert S. Goldberg, "Victims of criminal violence in the workplace: An assessment of remedies in the United States and Great Britain", in *Comparative Labor Law Journal*, Vol. 18, No. 3, Spring 1997.

At the European level, a Council Directive on the Introduction of Measures to Encourage Improvements in the Safety and Health of Workers at Work calls for the prevention of occupational risks, the protection of safety and health, and the elimination of risks and accident factors.[26] Article 6 of the Directive is reproduced in a box, below.

---

[26] Council Directive 83/391/EEC of 12 June 1989, in *Official Journal of the European Communities*, Vol. 32, 29 June 1989.

European Directive on the Safety and Health of Workers 1989: Employer's Responsibilities

1. Within the context of his responsibilities, the employer shall take the measures necessary for the safety and health protection of workers, including prevention of occupational risks and provision of information and training, as well as provision of the necessary organization and means.

   The employer shall be alert to the need to adjust these measures to take account of changing circumstances and aim to improve existing situations.

2. The employer shall implement the measures referred to [above] ... on the basis of the following general principles of prevention:

   (a) avoiding risks;

   (b) evaluating the risks which cannot be avoided;

   (c) combating the risks at source;

   (d) adapting the work to the individual, especially as regards the design of workplaces, the choice of work equipment and the choice of working and production methods, with a view, in particular, to alleviating monotonous work and work at a predetermined work-rate, and to reducing their effect on health;

   (e) adapting to technical progress;

   (f) replacing the dangerous by the non-dangerous or the less dangerous;

   (g) developing a coherent overall prevention policy which covers technology, organization of work, working conditions, social relationships and the influence of factors related to the working environment;

   (h) giving collective protective measures priority over individual protective measures;

   (i) giving appropriate instructions to the workers.

3. [...] The employer shall, taking into account the nature of the activities of the enterprise and/or establishment:

   (a) evaluate the risks to the safety and health of workers, *inter alia* in the choice of work equipment, the chemical substances of preparations used, and the fitting-out of workplaces.

   Subsequent to this evaluation and as necessary, the preventive measures and the working and production methods implemented by the employer must:

   — assure an improvement in the level of protection afforded to workers with regard to safety and health;

   — be integrated into all the activities of the undertaking and/or establishment and at all hierarchical levels;

   (b) where he entrusts tasks to a worker, take into consideration the worker's capabilities as regards health and safety;

   (c) ensure that the planning and introduction of new technologies are the subject of consultation with the workers and/or their representatives, as regards the consequences of the choice of equipment, the working conditions and the working environment for the safety and health of workers;

   (d) take appropriate steps to ensure that only workers who have received adequate instructions may have access to areas where there is serious and specific danger.

Source: "Council Directive of 12 June 1989 on the introduction of measures to encourage improvements in the safety and health of workers at work", 89/391/EEC, in *Official Journal of the European Communities* (Brussels), Vol. 32, 29 June 1989, Article 6, pp. L 183/3 to L 183/4.

PREVENTION THROUGH ENVIRONMENTAL MEASURES

Environmental legislation and regulation is being seen as an effective and increasing means of preventing violence at work. Measures of this type facilitate the identification of the causes of violence, the understanding of violence-related problems, and the adoption of remedial strategies. By encouraging a preventive approach to violence, these measures set the scene for the development of policies, guidelines and practices which in growing numbers are targeted at eliminating the causes of violence at work rather than merely alleviating its consequences.

In 1994, the Netherlands added provisions to its 1980 Working Environment Act aimed at preventing sexual intimidation, aggression and violence at work.[27] Under these new provisions, aggression and violence occur when the worker is mentally or physically harassed, threatened or attacked in circumstances directly connected with the performance of his or her work. The responsibility of the employer regarding the safety, well-being and health of staff is extended to cover such behaviours, including those perpetrated by "clients". The impact of these new provisions is currently being monitored.

Monitoring the impact of anti-violence legislation in the Netherlands

In the context of the above-mentioned amendment to the [1980 Working Environment Act], the first of a series of surveys was carried out in the casualty department of a teaching hospital in the Randstad (the urban conurbation of Western Holland). In all, 38 people, directly or indirectly involved with patients arriving in the casualty department, were interviewed and given questionnaires. Aggressive behaviour by patients mainly involves swearing at staff and threatening them with words and gestures (verbal aggression). As one worker explained, "verbal violence happens every day, but physical violence (fighting) is rare". The survey highlighted the potential causes of aggression and violence, the measures already in force to combat it, and the attention given to the problem within the organization.

Causes
Staff mentioned a number of causes of aggressive behaviour by patients. From the patient's side, these include annoyance at being kept waiting, dissatisfaction with treatment, intoxication (through drink or drugs), and the continuation of incidents which began outside the hospital (e.g. fights).

Staff also mentioned a number of factors from their own side which could possibly make patients aggressive. For example, the pressure on them from being understaffed could make them irritable and snappy with patients. Patients who were already feeling annoyed, perhaps from being kept waiting, could then quickly become aggressive.

Other factors liable to cause aggression include no-smoking rules in waiting-rooms, impersonal waiting-rooms and small treatment-rooms. Aggressive behaviour by patients is commonest at weekends, on public holidays and on late-shopping nights. Aggression is worst in the late evening, after the pubs have shut.

---

[27] Article 3, part 2 of the Working Environment Act, dated 8 November 1980 (Staatsblad, No. 664, 1980), as amended up to Act dated 21 February 1996 (Staatsblad, No. 133, 1996).

Prevention and follow-up

Various preventive measures have been taken to protect staff from aggressive patients in the casualty department. According to the staff, the most effective are an extra nurse during the night shift, a silent alarm, and security surveillance of the department.

Support for staff who have been the victims of a violent incident comes from talking the matter through with their colleagues and boss. Confrontations with aggressive patients can adversely affect both the individual workers concerned and the organization as a whole. [...]

In addition to the existing measures, there appears to be a strong demand for alternative measures to counter aggression and violence, such as the acquisition of social skills, the recording and reporting of incidents, the introduction of additional technical measures, and agreement on what constitutes unacceptable aggressive behaviour.

The most prominent of these are the need for additional technical measures and the acquisition of social skills. This indicates that the casualty staff see the work as dangerous and anticipate even more aggression and violence in the future.

Source: E.V. Boom et al., "Violence and aggression: Not just a problem for the individual worker", in *Janus* (Luxembourg), No. 20-II-1995, pp. 5-6, with permission from the General director of NIA-TNO B.V., Amsterdam.

Also in line with this approach, innovative environmental laws in Norway and Sweden highlight the importance of a work environment designed for the people working in it; the key role of work organization and job design in reducing risks; the relevance of both physical and psychological factors at work; the need to provide each worker with a meaningful occupation and with opportunities for occupational development, as well as for self-determination and occupational responsibility; and the need to ensure that workers are informed and involved in all matters concerning health and safety.

All these factors that have a direct bearing on preventing violence at work are illustrated in the following Provisions of the Swedish Work Environment Act.[28]

Working conditions shall be adapted to people's differing physical and mental aptitudes.

The employee shall be given the opportunity of participating in the design of his own working situation and in processes of change and development affecting his own work.

Technology, work organization and job content shall be designed in such a way that the employee is not subjected to physical or mental strains which can lead to illness or accidents. Forms of remuneration and the distribution of working hours shall also be taken into account in this connection. Closely controlled or restricted work shall be avoided or limited.

Efforts shall be made to ensure that work provides opportunities of variety, social contact and cooperation, as well as coherence between different working operations.

Furthermore, efforts shall be made to ensure that working conditions provide opportunities for personal and vocational development, as well as for self-determination and professional responsibility.

The linkage between the working environment and violence at work is becoming much more explicit in this type of legislation. Recent amendments to Norwegian legislation, for example, have made clear the right of the employee "not to be subject to harassment or other improper conduct"[29] within the work environment.

---

[28] See Section 1, Chapter 2 of the Work Environment Act, Act No. 1160, dated 19 December 1977 (*Svensk författningssamling*, No. 1160, 1977), as amended up to Act No. 667, dated 31 March 1991 (*Svensk författningssamling*, No. 667, 1991) [LS 1977-Swe. 4].

[29] Paragraph 12, point 2 of Act No. 4 respecting workers' protection and the working environment, dated 4 February 1977 (*Norsk Lovtidend*, Part I, No. 4, 14 February 1977), as amended up to Act No. 2, dated 6 January 1995 (*Norsk Lovtidend*, Part I, No. 12, 1987) [LS 1977-Nor. 1.].

SPECIFIC MEASURES AGAINST VIOLENCE AT WORK

Reflecting the growing awareness of and concern about violence at work, new measures are now being introduced which address this problem in a much more focused way. In 1993, for example, the Canadian province of British Columbia adopted a regulation relating to the "Protection of Workers from Violence in the Workplace". The regulation requires a violence risk assessment to be performed in any place of employment and, if a risk is thus identified, the development of policies, procedures and work environment arrangements to eliminate this risk.[30]

Also in 1993, the National Board of Occupational Safety and Health in Sweden issued two comprehensive and innovative ordinances on workplace violence under the authority of its Work Environment Act.[31] These ordinances cover violence and menaces in the working environment and victimization at work.[32]

These are valuable measures, each ordinance being accompanied by practical guidance on how to implement their provisions and tackle the problem of violence at work. The emphasis is on a combination of prevention strategies that deal with violence in the context of environmental and organizational issues, rather than through its containment at the level of the individual. The ordinances require employers to plan and organize work in a way which seeks to prevent the occurrence of violence and victimization. They must also make it clear that violence will not be tolerated in the workplace. The following box illustrates the key points contained in the first of these two ordinances:

Swedish Ordinance on measures for the prevention of violence and menaces in the working environment

The Ordinance applies to work where there may be a risk of violence or the threat of violence. Examples include having access to cash, goods or valuables. The Ordinance places specific responsibilities on employers, accompanied by considerable guidance on possible action.

Employers are responsible for investigating the risks of or threat of violence, and taking such measures as may be occasioned by the investigation. Work and workplaces are to be arranged and designed to avert the risk of violence or threats of violence as far as possible. There are to be special security routines for work with risks of violence, and these must be made known to all employees. Employees are to be given sufficient training, information and instruction to be able to do their work safely. If there is a risk of recurrent violence or threats of violence, employees are to receive special support and guidance. Employees should be informed at the time of hiring, or before being transferred to work where such work is known to entail certain risks.

---

[30] Workers' Compensation Board – Regulations: Protection of Workers from Violence in the Workplace, effective November 1, 1993. The regulation states that violence is the exercise of physical force and any threatening statement or behaviour, causing or likely to cause injury.

[31] Work Environment Act, Act No. 1160, dated 19 December 1977 (*Svensk författningssamling*, No. 1160, 1977), as amended up to Act No. 1239, dated 30 November 1995 (*Svensk författningssamling*, No. 1239, 1995) [LS 1977-Swe. 4].

[32] Statute Book of the Swedish National Board of Occupational Safety and Health, Ordinance (AFS 1993:2) on Violence and Menaces in the Working Environment, 14 January 1993, and Ordinance (AFS 1993:17) on Victimization at Work, 21 September 1993.

> Employees must have the possibility of summoning prompt assistance in a violent or threatening situation, and employers must ensure that alarm equipment and other necessary technical aids are provided, maintained and their use adequately explained, as well as having fixed routines for security and alarm calls which are practiced regularly. The use of technical aids such as intercom telephones, hidden telephones or optical surveillance in the form of a still camera, video monitoring or observation mirrors, however, is subject to legislation governing the use of such devices.
>
> Specific measures are spelled out for operations involving the transport of money, securities and other valuables. There are also provisions for recording, investigating and following up on violent incidents including threats, as well as notifying the Labour Inspectorate of serious injuries or incidents involving violence. Finally, employers must assure prompt assistance and support to employees who are subjected to violence or threats of violence, to prevent or alleviate both physical and mental injury; they must have special routines for this purpose. It is suggested that large workplaces have a special emergency or crisis group to act in serious emergencies. Both medical and psychological attention is required when an employee is involved in a traumatic event.

The current and continuing trend towards the enactment of specific legislation and regulations on violence at work has been accompanied by similar developments in regard to specific risk factors, occupations particularly at risk and special types of violence. Some examples of these developments follow, described under each of these headings.

Specific risk factors: Working alone

The Canadian Labour Code addresses a particular risk factor for violence created by the organization of work, that of *working alone*. It provides that:

> It remains the responsibility of the employer to ensure the safety and health of every employee at work. Through discussion with the safety and health committees, the affected worker(s), and examination of the work site, many different alternatives may be found to be available to ensure that the solitary worker would not be placed in a situation of undue risk, by virtue of their solitude.[33]

Occupations particularly at risk: Health care and social service workers

Due to the severity and frequency of violence in the health care industry in the United States, the Occupational Safety and Health Authority (OSHA) has published violence prevention guidelines for health care workers and social service workers.[34] Similar guidelines are being prepared for workers in night retail establishments, which are among those exposed to a higher risk of violence. The legal bearing of these types of guidelines has already been assessed (see box on "The role of OSHA guidelines").

Special types of violence: Sexual harassment

The law on sexual harassment is in a state of rapid change. In many countries there is still no law concerning sexual harassment as a legally distinct and prohibited activity.

---

[33] Canadian Labour Code, 1966, as amended up to 23 June 1993 (*Revised Statutes of Canada,* Ch. 42, 1993).

[34] OSHA, 1996(a) on Web site: http://www.osha.gov/oshpubs/workplace. Retrieved on 15 August 1996.

Equal opportunity, labour, tort and criminal laws may all be applied separately or in combination to deal with this behaviour.[35]

When equal opportunity law is utilized to deal with sexual harassment it is equated with a type of discriminatory employment practice. Labour laws, tort and criminal laws frequently address the issue in terms of an abuse of power, or an unacceptable affront to the dignity and privacy of the individual. The question of legal liability for sexual harassment is not always clear – it can fall on the employer, the harasser alone, or both.

Where specialized institutions exist to deal with complaints of sexual harassment, the worker has an avenue outside the workplace to pursue a case. This may result in the resolution of the issue through conciliation, or in an enforcement action against the employer or alleged harasser. Remedies for sexual harassment can include payment of damages, and court orders against employers or harassers to stop the harassment complained of. Employers may also be ordered to repair the damage caused by the harassment, including reinstatement of the complainant or transfer of the harasser, and be required to implement a policy to prevent future sexual harassment. In terms of internal sanctions, employers can discipline harassers, including ordering their dismissal, depending upon the seriousness of the offence.

In a growing number of countries, however, these issues have now been addressed by specific initiatives relating to sexual harassment. In common law jurisdictions like Australia, Canada, New Zealand, the United Kingdom and the United States, sexual harassment measures are now well developed, either by statute or case law. In France, Spain and Sweden there are either labour or penal statutes which expressly address sexual harassment issues. In several other European countries, including Austria, Belgium, Finland, Germany, Italy, the Netherlands and Switzerland, specific action has also been taken in this field in recent years.

There has also been a major increase in legislative attention to this question in developing countries. Thus Argentina, Costa Rica, the Republic of Korea and the Philippines have each adopted specific legislation declaring sexual harassment to be a prohibited activity, or general legislation covering sexual discrimination under which protection from sexual harassment can be provided. Some of this new legislation is particularly advanced.

Philippines Anti-Sexual Harassment Act of 1995 (excerpts)

Declaration of policy
The State shall value the dignity of every individual, enhance the development of its human resources, guarantee full respect for human employees, applicants for employment, students or those undergoing training, instruction or education. Towards this end, all forms of sexual harassment in the employment, education or training environment are hereby declared unlawful.

Work, education or training-related sexual harassment
Work, education or training-related sexual harassment is committed by an employer, employee, manager, supervisor, agent of the employer, teacher, instructor, professor, coach, trainer, or any other person who, having authority, influence or moral ascendancy over another in a work or training or

---

[35] See Aeberhard-Hodges, 1996, in regard to contemporary and comparative legal developments concerned with sexual harassment in the workplace.

97

education environment, demands, requests or otherwise requires any sexual favour from the other.

In a work-related or employment environment, sexual harassment is committed when:

- The sexual favour is made as a condition in the hiring or in the employment, re-employment or continued employment of said individual, or in granting said individual favourable compensation, terms, conditions, promotions, or privileges; or the refusal to grant the sexual favour results in limiting, segregating or classifying the employee which in any way would discriminate, deprive or diminish employment opportunities or otherwise adversely affect said employee;
- The above acts would impair the employee's rights or privileges under existing labour laws; or
- The above acts would result in an intimidating, hostile, or offensive environment for the employee.

Duty of the employer

It shall be the duty of the employer to prevent or deter the commission of acts of sexual harassment and to provide the procedures for the resolution, settlement or prosecution of acts of sexual harassment. Towards this end, the employer shall promulgate appropriate rules and regulations in consultation with and jointly approved by the employees, through their duly designated representatives, prescribing the procedure for the investigation of sexual harassment cases and the administrative sanctions therefor. The employer shall also create a committee on decorum and investigation of cases on sexual harassment. The committee shall conduct meetings, as the case may be, with officers and employees, to increase understanding and prevent incidents of sexual harassment. It shall also conduct the investigation of alleged cases constituting sexual harassment.

Liability of the employer

The employer shall be liable for damages arising from the acts of sexual harassment committed in the employment, education or training environment if the employer, or head of office, is informed of such acts by the offended party and no immediate action is taken thereon.

Independent action for damages

Nothing in this Act shall preclude the victim of sexual harassment from instituting a separate and independent action for damages and other affirmative relief.

Penalties

Any person who violates the provisions of this Act shall, upon conviction, be penalized by imprisonment of not less than one month nor more than six months, or a fine or both, such fine and imprisonment at the discretion of the court.

Source: Anti-Sexual Harassment Act, Act No. 7877, dated 14 February 1995, *Official Gazette* (Manila), Vol. 91, No. 15, 10 April 1995, pp. 2144-2146.

ENCOURAGING ACTION AGAINST VIOLENCE

In addition to measures targeted at the repression and punishment of violence at work, and those aimed at preventing such violence, increasing interest is being shown in a new type of legislation directed at supporting and encouraging workplace initiatives against violence. One of the first initiatives of this type is the United States

Workplace Violence Prevention Tax Credit Bill 1997, which encourages companies to establish workplace safety programmes to combat violence against women.[36]

A tax credit of 40 per cent of the cost would be granted for:

- Programmes ensuring the safety of women employees from violent crimes, including the hiring of new security personnel and the purchase or installation of lights and security systems for the purpose of addressing violent crimes against women.
- Programmes providing counselling to employees with respect to violent crimes against women, including the establishment of a hotline or direct counselling service for the use of employees.
- Programmes providing legal, medical or financial services to employees subjected to, or at risk from, violent crimes against women.
- Programmes designed to educate employees about the issue of violent crimes against women, including the establishment of training sessions or seminars, studies of the cost, impact and extent of domestic violence at the company, and publication of a regularly disseminated newsletter.
- Programmes implementing human resource or personnel policies initiated to protect employees from violent crimes against women, including leave policies that allow employees to go to court against assailants, flexitime policies that allow employees to adjust work hours to avoid batterers, and transfer policies that allow employees to change office locations within a company in order to escape a battering relationship.[37]

COLLECTIVE AGREEMENTS ON VIOLENCE AT WORK

Legislation on violence at work is sometimes anticipated or supplemented by collective agreements dealing with this issue. In the European Union, for example, EURO-FIET, the European Branch of the International Federation of Commercial, Clerical, Professional and Technical Employees, and its counterpart Euro Commerce, signed an important joint statement in 1995 on combating crime and violence in commerce. In this statement, EURO-FIET and Euro Commerce emphasized that the problem of crime and violence was a health and safety problem. They stressed the necessity for close cooperation between the social partners and public authorities at European and national levels in order to tackle these problems effectively.

In particular, national and local public authorities should be urged to pay attention to the problem; emphasis should also be placed on the obligations of employers to protect the health and safety of their employees, and to the benefits of continuous social dialogue at the European level; tripartite cooperation should be encouraged and guidelines for workplaces involved in commerce introduced to help employers and employees prevent and deal with violent incidents; employees should be given adequate training to deal with problems and be aware of their obligations; and particular information and guidelines should be provided about the risks of violence. The document also calls for effective procedures for the handling of cash and dealing with

---

[36] H.R. 1071 IH, 105th Congress, 1st Session. *A Bill to amend the Internal Revenue Code of 1986 to provide a credit for employers for certain costs incurred to combat violence against women.* Introduced by Congresswoman Lowey, 13 March 1997.

[37] Source: Congresswoman Lowey's Office, 18 March 1997.

suspected shoplifters and robbers, with priority being given to the safety of employees; the identification of risks and the recording and reporting of violent workplace incidents; and the development of proper after-care programmes.[38]

In Norway, the basic agreement of 1994 between the Norwegian Confederation of Trade Unions (LO) and the Confederation of Norwegian Business and Industry (NHO) establishes the express right for workers to refuse to work with persons who have exhibited such improper conduct.

> Employees have the right to refuse to work with, or under the management of, persons who have shown such improper conduct that, according to the norms of working or social life generally, it ought to justify their dismissal. Discussions between employers and shop stewards should be held immediately if such situations arise. If they fail to reach agreement, there shall not be any stoppage or other forms of industrial action.[39]

Model agreements on work-related violence have also been prepared. For example, in the United Kingdom UNISON has developed a Model Agreement on Tackling Violence in the National Health Service. The development and implementation of policies to tackle violence must be the subject of negotiation, and agreed at all stages between management and trade union representatives. Full use must be made of the safety representatives and safety committees. This must include adequate information and opportunities for additional union-approved training for safety representatives; adequate arrangements to investigate cases of violence and assault; and provision for safety committees to review the effectiveness of anti-violence policies.[40]

Along similar lines, the Manufacturing, Science and Finance Union (MSF) in the United Kingdom has published the *Guide to Prevention of Violence at Work*, which stresses that a successful strategy in this area can only be achieved if employees are fully involved in its development. The employer must consult fully with safety representatives over the strategy, and over the planning and organization of any training provided as part of that strategy.

The following model agreement is proposed by MSF to make operational such a strategy.

Model agreement on violence at work

The agreement on violence at work between ABC [...] (employer) and MSF explains procedures to deal with violence. It is part of the Health and Safety Policy and will be regularly reviewed and updated as appropriate. The next review date will be [...]

1. Definition of violence
The working definition of violence will be:
Any incident in which an employee is abused, threatened or assaulted by a member of the public in circumstances arising from his or her employment.

This includes verbal abuse and threats (with or without a weapon), rude gestures, innuendos, sexual and racial harassment, discrimination because of a person's disability or sexuality as well as physical assault, whether or not it results in injury. Physical assault includes being shoved or pushed as

---

[38] Euro Commerce and EURO-FIET statement on combating violence in commerce, March 1995.
[39] LO-NHO Basic Agreement, 1994, Paragraph 10.1.
[40] UNISON, *Violence in the National Health Service*, 1992, p. 7.

well as hit, punched, etc. When in a vehicle, it can also include another driver behaving in a threatening manner. Members of the public include patients, clients and co-workers.

2. ABC (employer)

i. recognizes the potential for violence arising from employment and undertakes to do all that is reasonably practicable to eliminate and/or reduce the risk of violence to employees;

ii. will develop a policy on the prevention of violence in consultation with the Health and Safety Committee and with union Safety Representatives and will develop local strategies and guidelines to all staff, based on this policy;

iii. affirms that employees are instructed not to take risks on behalf of the employer to protect the employer's property, etc., and affirms that the procedures for serious and imminent danger under Regulation 7 of the Management of Health and Safety at Work Regulations 1992 cover violence at work;

iv. undertakes to assess the potential for violence arising from the work, to identify any group of employees especially at risk, to take all practical steps to eliminate/reduce the risks, including the provision of training, work environment, information about potentially violent clients/customers (and those who may be with them) and information about the area/location in which the work is to be carried out;

v. requires full reporting of all incidents of violence, including abuse and near misses, and provides a reporting system;

vi. will investigate all incidents and report to the Health and Safety Committee;

vii. will provide support and aftercare, including counselling and professional help where appropriate, to those who have experienced violence;

viii. will agree to move the perpetrator of the violence where this is possible (recognizing that in many cases this may not be possible);

ix. will agree to a change of duties/location/redeployment for a person who is unable to undertake their former duties as a result of experiencing violence, without prejudice to future prospect or any detriment;

x. will in consultation with union Safety Representatives provide full training to employees who may be at risk from violence, enable them to recognize violent or potentially violent situations, and to provide re-training and training updates where appropriate;

xi. will take seriously and investigate report(s) from employees about the potential for violence, and will take preventive measures to reduce the risk;

xii. will regularly monitor and review the prevention of violence policy, in consultation with the Health and Safety Committee; and

xiii. will identify the person responsible for the implementation of the prevention of violence policy.

Source: *MSF Health and Safety Information Sheet*, No. 37 (Bishop's Stortford, Hertfordshire), April 1993, p. 9 and pp. 24-25.

FROM INTERVENTION TO ACTION

This chapter has now traversed a wide range of legislative and regulatory interventions taken over recent years to deal with violence in the workplace. The review has, however, concentrated deliberately upon broad trends and developments, without examining how specific governments, enterprises, trade unions and other bodies have sought to give practical meaning and direction to these legislative and regulatory dictates. A review at this more specifically focused level is now pursued in Chapter 5.

GUIDELINES AND BEST PRACTICE

5

Best practice: Case-studies

London Underground Limited (LUL)

The London Underground employs more than 7,000 operating staff on trains and at 274 stations in the London area. It carries more than 750 million passengers each year. Between January 1993 and August 1996 a total of 2,231 assaults on LUL staff were reported.[1]

As a public service, LUL accepts that it has to deal with a certain level of violence from the public.

It attributes [a] fall in the number of assaults over the last few years not to any single factor, but to a range of improvements: in policing, in awareness and publicity; in equipment and the design of stations and rolling stock; in public education, including poster campaigns and visits to schools; and in the information about services and delays which is provided to the public. Perhaps the most important aspects are a training system which at each stage teaches staff to deal with violence, and a determined effort to recruit temperamentally suitable employees.[2]

Midland Bank

Midland Bank employs more than 30,000 staff in about 1,750 branches and several office complexes across Britain. Its security department consists of about 20 professional security staff, as well as guards. One side of the security department deals with fraud and money-laundering, handling both preventative and investigative work, and taking responsibility for complying with regulatory requirements. The other half is responsible for the protection of people and property. It reacts to raids and other violent incidents when they occur, and takes preventative measures, surveying premises in order to conduct risk assessments.

Midland takes the view that its primary objective is to ensure the safety of its staff. If employees are alert to their own safety, the assets of the bank will be protected anyway. The policies and programmes the bank has initiated to improve safety include the development of a design guide for branches; special protection for cashiers; controlling access to offices; specific educational training for staff and the issue to all employees of a booklet on "Your Personal Safety and Security"; security strategies for use at home and while travelling to work; and aftercare counselling and advice.[3]

---

[1] Trident Consultants Ltd., 1997, p. 28. This research was initiated by LUL in order to help the company to adopt a risk assessment approach to assaults and to quantify the probability of assault by grade and location, using passenger flows and staff numbers. The findings from the research are also to be used to prioritize the use of resources, including assault-awareness training and the issue of personnel protective equipment, to those in greatest need. It is also intended to use the research to justify capital equipment purchases for security cameras and other protective devices.

[2] Incomes Data Services, 1994, p. 28.

[3] ibid., pp. 28-30.

Social Security Benefits Agency (BA)

The BA is the largest of the Department of Social Security's agencies, delivering the payment of state benefits in Britain through a network of around 500 district offices, which are linked to satellite offices in smaller towns. The agency employs more than 65,000 people.

The BA has a wide-ranging definition of violence which includes all types of assaults, serious threats, intimidation and "severe or persistent verbal abuse", as well as serious or persistent harassment.

Verbal assaults of varying degrees pose the main problem, outnumbering physical attacks by more than ten to one. The number of physical attacks has fallen in recent years, while other incidents rose sharply in 1995. This increase is mainly attributed to improved reporting procedures and the agency believes that the majority of incidents are now being recorded.

The agency's conditions of service manual, which is readily available to all staff and is publicized during induction training, includes its policy on violence. This defines violence and explains the necessity of reporting incidents. It outlines how staff should react, including the use of "reasonable force" to defend themselves, and the role of the police. The manual also contains the agency's counselling provisions and procedures for dealing with potentially violent people. Staff receive a wide range of training including being taught how to defuse situations which begin to get out of hand, and how to handle potentially aggressive situations. An extensive aftercare service is provided for staff.[4]

The United States Postal Service

The US Postal Service introduced an Integrated Framework of Strategic Anti-violence Initiatives in 1994.

The approach was shaped by the Service's particular experience with workplace violence. For example, while research showed that the Postal Service was not more dangerous than other businesses, co-workers appeared to be disproportionately responsible for homicides. The National Institute of Occupational Safety and Health (NIOSH) reported that 57 per cent of work-related homicides in the Postal Service were committed by co-workers or former co-workers between 1983 and 1989. This compared to only 4 per cent of work-related homicides being committed by this group industry-wide in 1992. The Service was also characterized by an authoritarian, top-down management style and objectionable disciplinary procedures.

Its new programme addressed both the issue of "problem employees" and organizational problems. Concerning problem workers, it introduced stricter pre-hiring criteria to obtain the right people at the beginning. A screening process was put in place which includes competency tests and background checks, as well as a no-tolerance policy for weapons on postal property or of threats of any kind. On organizational issues, the Service moved towards a more "participatory culture"; an improved work environment; enhanced support for employees through the employee assistance programme; a toll-free hotline for reporting threats or concerns; and a process of creating more effective policies and procedures for terminating employees and evaluating whether those dismissed could be dangerous. Security initiatives were also taken depending on decisions made by management in the various facilities, after assessing the measures that should be taken with the Postal Inspection Service, the law-enforcement arm of the Postal Service. In some facilities, these were limited to awareness programmes and training on how to report incidents, while other facilities employed security guards, required access badges or installed surveillance cameras on the premises.[5]

---

[4] Incomes Data Services, 1997, pp. 20-23.

[5] Information supplied to the ILO by the United States Postal Service, 13 June 1996. See also J.G. Karutz et al., "The United States Postal Service Employee Assistance Program: A multifaceted approach to workplace violence prevention", in VandenBos and Bulatao, 1996, pp. 343-352.

CHOOSING THE BEST APPROACH

These four brief contemporary case-studies illustrate how an extremely valuable body of knowledge is now being applied to the development of strategies to deal with workplace violence. Important sets of guidelines on this subject are emerging from government, trade unions, special study groups, workplace violence experts, employers' groups and specific industries. Despite different approaches and methods being used, these guidelines reveal common themes:

- preventive action is possible and necessary;
- work organization and the working environment hold significant keys to the causes and solutions to the problem;
- the participation of workers and their representatives is crucial both in identifying the problem and in implementing solutions;

The organizational model of managing occupational violence

This model is based on the recognition that employee problems associated with occupational violence are essentially human resource management issues and not problems of individual employee illness. They are not separate from the life of the organization nor from the responsibilities of those running it.

The essential features of this model are as follows:

(1) occupational violence management is a core human resource management issue;
(2) occupational violence should never be accepted as "part of the job";
(3) concentration on "sick" employees avoids the work organizational issues necessary to deal with the problem effectively;
(4) management activities should be centred around a risk management strategy, i.e. identifying and assessing risks and associated losses, and developing strategies for action;
(5) action on occupational violence should be part of mainstream corporate strategy;
(6) action on occupational violence should be part of mainstream line management responsibility;
(7) action on occupational violence should include employees and their formal representatives;
(8) the management of internal conflict will be facilitated by attention to achieving and maintaining clear and unambiguous communication throughout all levels of an organization;
(9) strategies for the prevention and management of conflict, assault, harassment and abuse should form part of organizational human resource management and occupational health and safety strategy, including training;
(10) potential areas of internal conflict, such as performance and disciplinary management, ought to be assessed in light of occupational violence management strategies;
(11) service organizations need to pay particular attention to occupational violence associated with public contact;
(12) any clinical/therapeutic services provided by the organization ought to be assessed as part of an overall management strategy, and not provided in place of that strategy.

Source: Toohey, 1993, pp. 16-17.

- the interpersonal skills of management and workers alike cannot be underrated;
- there cannot be one blueprint for action, but rather the uniqueness of each workplace situation must be considered; and
- continued review of policies and programmes is needed to keep up with changing situations.

The correct and preferable response to the issue of violence at work is seen increasingly to be an essential part of human resource management. It is also clear that government, trade unions, workers, occupational health and safety professionals, the mental health and public health communities and security professionals have important roles to play in developing, promoting and implementing strategies to prevent workplace violence, and dealing with its consequences when it does occur.

The guidelines developed in this area emphasize the importance of a **systematic** approach to violence at work. This involves several steps and the application of a "control cycle". The following steps have been identified.

The control cycle of violence at work

1. Find out if there is a problem
Violence at work is often an "unrecognized" problem. Organizations and people may be reluctant to, or incapable of accepting the very existence of violence at their workplace. The best way to tackle such a problem is to ask the views of workers (without creating anxiety or artificially creating a problem) and managers, to review accident reports, and to assign a person to deal with enquiries and reports of violence. Record all incidents and encourage employees to report them. Classify all incidents, types of incident and results, look for patterns and common cause.

2. Determine the relevance of the problem
Are there problems in similar sectors of activity? Are you engaged in work or situations which have experienced violence or located where violence is a risk? Determine where the greatest risks are, and analyse workplace injury statistics to determine the extent of violent incidents and the circumstances in which violence occurred.

3. Describe the problem
Once the nature of the problem is clear, it is important to assess it in detail. Look for common elements – for example, certain times or days of the week, in certain locations, in similar situations, particular types of aggression.

4. Analyse reasons for violence
Analyse the conditions that allow or facilitate particular types of violence; systematically study possible alternativee solutions.

5. Design a preventive strategy
Develop a coordinated programme to prevent and reduce aggression. The process would include the identification of the measures to prevent violence, which can involve physical environment, work organization, procedures, work design, training and selection of workers. The possible measures will have to be costed and their effectiveness estimated. There are many examples where the cheaper measures have been preferred, but which have had little effect. It may be that several measures combined together would be the most effective solution.

---

6. Implement the strategy
   Depending on cost and other factors, the methods and timing of implementation will vary. Employees will help in putting measures into practice. Implementation will take place in a way that permits evaluation.

7. Evaluate and monitor
   Once strategies have been implemented, it is vital that their effects be evaluated both in terms of their impact upon the initial problem and in terms of any broader organizational criteria. On the one hand, this may have the effect of identifying and sustaining effective strategies and, on the other, it may highlight those interventions in need of modification, replacement or removal.

Source: Various, but primarily Health and Safety Executive (United Kingdom), 1991, pp. 4-9.

Another approach suggested is one which provides a targeted response to violence at work according to the type of "hazardous agent" involved. The approach, which has been incorporated into official guidelines in the state of California,[6] identifies three main types of "hazardous agent":

Type I – Criminal intruder: The agent has no legitimate relationship to the workplace and usually enters the workplace to commit a robbery or other criminal act.

Type II – Dissatisfied client type: The agent is either the recipient or the object of a service provided by the affected workplace or the victim, e.g. the assailant is a current or former client, patient, customer, passenger, criminal suspect or prisoner.

Type III – Scorned employee: The agent has an employment-related involvement with the workplace. Usually this involves an assault by a current or former employee, supervisor or manager; by a current/former spouse or lover; a relative or friend; or some other person who has a dispute involving an employee of the workplace.[7]

Each of these types of **hazardous** agent requires a specific response, as was emphasized in Chapter 3, where the interactive model of violence at work was expounded.[8]

To many people, **Type I** workplace violence appears to be part of society's "crime" problem, and not a workplace safety and health problem at all. Under this view, the workplace is an "innocent bystander" and the solution to the problem is societal, not occupational.

The ultimate solution to Type I events may indeed involve societal changes, but until such changes occur, it is still the employer's legal responsibility to provide a safe and healthful place of employment for their employees.

Employers with employees who are known to be at risk – for Type I events – taxicab drivers, clerks in liquor stores, convenience stores, grocery stores or gas stations, all of whom may handle cash late at night, clerks in hotels or motels open late at night, jewellery store employees or security guards – are required to address workplace security hazards to satisfy the regulatory requirement of establishing, implementing and maintaining an effective Injury and Illness Prevention (IIP) Programme.

The first step in establishing and implementing an effective workplace security component of a IIP Programme is strong management commitment.

The cornerstone of an effective workplace security plan is appropriate training of all employees, supervisors and managers. Employers with employees at risk of workplace violence must educate them about the risk factors associated with the various types of workplace violence, and provide appropriate training in crime awareness, assault and rape prevention and in

---

   [6] California, 1994. Quotations given below are reproduced with permission from the Department of Industrial Relations, Division of Occupational Safety and Health, State of California.

   [7] ibid., p. 7.

   [8] See Chapter 3, figure 12, above.

defusing hostile situations. Also, employers must instruct their employees about what steps to take during an emergency incident.

Employers concerned with **Type II** events need to be aware that the control of physical access through workplace design is an important preventive measure. This can include controlling access into and out of the workplace, and freedom of movement within the workplace, in addition to placing barriers between clients and service providers. Escape routes can also be a critical component of workplace design.

Employers at risk for Type II events must also be attentive to communication problems and provide their employees with instruction in how to effectively defuse hostile situations involving their clients, patients, customers, passengers and members of the general public to whom they must provide services. In certain situations, the installation of alarm systems or "panic buttons" may be an appropriate back-up measure. Establishing a "buddy" system to be used in specified emergency situations is often advisable as well. The presence of security personnel should also be considered where appropriate.

Since **Type III** events are more closely tied to employer-employee relations than are Type I or II events, an employer's considerate and respectful management of his or her employees represents an effective strategy for preventing Type III events.

Some mental health professionals believe that verbally assaultive behaviour by an employee or by a supervisor, including belligerent, intimidating and threatening behaviour, is an early warning sign of an individual's propensity to commit a physical assault, and that monitoring of such behaviour is also a part of effective prevention.

Employers at risk of a Type III event need to establish and implement procedures to respond to workplace security hazards when they are present, and to provide training as necessary to their employees, supervisors and managers in order to satisfy the regulatory requirement of establishing, implementing and maintaining an effective IIP Programme.

To effectively prevent Type III events from occurring, employers need to establish a clear anti-violence management policy, apply the policy consistently and fairly to all employees, supervisors and managers, as well as to provide appropriate supervisory and employee training in workplace violence prevention.[9]

Guidelines for **occupations/situations at special risk; special types of violence;** and **special audiences** have proliferated in recent years. These provide a specific response to specific problems, while usually reflecting the main points contained in guidelines of a more general type. The list provided in the box below is merely indicative.

Published guidelines on violence – A selection

Guidelines for occupations/situations at special risk

American Federation of State, County and Municipal Employees, AFL-CIO: *Preventing workplace violence*, Washington, DC, 1998. (Web site http://www.igc.org/afscme/health/violtc.htm)

California, Department of Industrial Relations, CAL/OSHA: *Guidelines for security and safety of health care and community service workers*, San Francisco, 1993.

Crime Prevention Unit: *The prevention of robbery at building society branches*, Paper No. 14, London, 1988.

HSAC (Health Services Advisory Committee): *Violence to staff in the health services*, London, 1987.

HSC (Health and Safety Commission): *Violence to staff in the education sector*, London, 1990.

HSE (Health and Safety Executive): *Violence to staff*, London, 1991.

HSE: *Preventing violence to retail staff*, London, 1995. Department of Transport, *Protecting bus crews – A practical guide*, London, 1995 (July).

---

[9] See California, 1994, pp. 11-15.

HSE: *Prevention of violence to staff in banks and building societies*, London, 1993.

IATA: *Guidelines for handling disruptive/unruly passengers*, Geneva, 1999.

Suzy Lamplugh Trust: *Personal safety for social workers*, London, 1994.

Suzy Lamplugh Trust: *Personal safety for health-care workers*, London, 1995.

Suzy Lamplugh Trust: *Personal safety for schools*, London, 1996.

Suzy Lamplugh Trust: *Personal safety in other people's homes*, London, 1998.

MSF (Manufacturing, Science, Finance Union): *Working alone: Guidance for MSF members and safety representatives*, London, 1994.

Occupational Safety and Health Service: *Guidelines for the safety of staff from the threat of armed robbery*, Wellington, New Zealand, 1995 (Jan.).

OSHA (Occupational Safety and Health Authority): *Guidelines for preventing workplace violence for health care and social service workers*, Washington, DC, 1996.

OSHA (Occupational Safety and Health Authority): *Recommendations for workplace violence prevention programs in late-night establishments*, Washington, DC, 1998.

Royal College of Nursing: *Violence and community nursing staff: Advice for managers*, London, 1994.

B. Swanton; D. Webber: *Protecting counter and interviewing staff from client aggression*, Canberra, Australian Institute of Criminology, 1990.

UNISON: *Working alone in safety – Controlling the risks of solitary work*, London, 1993.

United States Departments of Education and Justice: *A guide to safe schools*, Washington, DC, 1998. (Web site http://www.ed.gov/offices/OSERS/OSEP/earlywrn.htm)

WorkCover Authority of New South Wales: *Armed hold-ups and cash handling: A guide to protecting people and profits from armed hold-ups*, Sydney, 1994.

WorkCover Corporation of South Australia: *Guidelines for aged care facilities*, Adelaide, 1996.

WorkSafe Western Australia Commission: *Working alone*, West Perth, 1999.

Guidelines for special types of violence

Commission of the European Communities: *How to combat sexual harassment. A guide to implementing the European Commission Code of Practice*, Brussels, 1993.

Department of Employment: *Sexual harassment in the workplace: A guide for employers*, London, 1992 (June).

Equal Opportunities Commission: *Sexual harassment at work: Consider the cost*, London, 1994 (Oct.).

MSF: *Bullying at work. Confronting the problem*, London, 1994.

TUC (Trades Union Congress): *Guidelines. Sexual harassment at work*, London, 1992.

TUC: *Racial harassment at work, A guide and workplace programme for trade unionists*, London, 1993.

UNISON: *Bullying at work. Guidance for safety representative and members on bullying at work and how to prevent it*, London, 1996.

UNISON: *Bullying at work. Guidelines for UNISON branches, stewards and safety representatives*, London, 1996.

Working Women's Centre: *Stop violence against women at work*, Adelaide, 1994 (June).

Guidelines for special audiences

Center for Occupational and Environmental Health, University of California: *Violence on the job: A guidebook for labor and management*, Berkeley, California, 1997.

HSE: *Violence at work: A guide for employers*, London, 1997.

Suzy Lamplugh Trust: *Violence and aggression at work: Reducing the risks. Guidance for employers*, London, 1994.

Suzy Lamplugh Trust: *Personal safety at work. Guidance for all employees*, London, 1994.

Occupational Safety and Health Service: *A guide for employers and employees on dealing with violence at work*, Wellington, New Zealand, 1995.

PERSEREC (Defence Personnel Security Research Center): *Guidance for employers*, Washington, DC, 1995.

UNISON: *Violence at work. A guide to risk prevention for UNISON branches, stewards and safety representatives*, London, 1997.

United States Office of Personnel Management: *Dealing with workplace violence: A guide for agency planners*, Washington, DC, 1997 (Oct.).

Workers' Compensation Board of British Columbia: *Take care – How to develop and implement a workplace violence programme – A guide for small business*, Vancouver, Canada, 1995.

PREVENTIVE STRATEGIES AND MEASURES

Much suffering can be averted by means of preventive measures, efficient routines and proper care of a person who has been subjected to violence or menaces.[10]

Preventive strategies

As has been seen in Chapter 4, governments, employers and workers to an ever-increasing degree now view incidents of workplace violence as potentially preventable, rather than as random acts of violence by criminals. Attention is consequently focusing on the elimination of the causes of violence, rather than the treatment of its effects, and on the positive implications, in terms of cost efficiency and longstanding results, of preventive strategies.

The prevention of violence in the workplace is of critical importance if employers want to continue the national trend towards increased productivity. Deming, the late founder of the quality improvement movement, extolled managers to "drive out fear". One source of fear that Deming did not anticipate was the fear of violence in the workplace. Yet it is clear that the aftermath of such violent episodes is associated with substantial drops in productivity as workers are traumatized, distracted by fear, and spend time seeking reassurance and social support. Thus, the prevention of violence is in the best interest of productivity and profitability. It also is in the best interest of management because, as Losey, chief executive officer of the Society for Human Resource Management (SHRM), noted, the firing manager and the human resources manager are the most likely targets of retribution by an employee going through the process of termination. Executives also have been the targets of kidnappers and terrorists. The motivation for prevention should be clear.[11]

Common elements of preventive strategies and prevention plans on violence usually include the involvement of all those concerned – "the best way to tackle violence is for the employer and the employees to work together to decide what to do"[12] – and a clear statement of intent which reflects a real commitment from all parties concerned to recognize the importance of the fight against violence at work. This

---

[10] Statute Book of the Swedish National Board of Occupational Safety and Health, Ordinance (AFS 1993:2) on Violence and Menaces in the Working Environment, adopted 14 January 1993, p. 9.

[11] Bush and O'Shea, 1996, p. 295.

[12] Health and Safety Executive, 1991, p. 4.

Violence-Free Campus Policy, Sonoma State University

Sonoma State University is committed to creating and maintaining a campus environment for all members of the university community that is free from violence.

Civility, understanding, and mutual respect towards all members of the university community are intrinsic to excellence in teaching and learning, to safety in the workplace, and to maintenance of a culture and environment that serves the needs of all campus constituents.

Sonoma State University will not tolerate violence and threats of violence on campus or at campus-sponsored events by members of the university community against other persons or property.

For the purposes of this policy, violence and threats of violence include, but are not limited to:

- any act that is physically assaultive; or
- any threat, behaviour or action which is interpreted by a reasonable person to carry the potential:
  - to harm or endanger the safety of others;
  - to result in an act of aggression; or
  - to destroy or damage property.

Any member of the university community who commits a violent act or threatens to commit a violent act towards other persons or property on campus or at campus-sponsored events shall be subject to disciplinary action, up to and including dismissal from employment or expulsion from the university, exclusive of any civil and/or criminal penalties that may be pursued, as appropriate.

It is the responsibility of every administrator, faculty member, staff member, and student to take any threat or violent act seriously, and to report acts of violence or threats of violence to the appropriate authorities.

Source: Sonoma State University, *Workplace violence: Prevention and response program*, 1991. Documentation supplied to the ILO by Human Services/Environmental Health and Safety, Sonoma State University, Sonoma, California, dated 28 April 1997.

---

will usually be accompanied by the establishment of a written policy, as in the case of the Violence-Free Campus Policy at Sonoma State University, California (see box).

Preventive measures

Experts emphasize the importance of a response which includes the largest possible number of the following measures, and combines them in the most appropriate mix according to the specific situation:

Selection and screening

Selection tools such as written tests, interviews, performance tests, psychological profiles and other prediction devices are commonly recommended. Selection and screening may have an important bearing in terms of violence prevention although, as noted in Chapter 4, these various predictive tools should be used and interpreted with care and caution. Selection may help in identifying those individuals who are more tailored to certain jobs, less likely to get stressed, frustrated or angered because of it, and consequently less prone to violent workplace responses. Alternatively, selection may be used to screen out the "bad apples" – those who have a violent profile and constitute a risk to the workplace.

Screening

Use a job application form that includes an appropriate waiver and release (permitting the employer to verify the information reported on the application). Prior to hiring any applicant, check references and inquire about any prior incidents of violence. In addition, conduct thorough background checks and use drug screening to the extent practicable.

Also evaluate the need for screening contract personnel who work at your facility. Vendors and service organizations whose personnel make frequent visits or spend long periods of time working at your facility should certify that those individuals meet or exceed your firm's safety and security requirements. Conversely, contractors who assign personnel to work at other organizations' facilities should also consider the host firm's safety and security policies and practices.

Source: PERSEREC, Defence Personnel Security Research Centre, Washington, DC, "Guidelines for employers" in *Combating workplace violence*. Web site: http://www.amdahl.com/ext/iaep/pslc1.toc.html. Retrieved on 22 July 1997.

The effectiveness of this screening has, however, been questioned, as have the limits that should be imposed on such a practice. In particular, **psychological, alcohol, drug** and **genetic** testing are under scrutiny.

Psychological testing may certainly help to clarify the personality of the applicant. However, while it is generally accepted that these tests might be employed, there are questions regarding their reliability and validity. Legal regulation, essentially based on principles of privacy and equal opportunity employment, often places major restrictions on psychological testing in a significant number of countries. These legal limitations frequently impose, on the one hand, an obligation on the employer to collect information that is relevant only to a given employment decision and, on the other hand, an obligation not to request information unjustifiably invasive of the privacy of an individual.[13]

One of the most controversial issues in screening is the use of **alcohol and drug tests**. Workers' and employers' organizations often have divergent opinions in this respect. The National Association of Manufacturers in the United States, for example, is of the opinion that while drug testing should be done in a fair and equitable manner, with due concern for the employee's privacy, it none the less opposes any legislation that would prohibit employers from testing applicants and employees for substance abuse, believing that a company's testing policy should be left to the company itself.

On the other hand, unions which have addressed the issue, such as the AFL-CIO and the Canadian Labour Congress, are on the whole opposed to it. They argue that many of the tests companies use to screen workers for drugs and alcohol are open to serious abuse by employers; are inaccurate and unreliable; cannot determine whether an employee is unable to perform job functions because of drug use; do not by themselves establish that the employee has a pattern of abuse; and can constitute an invasion of workers' rights and privacy.[14]

Concern has also been expressed in respect of **genetic screening** and recommendations made on the limits to such a type of selection. In Switzerland, the Union

---

[13] ILO, "Workers' privacy: Testing in the workplace", *Conditions of Work Digest*, Vol. 12, 2/1993, pp. 81-82.

[14] ILO, "Alcohol and drugs", *Conditions of Work Digest*, Vol. 6, 1/1987, p. 5.

of Swiss Trade Unions (USS) has argued that genetic tests, if applied to workers, could give a new and dangerous basis to medical tests which are already applied in the hiring process. There is a danger that genetic characteristics, which are called defects, could be considered as a sickness; and the persons concerned would be excluded from work and social benefits.[15]

The USS has argued that such tests would give an employer the possibility to use a "highly problematic selection process to identify and eliminate workers with a risk". The union has taken the position that no genetic analysis should be carried out for employment or insurance purposes, maintaining that "genetic information does not belong to employers, company doctors and social insurance bodies. Each individual should decide whether he or she believes it is appropriate that a genetic analysis be carried out by a physician of his or her own choice."[16]

In Germany, an investigative commission issued recommendations in 1988 on the subject of the risks and opportunities of gene technology. The commission's recommendations included the following:

- restricting the right to ask questions on genetic traits, as well as preventing doctors and medical institutions that have carried out genetic tests not required by law from furnishing such information to employers;
- excluding genetic screening which would permit a diagnosis of whether an individual might be predisposed to developing a disease, unless expressly allowed by legislation;
- specifying in law that co-determination between workers' representatives and employers is required for genetic diagnosis in the framework of medical examinations provided for by law;
- ensuring that only scientifically approved tests are used;
- requesting professional associations to state in their accident prevention regulations the methods to be used in such tests and the conclusions which can be drawn; and
- requiring that workers be informed of the nature of such tests and that written consent by the worker and the medical practitioner be obtained.[17]

Training

Regular and updated training is essential to violence prevention. Training involves instilling interpersonal and communication skills which defuse and prevent a potentially threatening situation; developing competence in the particular function to be performed; improving the ability to identify potentially violent situations and people; and preparing a "core group" of mature and specially competent staff who can take responsibility for more complicated interactions. Guidelines for specific occupations further identify the special training needs and skills required to prevent or cope with violence under different circumstances. For counter staff and interviewing officers, for instance, improved interpersonal relations skills are a vital element in reducing

---

[15] ILO, "Workers' privacy: Testing in the workplace", *Conditions of Work Digest*, Vol. 12, 2/1993, 1993, p. 62.

[16] idem.

[17] Op. cit., p. 63.

aggression. Employees should also have knowledge of the nature of client aggression, the motivations of aggressors, cues to impending aggression, how to conduct interviews properly and to adhere to prescribed procedures, and how to respond to emotional clients. Specific advice should be given on when and how contact with a client should be ended to protect the employee from violence.[18] Special training of employees who have responsibility for public safety is crucial. This is often the case at airports and other public transport facilities. Inadequate training or employee performance can lead to disasters.

Bus drivers become social actors
Experience from Montpellier (extracts)

Recent events have put problems of violence in urban transport high on the public agenda. Whether they like it or not, drivers are active participants in social questions, and new ideas and experiments are emphasizing their new-found role.

"If people would recognize the social and human dimension of drivers' work, we would get better results in terms of preventing conflict on public transport." (Y.B.). This has led to an experimental project by the Montpellier City Bus Company (SMTU). "Instead of trying to change society, we've simply tried to teach drivers to become quality social actors. In Montpellier, that has brought about a spectacular decline in the number of attacks taking place on our bus network – from 71 to five in three years." L.G., a training officer with SMTU since 1978, also believes in this approach: "A driver meets about 700 to 1,000 people per day. His or her main job is driving, but there's also a social component to the work. It can be minimal, but it is always there, and therefore requires some training; not to make them social workers, but to help them face the day-to-day problems they encounter."

Source: "Transports urbains – Un terrain possible pour les travailleurs et les intervenants sociaux", in *L'observation des nouveaux risques sociaux*, No. 13, November 1998, p. 6.

Information and communication

Circulation of information, open communication and guidance can greatly reduce the risk of violence at work by defusing tension and frustration among workers.

Violence at the two plants of Wainwright Industries in the US "is just nonexistent", says David Robbins, the company's vice president and a co-owner with his two brothers-in-law. "Knock on wood, it's just never been a problem. I attribute that in no small part to our very, very open communications." "Employees may still get frustrated sometimes", he says, "but there is always an avenue to talk it out".[19]

Circulation of information is of particular importance in removing the taboo of silence which often surrounds cases of sexual harassment, mobbing and bullying. Information sessions, personnel meetings, office meetings, group discussions and problem-solving groups can prove very effective in this respect.[20]

Effective communication can also do much to prevent violence in contacts with clients and the public. Thus the provision of information to patients, their friends and relatives is crucial in lessening the risk of assault within hospitals. This is particularly

---

[18] Swanton and Webber, 1990, p. 41.

[19] "Creating a violence-free company culture", in *Nation's Business* (Washington, DC), February 1995, p. 22.

[20] Beermann and Meschkutat, 1995, pp. 31 and 38.

the case in situations involving distress and long waiting periods, as often occurs in accident and emergency departments. Even the usually well-balanced individual may be apprehensive and anxious about unfamiliar surroundings and procedures. In such situations, people are less worried when they have sufficient information to reduce uncertainty. Many staff, having become accustomed to the hospital environment, fail to appreciate how disconcerting it is to patients who are experiencing that environment for the first time, often when in a state of distress or apprehension.[21]

It is also recommended that staff are informed in the best way possible to cope with aggression, by providing guidelines and staff development programmes, devoted particularly to violence at work. Assistance from supervisors and co-workers should be available if a client or member of the public becomes aggressive or physically violent. Mutual support among the staff members should be emphasized.[22]

Physical environment and layout

In the context of possible violence and aggression in the workplace, the design of workplaces can be viewed from different perspectives: design of the environment in general and protection-specific design.

General factors to consider at the design stage include ventilation and thermal control; seating, which is crucial, especially where waiting is involved; comfort and size of waiting rooms; noise level; colour and light; and toilet facilities. Other design factors include controlled entrances, alarms, security screens, security guards, protective barriers, surveillance cameras and systems to alert co-workers that urgent help is needed.[23]

As to protection-specific design, conditions vary greatly between locations and industries. While, for example, in cash-handling businesses it is suggested to position the bulk cash-handling areas as far as possible from the entrance and exits,[24] in educational institutions it is suggested that the reception area be located close to the premises' main entrance.[25]

Special protection is needed by people working alone, particularly those operating in transport services, such as bus drivers.

However, the acceptability and perceived effectiveness of certain measures can differ. While in British studies, screens around drivers reduced assaults on drivers, in France enclosing the seat in this way has not always been believed to be effective, nor has it been received positively by passengers. In Australia, New South Wales State Transit experimented with partitions at night, but discarded them in favour of emergency buttons and hidden microphones linked to the bus office, which were found to be of greater deterrent value. Radios can also be connected to police sources or street supervisors. However, the potential for radios, silent alarms, flashing lights and cameras to prevent assault depends upon the drivers' ability to reach the particular apparatus, and the speed of the response by police. Other elements of bus design and special procedures have proved effective. For example, exit doors in the centre can reduce

---

[21] Health Services Advisory Committee, 1987, p. 8.
[22] Swanton and Webber, 1990, p. 35.
[23] idem, pp. 11-38.
[24] Department of Labour (New Zealand), 1995b, p. 9.
[25] Health and Safety Commission (United Kingdom), 1990, p. 4.

Protecting bus drivers against attacks

Installing appropriate equipment can help to protect staff and passengers from attack, as well as to improve services and the company's public image. Here are four examples:
1. Two-way radios. Fitting such radios to vehicles enables staff to communicate rapidly with the control point and from there with the police. Staff find the radios helpful. They give greater confidence and may well act as a deterrent against assaults. Radios can also be used for tracking a vehicle's progress, giving the added benefit of improved service quality and reliability. Where radios are installed, staff must be properly trained to use them.
2. Protective screens for drivers. Some versions are fixed, while others can be closed by the driver.
3. Alarm systems. These have proved to be of value. There are two main types: those fitted to the vehicle, which sound a siren or flash the lights; and pocket-sized, personal alarms which can be carried by the individual staff member.
4. Video cameras, CCTV etc. Video cameras and closed circuit TV can help identify assailants and vandals. They also act as a deterrent. Dummy cameras can also be fitted. Ensure that the equipment is visible, and fit warning notices to enhance the deterrent effect.

Source: Department of Transport (United Kingdom), 1995, p. 8. Crown copyright, reproduced with the permission of the Department of the Environment, Transport and the Regions.

---

assaults which occur when passengers disembark; fare systems where drivers have a minimal amount of money reduce the risk of theft; fare systems based on zones and pass systems reduce a common source of assaults – disputes over fares; having the number of buses geared to the volume of passengers reduces frustration over lengthy waits; and training drivers can help them defuse potentially aggressive interaction.[26]

Work organization and job design

Work organization and job content are key issues in developing preventive strategies against workplace violence. Engineering out the organizational problem at the source usually proves much more effective and less costly than increasing the coping capacity by means of protective intervention at the individual level.

Unsolved, persistent organizational problems cause powerful and negative mental strain in working groups. The group's stress tolerance diminishes and this can cause a "scapegoat" mentality and trigger acts of rejection against individual employees.[27]

Ensuring that staffing levels are appropriate, that tasks are assigned according to experience and competence, that tasks are clearly defined, that working hours are not excessive and that shifts are adequate to the particular situation, are all effective means to reduce tension and avoid aggression between workers and in their contact with the public.

Changing work practices to limit dissatisfaction from clients is also extremely important. The most influential factors for reducing client aggression are speedy and efficient service, which can be stimulated by various strategies such as staff rotation

---

[26] Easteal and Wilson, 1991, p. 39.

[27] Swedish National Board of Occupational Safety and Health, Ordinance (AFS 1993:17) on Victimization at Work, 21 September 1993, p. 5.

for particularly demanding jobs, rostering more staff at peak periods, designing how staff move between different working areas, tailoring client flow systems to suit needs and resources, and keeping waiting times to a minimum.

Organizational solutions can also help in reducing the risks of exposure to criminal attack. These may include changing the job or system of work to give less face-to-face contact with the public, thus limiting the opportunity for violent and threatening behaviour. The improvement of cash-handling procedures and the introduction of automatic ticket dispensers/collectors and cash machines can also assist, but, at the same time, it is important that these measures do not make violence a greater risk for members of the public instead, because staff are less visible or vulnerable.

A combination of different measures is usually recommended. Since every working situation is unique, so is the mix of measures which can best respond to that situation.

A mix of measures will often work best

Try to balance the risks to your employees against any possible side-effects to the public. An atmosphere that suggests employees are worried about violence can sometimes increase its likelihood.

Here are measures that have worked for some organizations:

- Changing the job to less face-to-face contact with the public, for example, introducing automatic ticket dispensers/collectors and cash machines. (Care should be taken that such measures do not increase the risks of violence to members of the public because there are no visible staff.)
- Staff who have to wear a company "uniform", e.g. bank or building society staff' are encouraged not to wear it (or at least to cover it up) when travelling to and from work.
- In one housing department, it was found that protective screens made it difficult for staff and the public to speak to each other (deaf people for instance can find screens a real problem). This caused tension on both sides. Management and trade unions agreed a package of measures, including taking screens down, providing more comfortable waiting areas and better information on waiting lists. These measures reduced tension and violent incidents.
- Using cheques, credit cards or tokens instead of cash can make robbery less attractive. For example, some milk delivery staff now operate a token system.
- Checking the credentials of "clients" and, if possible, the place and arrangements for meetings away from the office. This is standard practice now for some estate agents.
- Making sure that staff can get home safely. The threat of violence does not stop when work has ended. The Health and Safety at Work Act requires employers to protect employees only while they are at work, but some employers will take further steps where necessary. For example, if your staff work late, try and arrange for them to be able to drive to work and park their cars in a safe area. Many publicans [pub managers] arrange transport to take their staff home.
- Training your employees, either to give them more knowledge and confidence in their particular jobs, or to enable them to deal with aggression generally, by spotting the early signs and avoiding or coping with it.
- Changing the layout of public waiting areas. Better seating, decor, lighting and more regular information about delays have helped to stop tension building up in some hospital waiting rooms, housing departments and benefit offices.

- Using wider counters and raising the height of the floor on the staff side of the counter to give staff more protection. Some pubs have done this.
- Installing video cameras or alarm buttons. On buses, cameras have protected staff *and* reduced vandalism and graffiti.
- Putting protection screens around staff areas, as in some banks, social security offices and bus drivers' cabs.
- Using "coded" security locks on doors to keep the public out of staff areas.

Source: Suzy Lamplugh Trust, 1994(a), pp. 6-7. The Trust is a registered charity specializing in personal safety. For further information contact +44 181 876 0305.

DEALING WITH VIOLENT INCIDENTS

While prevention is by far the best way to deal with violence at work, and every effort should be made to tackle the causes of violence rather than its effects, it is important that workers are prepared and procedures are established to defuse difficult situations and to avoid violent confrontation.

Defusing aggression

Even in the most difficult circumstances, there is often some room for manoeuvre before violence is released. Control of a situation may not be easy, but many guidelines recommend ways of minimizing the risk of a violent incident taking place. Personal attitudes and behaviour are extremely important:

Advice on defusing aggression

Fear is information. It tells you something is threatening you. So if you feel your hair prickling at the back of your neck, stop and assess the situation. It may be a natural reaction to change, or fear of the unknown – or it might be something more. So when you are frightened, ask yourself:
- Is this person's anger/hostility directed at me, the organization, or themselves? Is it a form of distress?
- Am I in danger? If you think you are, leave and get help immediately.
- Am I the best person to deal with the threat? If you find a particular situation difficult, perhaps someone else could handle it more effectively. This is a positive step, not a cop-out [means of escape].

Never underestimate a threat, but do not respond aggressively. This will increase the chance of confrontation.
- Stay calm, speak gently, slowly and clearly.
- Do not be enticed into an argument.
- Do not hide behind your authority, status or jargon.
- Tell the person who you are, ask their name and discuss what you want him, or her, to do.
- Try to defuse the situation by talking things through as reasonable adults, while remembering your first duty is to yourself.
- Avoid an aggressive stance. Crossed arms, hands on hips, a wagging finger or a raised arm will challenge and confront.
- Keep your distance and try to avoid looking down on your aggressor.
- Never put a hand on someone who is angry.

A person on the brink of physical aggression has three choices: to attack, to retreat or to compromise. You need to guide them towards the second or third. Encourage them to move, to walk, to go to see a colleague. Offer a compromise such as talking through the problem. Or divert their aggression into actions like banging on a table or tearing up paper.

> If violence is imminent, avoid dangerous locations such as the top of staircases, restricted spaces, or places where there is equipment which could be used as a weapon. Keep your eye on potential escape routes. Keep yourself between the aggressor and the door and, if possible, behind a barrier such as a desk.
>
> Never turn your back, be prepared to move very quickly if necessary, and never remain alone with an actively violent person. To leave, move backwards gradually.
>
> If you manage to calm the situation, re-establish contact cautiously.
>
> Source: Suzy Lamplugh Trust, 1994(b), p. 3.

General advice of this nature has been more finely tuned and adapted for occupations at special risk. In the case of teachers, for example, the following recommendations have been given:

Teachers dealing with aggression

- Avoid confrontation in front of an audience, particularly groups of pupils. The fewer people that are involved in an incident, the easier it is for the aggressor to back down without losing face;
- Ask another, preferably senior, member of staff to help talk things through with the visitor;
- Stay calm, speaking slowly, so as not to be drawn into heated argument;
- Avoid aggressive body language such as hands on hips, wagging fingers, looking down on the aggressor.

Source: Health and Safety Commission, 1990, p. 5. Crown copyright.

Immediate action after violent incidents

Depending on the nature and gravity of the violence, police intervention may be required, especially in the case of major incidents. Guidelines often provide special recommendations relating to such incidents, particularly robberies.

Reporting incidents to the police

Notifying the police

The police must be notified as soon as it is safe to do so, before any other action is taken. The police will require to be told:

- the type of crime – armed robbery, etc.;
- the identity of the caller;
- the exact location of the crime for easy identification, not just the street number;
- whether anyone has been injured;
- description of events;
- the number of offenders, whether any are still present and, if they have left, the direction of escape;
- a brief description of offenders and any vehicles used; and
- whether firearms or other weapons have been seen or used.

If possible, the telephone line with the police should be left open until the police arrive, in order to maintain contact and enable instructions and information to be passed without delay.

Awaiting the police
While waiting for the police to arrive, the following basic measures need to be followed:
- If required, first aid should be rendered to any victims, and confirmation given that professional help is on the way.
- Shut and lock the outside doors, and post a member of staff there to allow urgent access to the emergency services when the police arrive.
- Preserve the scene and the evidence. As far as possible, avoid touching anywhere the robbers may have left fingerprints, footmarks or other evidence.
- Discourage witnesses from leaving before the police have arrived and spoken to them, or take their names and addresses and give them to the police.
- Ensure that those present do not discuss the events prior to being interviewed by the police. Written descriptions of the offender(s), such as height, build, clothing, footwear, speech, mannerisms, name(s) used, jewellery worn, other distinguishing features such as tattoos, description of weapon(s), vehicle(s) used and registration number(s) should be separately recorded by each witness.

On arrival at the scene of the incident
When the police arrive:
- Help them as much as possible.
- They will need to interview all witnesses including staff as appropriate. They will, however, ensure that private details of staff are not released to defence counsel, the media or through the court process. Police should be asked to ensure that the amount stolen is not released to the media.
- Make an inventory of stolen money or property, and give it to the police as soon as possible.
- Discuss and agree arrangements for liaison with the media.
  Staff should be told that in order to preserve the scene, the police may ask to conduct all interviews at a police station or in a place away from the premises that have been robbed.

Source: With the permission of the Department of Labour, Occupational Safety and Health Service (New Zealand), 1995, p. 15.

While police will normally lay charges against an aggressor where an offence is evident, it does not always happen. In situations like this, a victim may wish to institute personal proceedings against the aggressor. In those cases where criminal proceedings are instituted, staff will need particular care and support. Many will not have any experience of the criminal justice system, and will be worried about dealing with the police and giving evidence. It is recommended that help and advice start at the initial response stage, and be followed through with support for the police investigation and court hearing. Issues to consider will include additional support for staff called as witnesses or involved in identification parades; such tasks can often re-awaken bad memories of the incident itself.

Post-incident management

The first error many organizations make is failing to plan and prepare for traumatic incident management. After this, the most striking error is a failure to take appropriate action after the event because staff problems are not grossly evident or observable.[28]

---

[28] Conference Clearing House (CCH) International, "Managing violence and traumatic incidences at work", 1991, Ch. 42, Section 39, 823.

Victims of violence can experience a wide range of disturbing reactions such as anxiety, feeling of vulnerability and helplessness, disturbed sleep, difficulty in concentrating, increased fear, irritability, obsessive thoughts and images, feelings of shame, anger, frustration, guilt, changes in beliefs and values and a desire to retaliate. Experts emphasize the necessity of psychological help for victims of violence, to deal with the distressing and often disabling after-effects of a violent incident, as well as to prevent severe psychological problems from developing later. The quicker the response, the more effective and less costly it will be.

Debriefing is recommended in all but the most trivial cases. It usually involves meetings, preferably run by staff, and as many people as possible who were involved in the incident. This will give the victims of violence an opportunity to let out their feelings and to share the traumatic experience with others, as the following case illustrates:

Chain of care and support policy – "Time to talk" British Rail safety directive

What is the purpose of the safety directive?
To ensure that every member of staff who has been involved in a distressing incident is looked after properly. After such an incident, it will be normal procedure for staff to be offered the services of a trained debriefer to talk about what has happened.

Who is the debriefer?
A member of staff who has been trained to support people after a distressing incident. Anything you say to a debriefer is confidential. Debriefers do not pass reports to management unless you want further help. In this case, the manager will make the necessary arrangements with the Occupational Health Service.

What is a distressing incident?
It is difficult to give a complete list – some people are distressed by events which leave others unaffected – but it would include accidents, suicides, near misses, vandalism, robbery, assault. Staff affected may have been directly or indirectly involved.

Why do we need a safety directive?
Railway workers have very high demands placed upon them. Incidents that can be everyday occurrences on the railway bring sights and experiences which most people would not encounter in a lifetime. A distressed reaction can be normal, and managers must make sure staff are supported, so that they can continue to work safely and effectively.

What good is talking?
Going over a distressing incident can help to put it in perspective. After a trespasser fatality, for example, many people ask themselves – is there anything I could have done? Why did it happen to me? Will it happen again? They may start to think about death and dying. A debriefer will understand that these feelings can be quite normal and, for most people, such feelings will lessen over time.

Isn't it better just to forget it?
If a member of staff has been upset by a distressing incident, they cannot just forget it. Everyone reacts differently. There is evidence that bringing a

---

problem out "into the open" straight away can help prevent problems later on.

I am still upset by an incident that happened some time ago. Can I talk to a debriefer about it?
Yes. This can be arranged through your manager or supervisor, or by approaching the debriefer directly.

Source: Information supplied to the ILO by British Rail, dated 4 April 1996.

Depending on the gravity of the violence, it is recommended that the managers responsible for the area or people affected by it, as well as management with special information or relevant expertise on violence, be present. External consultants may also be involved in debriefing activities.

It is also recommended generally that trauma-crisis **counselling** be incorporated into the post-incident response. Certified employee assistance professionals, psychologists, psychiatrists, clinical nurse specialists or social workers could provide this counselling, or the employer can refer staff victims to an outside specialist. In addition, an employee counselling service, peer counselling, or support groups may be established.

In any case, counsellors must be well trained as well as having a good understanding of the issues and consequences of assaults and other aggressive, violent behaviour. Appropriate and promptly rendered post-incident counselling reduces acute psychological trauma and general stress levels among victims and witnesses. In addition, such counselling educates staff about workplace violence and positively influences workplace and organizational cultural norms, thus reducing trauma associated with future incidents.

When serious incidents occur, what happens afterwards is very important, as both the Dunblane and Port Arthur tragedies illustrate. Numerous sources emphasize and recommend the preparation of **plans** for handling situations after a violent incident. A plan which details the organization's incident response – how these events are to be managed – can help to bring the confusion and uncertainty of such episodes under control quickly. Post-incident planning can consider a variety of levels of response, as indicated in the box below:

Post-incident planning

Action immediately taken by readily available managers
An appropriate role for such managers would be to take control of the situation; to notify the organization's support staff; to support and relieve staff who were victims of abuse, while maintaining them within the work environment, if at all possible; to take responsibility for internal communications, and for liaison with police and counsellors for debriefing of traumatized staff.

Organizational and administrative intervention policies
Organizational and administrative policies aimed at minimizing the impact of traumatic events on the organization's human resources are also required.

Matters which need to be considered include the following:
• Provision of information and support for families of the people involved.
• Provision of information to the media. Ill-informed media reports have added to the trauma. Who will brief the media and when?

- Management should communicate directly with each person involved in an incident to express the organization's gratitude for the person's efforts. The manager's role is to take an interest, not to counsel. While some managers are hesitant about dealing with people who are emotional, it is better to say something, particularly to those who are most distressed, rather than to ignore these employees.
- Necessary investigatory procedures following an incident need to be fully explained to those involved. People otherwise commonly fear being "dumped" by the employer and/or being made a scapegoat.

Policy development
The organization's policy should detail the entitlements and support provided for employees who are victims of trauma. A clear policy of support and action may help to alleviate trauma and mitigate grievances.

The policy can outline how support will be provided in terms of provision of paid leave, dealing with medical expenses, other losses incurred by the employee for transfer or alteration of duties, provision of specialist trauma counselling services, legal representation, pursuing charges or seeking compensation against offenders.

Policy and procedures should be interpreted into safety, personnel and operations manuals.

Regular policy and procedures reviews are needed, as the type and extent of problems change over time.

Source: Conference Clearing House (CCH) International, "Managing violence and traumatic incidences at work", 1991, Ch. 42, section 39, 761.

The importance of **recording and reporting** workplace violence is emphasized by all experts. It is recommended that recording and reporting extends to all incidents, including both minor and potential incidents where no actual harm has resulted. Apparently trivial events should not be neglected, since they may become relevant later, assisting in detecting persistent patterns of behaviour or identifying an escalation in aggression.

Employers, in particular, are encouraged to record and report violent incidents. Minor incidents may be wrongly considered to be not worthwhile recording.

Employers may be reluctant to record workplace homicides, and some non-fatal assaults, because they often represent criminal law violations. However, the employer's recording of an injury or illness does not necessarily imply that the employer or employee was at fault, or that the injury or illness is compensable under workers' compensation or other systems, or that a violation of a Title 8 Safety Order or, more important, a Penal Code section, has occurred.[29]

It is also recommended that all employees should know how and where to report violent acts or threats of violence, without fear of reprisal or criticism. Employees should also be encouraged to report on conditions where they are subjected to excessive or unnecessary risk of violence; and to make suggestions for reducing the risk of violence or improving negative working conditions.

Some victims, especially in the case of major violent incidents, may need **long-term support**. Depending on the specific situation, such support will include extended professional counselling to help such victims to come to terms with the long-term effects of the incidents and enable them to return to work. It may also include legal assistance to facilitate the often complex and long-lasting procedures for compensation. Long-term rehabilitation and help in relocation of employment may also be required.

---

[29] California, 1993, p. 15.

Reporting and recording incidents

A formal system for reporting and recording incidents will be needed to:
(a) devise appropriate preventive strategies; and
(b) monitor whether these strategies are effective.

Staff will need to be positively encouraged to report incidents, if a true picture of their nature and frequency is to be built up.

Some staff, such as teachers, may be reluctant at first to report matters such as verbal abuse, for fear that this may reflect on their professional ability to manage classes. For this reason, it is important that the statement of intent makes it clear that reporting must not be linked adversely with ability to do a particular job.

A report form needs to contain sufficient detail to help identify appropriate preventive measures, and to help assess whether those measures were successful. Suggested details include information on:
(a) where the incident occurred, including physical environment;
(b) the time of day;
(c) activity at the time of the incident;
(d) details of assailant;
(e) relationship between victim and assailant;
(f) account of what happened;
(g) outcome;
(h) if preventive measures have been introduced, were they of help?

Good in-house reporting and recording systems are essential for identifying places and work activities where violence can be a problem.

Source: Health and Safety Commission, 1990, p. 3. Crown copyright.

Finally the need to **review and check** the effectiveness of new anti-violence measures after they have been introduced is strongly emphasized:

- Monitor the results of changes that have been introduced, using a system where employees can provide regular feedback, to check how well they are working and to make more modifications as necessary.
- Careful monitoring of the situation not only allows the effects of each change to be assessed, it also ensures that any remaining problems or change in the nature of the problem can be identified.
- It may be appropriate to hold joint management-employee meetings to discuss the measures put in place.
- If the measures work well, keep them up. If violence is still a problem, try something else. Go back through steps two and three and identify other preventative measures that could work.
- Review the management plan on a regular basis.[30]

Guidelines also provide special recommendations for monitoring and evaluation in specific sectors, such as banking. In principle, the higher the risk of violence at work, the more important the preventive measures to be adopted, and the more frequent and intense the monitoring and evaluation of such measures.

---

[30] Department of Labour (New Zealand), 1995(b), p. 15.

Monitoring and evaluation of anti-violence measures in banks

Monitoring is essential to maintain and improve the effectiveness of any policy or system. It is as important to monitor post-robbery procedures (for example, to determine whether counselling services are meeting individual and organizational needs) as it is to monitor security policy (for example to see whether a particular strategy has the effect of reducing the number of incidents).

Two complementary types of monitoring might be appropriate:
- **active systems** monitor achievement of plans and the extent to which predetermined performance standards have been complied with;
- **reactive systems** monitor incidents.

Both systems generate management information on levels of performance. Effective systems for reporting, investigating, recording and analysing the data are necessary to support them.

Information gained from monitoring systems should be analysed and evaluated regularly with the aim of:
- identifying common features or trends, or weaknesses or failure in performance, and their immediate or underlying causes;
- referring the results of evaluation to the level of management with the authority to initiate any remedial action, including organizational or policy changes.

Source: Health and Safety Executive (United Kingdom), 1993, p. 23. Crown copyright is reproduced with the permission of the Controller of Her Majesty's Stationery Office.

FROM NATIONAL TO CROSS-NATIONAL APPROACHES

The rich and diverse material reviewed so far in this part of the report has been largely concerned with ways of dealing with workplace violence in the setting of country-based interventions and initiatives. One noted exception to this approach was the European Directive on the Safety and Health of Workers referred to in Chapter 3. The European Union is not, however, alone in pursuing such a cross-national or regional strategy in response to violence at work. In Chapter 6 an examination is made of a number of actions taken at the international level which relate to this issue.

INTERNATIONAL ACTION

6

Violence: A global health problem

Given the many forms, circumstances and consequences of violence, measurement of the magnitude of the problem, until now, has been very unsatisfactory. Analysis of cause- and age-specific mortality statistics has been the most widely used approach, but deaths from violence are only the tip of the iceberg, merely suggesting the scale of the underlying problem. Data on morbidity, other consequences like unwanted pregnancy and family dissolution, disabilities, and socio economic costs are scarce and often unreliable.

In 1990 there were almost two million violent deaths in the world from homicide, suicide and war. Some 800,000 people took their own lives, 560,000 died as the result of homicide, and 500,000 were victims of wars and civil unrest. These statistics obscure the disproportionate impact of violence on specific subgroups throughout the world, most notably young people (and especially young adult males) women and children, and socially and economically deprived groups. In many developing and developed countries between 20 per cent and 40 per cent of deaths in males from 15 to 31 years of age are from homicide or suicide.[1]

Violence: A humanitarian aid issue

[In] today's conflicts and disturbances, the context in which the [International Committee of the Red Cross] ICRC has to operate is less and less well defined. Violence manifests itself in many different ways. Contacts have to be maintained with many different people, on account of the fragmentation of public authority, when there is any; persons not taking part in the hostilities, old people, children, are all potential targets; the limits to violence, which stem from the humanitarian values found in all great civilizations, are being constantly eroded by the choice of methods used by the parties to achieve their aims, such as summary executions, hostage-taking and torture…

The ICRC has endeavoured to respond to humanitarian problems of a new type and magnitude, by developing and diversifying its activities. Visits to detainees are now only one of the facets – albeit an extremely important one – of its mandate.

The ICRC's main task is not to take action itself, but to approach those in power to ensure that they are aware of and meet their humanitarian responsibilities both inside and outside places of detention.[2]

---

[1] World Health Organization (WHO), "Prevention of violence", Provisional Agenda Item 19, 50th World Health Assembly [A50/INF. Doc./4 12 March 1997], paragraphs 3-4. Reproduced with the permission of the WHO.

[2] M. Harroff-Tavel, "Action taken by the International Committee of the Red Cross in situations of internal violence", *International Review of the Red Cross* (Geneva), 1993, No. 294, pp. 219-220.

Violence: An international peacekeeping issue

On August 19th at 15.30 hours, Memisa's small Suzuki jeep with three persons inside was destroyed by an anti-tank mine near Kiziza, one kilometre
from their job, the Murunda hospital, before reaching the bridge at the junc-
tion with Gisenyi Kibuye road.The people at the hospital heard the blast and
went immediately to help them.

    One nurse died instantly due to the multiple injuries, and the driver one-
and-a-half hours later. The third person, an 8½ months pregnant lady sustained burns in around the half of her body's surface, a fracture on one wrist
joint and other injuries. She, as the driver, received resuscitation aid. She
was evacuated with a UNAMIR [United Nations Assistance Mission to
Rwanda] helicopter to Kigali for further aid.[3]

THE HAZARDS OF A GLOBAL WORKPLACE

Violence is a health problem of global dimensions, as the WHO statement cited above
illustrates. It is also a problem which impacts directly upon the work, and the personal health and safety, of the many thousands of individuals who seek to provide
humanitarian aid and assistance to the victims of this violence around the world.
For these workers, like those of the ICRC, who risk their lives in the service of international agencies or non-governmental organizations (NGOs), the workplace is
global in its dimensions and hazards.

    Action at the international level to combat global violence has included a num-
ber of new and important initiatives which relate directly to violence at work. These
initiatives form the principal subject matter of this chapter which looks initially at
violence at work in the context of human rights. Attention is then turned to the efforts
made by various international bodies, including the UN, to deal with this form of violence. The findings obtained from a small survey of a number of international agencies about their own internal policies regarding violence at work form part of this
analysis, as does a consideration of the regional activities of the European Union.
Finally, an account is given of some of the actions taken by multinational corporations in regard to violence which impinges upon their places of work.

VIOLENCE AT WORK IN THE CONTEXT OF HUMAN RIGHTS

The **Universal Declaration of Human Rights**, adopted by the UN General Assembly
on 10 December 1949, proscribes discrimination of any kind (art. 2); asserts the right
of everyone to life, liberty and security of their person (art. 3); and provides that no
one should be subject to torture or to cruel, inhuman or degrading treatment or punishment (art. 5). These fundamental rights were restated and further elaborated by the
International Covenant on Civil and Political Rights and the **International
Covenant on Economic, Social and Cultural Rights**, both of which were adopted by
the UN General Assembly on 16 December 1966. This last instrument, in particular,
expressly required the States which were parties to the Covenant to recognize the right
of everyone to the enjoyment of "safe and healthy working conditions" (art. 7(b)).

    However, it was not until the adoption by the UN General Assembly on
18 December 1979 of the **Convention on the Elimination of All Forms of Dis-**

---

[3] UNAMIR, *Special mines awareness* (Kibombobombo, Rwanda), no date, p. 2.

crimination against Women that the issue of violence at work was addressed in a specific way. Article 1 of the Convention states:

> For the purposes of the present Convention, the term "discrimination against women" shall mean any distinction, exclusion or restriction made on the basis of sex which has the effect or purpose of impairing or nullifying the recognition, enjoyment or exercise by women, irrespective of their marital status, on a basis of equality of men and women, of human rights and fundamental freedoms in the political, economic, social, cultural, civil or any other field.

Article 11 of the Convention requires ratifying States to "take all appropriate measures to eliminate discrimination against women in the field of employment". It was against this general background that in January 1992, the Committee on the Elimination of Discrimination against Women (**CEDAW**), set up under the Convention, adopted General Recommendation No. 19 on violence against women. The Recommendation, in particular, addressed the problem of sexual harassment providing, for the first time, a clear definition of this behaviour and listing actions to be taken against this form of violence by States.

- (Para.) 17. Equality in employment can be seriously impaired when women are subjected to gender-specific violence, such as sexual harassment in the workplace.
- (Para.) 18. Sexual harassment includes such unwelcome sexually determined behaviour as physical contact and advances, sexually coloured remarks, showing pornography and sexual demands, whether by words or actions. Such conduct can be humiliating and may constitute a health and safety problem; it is discriminatory when the woman has reasonable grounds to believe that her objection would disadvantage her in connection with her employment, including recruitment or promotion, or when it creates a hostile working environment.
- (Para.) 24. In light of these comments, the Committee on the Elimination of Discrimination against Women recommends that:
  - (j) States parties should include in their reports information on sexual harassment, and on measures to protect women from sexual harassment… in the workplace; …
  - (t) States parties should take all legal and other measures that are necessary to provide effective protection of women against gender-based violence, including, inter alia:
    - (i) Effective legal measures, including penal sanctions, civil remedies and compensatory provisions to protect women against all kinds of violence, including … sexual harassment in the workplace;
    - (ii) Preventive measures, including public information and education programmes to change attitudes concerning the roles and status of men and women.[4]

In June 1993, the World Conference on Human Rights held in Vienna, Austria, stressed the importance of working towards the elimination of violence against women in public and private life. One outcome of the Conference was the appointment of a Special UN Rapporteur on Violence Against Women. The Rapporteur who was to examine the causes and consequences of violence against women and recommend ways and means to eliminate them, now reports on an annual basis to the UN Commission on Human Rights.

In December 1993, the General Assembly adopted a landmark resolution on gender violence called the **Declaration on the Elimination of Violence against Women**. This Declaration defines what constitutes an act of violence against women, and calls on governments and the international community to take specific measures to prevent such acts. Violence against women is defined as:

---

[4] United Nations, "Report of the Committee on the Elimination of Discrimination against Women: Eleventh Session", General Assembly, *Official Records*, 47th Session, Supplement No. 38, A/47/38, New York, 1992, pp. 1-6.

any act of gender-based violence that results in, or is likely to result in, physical, sexual or psychological harm or suffering to women, including threats of such acts, coercion or arbitrary deprivation of liberty, whether occurring in public or in private life.[5]

The Declaration also lists abuses that are encompassed by the term "violence against women":

(a) Physical, sexual and psychological violence occurring in the family, including battering, sexual abuse of female children, dowry-related violence, marital rape, female genital mutilation and other traditional practices harmful to women, non-spousal violence and violence related to exploitation;

(b) Physical, sexual and psychological violence occurring within the general community, including rape, sexual abuse, sexual harassment and intimidation at work, in educational institutions and elsewhere, trafficking in women and forced prostitution;

(c) Physical, sexual and psychological violence perpetrated or condoned by the State, wherever it occurs.[6]

In September 1995, at the Fourth World Conference on Women held in Beijing, this definition was confirmed and action to be undertaken to combat violence against women was further specified.

Fourth World Conference on Women – Beijing, 1995: Call for action to combat violence against women at work

Actions to be taken by Governments:
"Enact and/or reinforce penal, civil, labour and administrative sanctions in domestic legislation to punish and redress the wrongs done to women and girls who are subjected to *any form of violence*, whether *in* the home, *the workplace*, the community or society;" (para. 124.c)

Actions by Governments, NGOs, educational institutions, enterprises, etc.:
"Recognize the vulnerability to violence and other forms of abuse of women migrants, including women migrant workers, whose legal status in the host countries depends on employers who may exploit their situation;" (para. 125.c)

Actions by Governments, employers, trade unions, etc.:
"Develop programmes and procedures to eliminate sexual harassment and other *forms of violence against women* in all educational institutions, *workplaces* and elsewhere;" (para. 126.a)

"Take special measures to eliminate *violence against women, particularly* those in vulnerable situations, such as young women, refugee, displaced and internally displaced women, women with disabilities and *women migrant workers*, including enforcing any existing legislation and developing, as appropriate, new legislation for women migrant workers in both sending and receiving countries;" (para. 126.d)

Actions by Governments, the private sector, NGOs, trade unions and the UN:
"Enact and enforce laws against sexual and other forms of *harassment in all workplaces*." (para. 180.c)

Source: United Nations, 1995, pp. 54, 56 and 82.

---

[5] United Nations, "Declaration on the Elimination of Violence against Women", in General Assembly, *Official Records*, 48th Session, A/RES/48/104, 20 December 1993, art. 1.

[6] ibid., art. 2.

Against this background the reports to the Commission on Human Rights by the Special Rapporteur on Violence Against Women have greatly contributed to highlighting the dimensions of the problem, with particular attention to sexual harassment and violence against women migrant workers. The Special Rapporteur's 1997 report contains a detailed analysis of these two issues:

Sexual harassment at work

The mere prohibition of sexual harassment is not adequate to assist victims of violence. It is imperative that institutions, whether public or private, educational or industrial, have internal procedures that ensure redress in cases of sexual harassment. The Canadian Federal Labour Code serves as a model in this regard. It requires employers to issue a sexual harassment policy, that condemns sexual harassment, indicates that disciplinary measures will be taken against transgressors, provides for procedures to deal with instances of harassment and informs employees of their rights.

Most private companies have been slow to respond to victims' needs since the company's first priority generally is seeking to avoid negative publicity. In some companies, informal mechanisms to address employees' complaints have been institutionalized. Internal mechanisms, if not implemented or enforced vigorously, may, however, serve to privatize the violation and impede the victim's recourse. Often such mechanisms are designed to resolve conflicts through mediation rather than to address the victim's needs and hold the perpetrator accountable. Such practices add pressure to the victim in deciding whether or not to pursue a claim against the harasser. With little or no institutional support for reporting, the victim's concerns about her own job status may encourage silence. In this connection, some jurisdictions render the employer vicariously liable for sex discrimination if he or she does not take adequate preventive measures.

Women migrant workers

"In astonishingly large numbers, women are migrating great distances across international boundaries to engage in poorly remunerated labour that isolates them in a subordinate position in a private realm, exposing them to acute risks of physical or psychological violence and to expropriation of their economic gain." [Joan Fitzpatrick, "Challenging boundaries: Gendered aspects of migration", unpublished document submitted to the Special Rapporteur, p. 9.]

The largely unregulated informal sector is the site of numerous violations of women's human rights. More than 2,000 cases of ill-treatment and abuse of migrant domestic workers in the United Kingdom have been documented. The abuses have included confiscation of passports, enforced change of contract, withholding of wages, deprivation of food and malnourishment, lack of access to medical and health services, imprisonment in the home of the employer, prohibition on engaging in social contacts, the interception of letters from home, and physical and sexual violence. …

In Latin America and the Caribbean, domestic labour migration has an extensive history plagued by reports of violence and abuse. In Asunción, there are roughly 15,200 domestic workers between the ages of five and 18 who have migrated from rural areas and work for free. Many of the girls receive education and accommodation in lieu of a salary. Such domestic arrangements increase their vulnerability to exploitation and violence. …

Similar conditions and consequences are reported among Colombia's *floristerias* (female workers in the flower export industry) who are also exposed to pesticides. In Guatemala, internal women migrants either work as domestic labourers or work in *maquilas* (garment assembly factories). In order to encourage foreign investors, *maquilas* are exempt from regulations guaranteeing workers' rights; women are subject to sexual violence and harassment, forced overtime, intimidation and generally poor working conditions.

In Morocco, young rural girls are placed with wealthy urban families as domestic servants. Despite promises of education and a better standard of living, the girls are often subjected to inhumane working conditions and forced to live in a state of indentured servitude. This situation is exacerbated in cases of "adoptive servitude", in which wealthy families adopt orphan girls for the explicit purpose of providing labour and there are widespread reports of physical abuse of the girls. Conditions in Asian countries with migrant domestic worker populations, including Japan, Malaysia, Cambodia and Singapore and in Hong Kong, are often characterized by such abuse.

In countries of the Persian Gulf, the estimated 1.2 million domestic workers constitute 20 per cent of the estimated six million migrants on whom these countries rely heavily. Sri

Lanka, Indonesia, India, and the Philippines are the primary sending countries to the Gulf region. The often violent and inhumane conditions in countries such as Saudi Arabia and Kuwait have been widely documented.[7] (Chapter V)

A closely related issue, violence against women in the family, is addressed in the 1999 Special Rapporteur's report. The link between violence at work and in the family, and their cumulative impact on victims, are emerging as a key to understanding the dramatic magnitude of overall violence against women. States and enterprises are beginning to realize the importance of the problem. However, as the report highlights:

Overwhelmingly, States are failing in their international obligations to prevent, investigate and prosecute violence against women in the family. While there are encouraging moves to create and implement new policies, procedures and laws with respect to violence against women generally, and domestic violence specifically, such violence does not appear to command Governments' attention. National policies continuously fail to give priority and force to women's human rights. Women continue to be viewed and treated as second-class citizens with a secondary rights status. Violence against women is overwhelmingly viewed as a "women's" issue rather than a serious human rights issue which affects a large percentage of any country's population. With few exceptions, domestic violence continues, to varying degrees, to be treated by Governments as a private family matter.[8]

Twenty years after the adoption of the Convention on the Elimination of All Forms of Discrimination against Women, a new UN instrument makes it possible for individual women or groups of women to submit claims directly to the Committee on the Elimination of Discrimination against Women in cases, inter alia, of violence at the workplace.

Optional Protocol adopted

On 12 March 1999 the forty-third session of the Commission on the Status of Women adopted an Optional Protocol to the Convention on the Elimination of All Forms of Discrimination against Women, at the recommendation of its Working Group. The Protocol contains two procedures: a communications procedure allowing individual women, or groups of women, to submit claims of violations of rights to the Committee on the Elimination of Discrimination against Women; and an inquiry procedure enabling the Committee to initiate inquiries into situations of grave or systematic violations of women's rights. In either case, States must be party to the Protocol.

The Protocol is the result of four years of negotiations in the Working Group. It will be submitted to the General Assembly of the United Nations for adoption in late 1999, and should be open for signature, ratification and accession in 2000. The Protocol will enter into force once ten States parties to the Convention have ratified, or acceded to, it.

Angela King, the Special Adviser to the Secretary-General on Gender Issues and Advancement of Women said that "the adoption of the Optional Protocol is particularly significant as 1999 is the 20th anniversary of the adoption of the Convention on the Elimination of All Forms of Discrimination against Women. Together with the achievement of the goal of universal ratification of the Convention by the year 2000, the Optional Protocol is a major step forward in Governments' commitment to the realization of women's human rights".

Source: United Nations Division for the Advancement of Women, New York, press release.
Retrieved from: http://www.un.org/womenwatch/daw/cedaw/protocol/adopted.htm, 26 April 1999.

---

[7] United Nations, 1997.

[8] United Nations, *Report of the Special Rapporteur on violence against women, its causes and consequences, Ms. Radhika Coomaraswamy*, Geneva, United Nations Commission on Human Rights, E/CN.4/1999/68, 1999 (10 March).

The protection of migrant workers is the specific object of another UN instrument, the **International Convention on the Protection of the Rights of all Migrant Workers and Members of their Families**, adopted by the General Assembly in 1990. The Convention extends the protection of fundamental human rights to all migrant workers and their families, irrespective of whether they are legal or illegal residents of the host country. Legally resident migrants are ensured, in addition, equality of treatment with nationals of the host country in a number of legal, political, economic, social and cultural areas. In particular, art. 7 explicitly provides that non-discrimination with respect to rights shall exist

without any distinction of any kind, such as sex, race, colour, language, religion or conviction, political or other opinion, national, ethnic or social origin, nationality, age, economic position, property, marital status, birth or other status.

Article 16.2 of the Convention specifically grants to migrant workers and members of their families "effective protection by the State *against violence, physical injury, threats and intimidation*, whether by public officials or by private individuals, groups or institutions".

Since its adoption, this UN Convention has been ratified by only seven states, most of them being nations which primarily send migrants abroad. The Convention will only enter into force after it has received at least 20 ratifications or accessions.

A third UN instrument which is relevant in regard to violence at work is the **International Convention on the Elimination of All Forms of Racial Discrimination**. Adopted in 1965, this Convention calls on States to condemn racial discrimination, to pursue by all appropriate means and without delay a policy of eliminating racial discrimination in all its forms, and to promote understanding among all races. The Convention prohibits, in particular, all forms of racial discrimination in respect of

the rights to work, to free choice of employment, **to just and favourable working conditions**, to protection against unemployment, to equal pay for equal work, to just and favourable remuneration. (Art. 5 (e)(i)).

ACTION BY INTERNATIONAL AGENCIES

In addition to the UN bodies operating in the area of human rights, a number of UN agencies and other international bodies are becoming increasingly active in the fight against violence at work. Depending on the nature of the agency or body, violence at work is tackled as a labour, health and safety, or a criminal justice issue.

Violence at work as a labour issue
The **ILO**'s concern and action in areas closely related to violence at work have already been highlighted in Chapter 1.

Violence at work as a health and safety issue
In 1996 the **WHO**, at its 49th World Health Assembly, adopted a Resolution which – in recognizing the serious immediate and future long-term implications for health and psychological and social development that violence represents for individuals, families, communities and countries – declared violence to be a leading worldwide public health problem.[9] As requested in the Resolution, a plan of action for progress towards

---

[9] WHO, 1996.

a science-based public health approach to violence prevention was presented to, and approved by, the WHO Executive Board in January 1997. The plan highlights the dramatic dimensions and consequences of violence, including violence at work, and indicates priorities and means of action to deal with the problem.

WHO plan of action against violence (excerpts)

Introduction

1. The burden of ill-health caused by violence is staggering. Violence undermines the social and economic conditions of communities. The atmosphere generated by frequent and severe personal or organized violence discourages investment, destabilizes national labour and industry, discourages tourism, and contributes to the emigration of skilled citizens. Violence in the home, on the street, and in the classroom disrupts education and the provision of basic services; it inhibits the delivery of curative and preventive health care. As an expression of power, it increases gender-based and social inequity. For various reasons the attitude of the health sector to violence has been until now ambivalent, insufficiently committed to preventing it and resorting to ad hoc solutions. Without a new public health vision to tackle the growing problem of violence, the cost to society can only increase.

2. While there is no universally accepted typology of violence, the groupings commonly used are:

Self-inflicted violence, for which suicide represents the fatal outcome. Other types include attempts to commit suicide and non-lethal self-mutilation.

Interpersonal violence occurs in many forms and can best be classified by the victim-offender relationship: domestic violence (family and intimate partners), violence among acquaintances, and violence involving strangers. It may also be specified according to the age or sex of the victim (child abuse, or rape). *Social institutions may be the setting for violence: bullying, harassment or criminally linked violence may be found in schools, the workplace, the commercial sector, and the military.*

Organized violence is violent behaviour of social or political groups motivated by specific political, economic or social objectives. Racial or religious conflicts are other forms of violence occurring among groups. Armed conflict and war are the extreme form of organized violence.
[...]

5. The consequences of violence extend far beyond physical injury: violence has profound psychological implications for its victims, perpetrators and witnesses, as well as close surviving relations and friends. For others, such as women and children who live under the daily threat of violence from partners or parents, the quality of life is drastically affected.

WHO integrated plan of action on violence and health

6. This plan is the first step in consolidating the activities of several WHO programmes concerning violence, and in building a coherent WHO public health approach to violence and health. During the first three years, the first objective and the highest priority will be better to define the problem.

Objective 1. To describe the problem (first priority) [...]
Objective 2. To understand the problem: conduct risk-factor identification and research: to promote research and increase information on determinants and consequences of violence through all appropriate technical programmes of the Organization. [...]
Objective 3. Identification and evaluation of interventions: to determine measures and programmes aimed at preventing violence and mitigating its effects, and to assess their effectiveness. [...]

> **Objective 4. Programme implementation and dissemination:** to strengthen the capacity, primarily of the health system but also of all concerned parties on the basis of the evaluation of existing activities, in order to implement coherent programmes.
>
> Source: WHO Executive Board, 99th Session, Provisional Agenda Item 13, "Prevention of violence", Document EB99/INF. Doc/3, 7 January 1997, pp. 1-4.

Violence at work as a criminal justice issue

The **Commission on Crime Prevention and Criminal Justice** in Vienna has been active in this area, with particular attention being given to the elimination of violence against women. In reiterating the importance of the problem, the Secretary-General, in his last report to the Commission, recommended that

measures relating to criminal law and procedure and other legal provisions should be taken as appropriate, which prohibit by criminal law all acts of violence against women, including, as applicable, **threats or coercion**, wherever they occur, **in the workplace**, in the home, in schools and other institutions, in society and elsewhere, and irrespective of the perpetrator or his relationship with the female victim.[10]

The UN Interregional Crime and Justice Research Institute, **UNICRI**, an autonomous body based in Rome which operates as the interregional research and training arm of the UN crime and criminal justice programme, has been involved in the conduct of the International Crime Victim Survey (ICVS), a comparative research exercise that has so far involved more than 50 countries. The results obtained from this survey in relation to violence at work have already been fully described in Chapter 2.

INTERNAL ACTION WITHIN THE UNITED NATIONS SYSTEM

To obtain more direct information about current internal policies, practices and actions regarding violence at work among international agencies, a small survey was conducted by the ILO on this subject. A short questionnaire was distributed in April 1997 to 32 organizations within the United Nations System of Organizations.[11] A list of these organizations appears below. It will be seen that 15 of these bodies provided a response to the questionnaire, including several employing large numbers of international civil servants.

Violence at work: Organizations surveyed*

Name of organization

Economic Commission for Africa
Economic Commission for Europe
Economic Commission for Latin America and the Caribbean
Economic and Social Commission for Western Asia and for Asia and Pacific
Food and Agriculture Organization
International Atomic Energy Agency
International Civil Aviation Organization

---

[10] Commission on Crime Prevention and Criminal Justice, 1997, p. 16.

[11] United Nations, *United Nations System of Organizations and Directory of Senior Officials*, New York, March 1995. A number of organizations were excluded because of their small size, very specialized role, or a combination of both.

International Fund for Agricultural Development
International Maritime Organization
International Monetary Fund
International Telecommunication Union
United Nations Centre for Human Settlements
United Nations Children's Fund
United Nations Conference on Trade and Development
United Nations Development Programme
United Nations Educational, Scientific and Cultural Organization
United Nations Environment Programme
United Nations Headquarters
United Nations High Commissioner for Refugees, Office of
United Nations Industrial Development Organization
United Nations International Drug Control Programme
United Nations Office at Geneva
United Nations Office at Vienna
United Nations Population Fund
United Nations University
Universal Postal Union
World Bank/International Finance Corporation
World Food Programme
World Health Organization
World Intellectual Property Organization
World Meteorological Organization
World Tourism Organization

* Responding organizations (15) are shown in bold.

The questionnaire included the following questions:

Question 1: Is violence at work a concern in your Organization?
Question 2: If "yes" under which form? ❐ physical attacks; ❐ sexual harassment; ❐ bullying/mobbing; ❐ verbal aggression; ❐ threats;
❐ other?
Question 3: Do you have any of the following anti-violence initiatives?
(planned or implemented) ❐ policies; ❐ employees' assistance
programmes; ❐ codes of practice; ❐ guidelines?
Question 4: Do you have any statistics available on the extent of violence
at work in your Organization?

The results of the survey showed that violence at work was said to be of concern to almost half of the organizations responding (see figure 13), although to different degrees between organizations and even within the same organization, depending on the type of violence and the geographical location of the workplace. As shown in figure 14, sexual harassment was indicated as being of most widespread concern (33 per cent), followed by verbal aggression (29 per cent), physical attacks (14 per cent), bullying and mobbing (14 per cent) and threats (10 per cent). Multiple answers were allowed.

Almost all of the responding organizations said that they had planned or implemented some form of anti-violence initiative (see figure 15), including policies (32 per cent), employees' assistance programmes (32 per cent) and codes of practice/ guidelines (36 per cent). Almost none of the answering organizations had statistics available on the extent of violence at work among their employees. The survey findings are summarized in the following figures.

These findings, while not representative of the general situation among United Nations organizations, should provide a starting point for a much more detailed review of a still largely unexplored area. Recognizing the need for such a review, the UN has launched an extensive harassment survey within the organization.[12] Further action of this type is clearly required in order to put in place appropriate anti-violence policies and programmes.

Figure 13.   1997 ILO survey on violence at work among United Nations organizations: Is violence at work a concern?

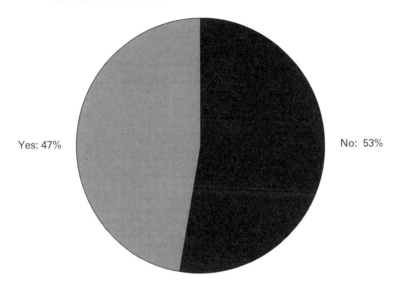

Yes: 47%   No: 53%

[12] United Nations, "United Nations Harassment Survey", Circular ST/IC/1997/37, New York, 24 June 1997.

Violence at work

Figure 14.   1997 ILO survey: Violence at work: Type of concern*

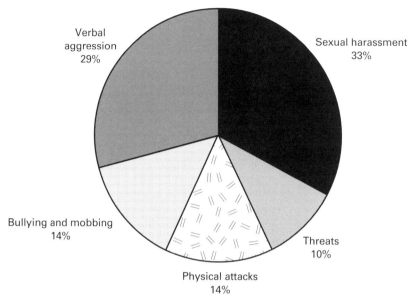

* Based on positive answers only.

Figure 15.   1997 ILO survey: Violence at work: Action taken*

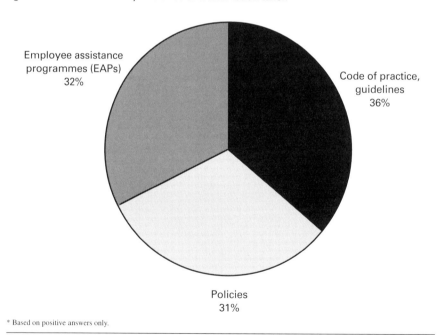

* Based on positive answers only.

REGIONAL INITIATIVES TO COMBAT VIOLENCE AT WORK

In June 1994, in Bélem do Pará, Brazil, the 24th Ordinary Session of the General Assembly of the Organization of American States adopted the **Interamerican Convention to Prevent, Sanction and Eradicate Violence against Women**. Article 2 of the Convention extends the scope of this instrument to *sexual harassment at the workplace*. The instrument includes important provisions specifying the fundamental rights of women in this area, the duty of the ratifying States to make such rights effective, and the mechanisms to implement the provisions of the Convention.

The issue of violence at work has also been high on the agenda of the **European Union** in recent years. In 1986, the European Parliament tackled the problem with a Resolution on Violence Against Women which included extensive recommendations and calls for action in respect of sexual harassment.[13] This position has been reiterated and reinforced in the Resolution on the need to establish a European Union wide campaign for zero tolerance of violence against women (September 1997). In 1990, a Resolution from the Council of the European Communities concerning the protection of the dignity of women and men at work[14] called for action by the Member States to fight sexual harassment, and asked the Commission of the European Communities to produce a **Code of Practice on Measures to Combat Sexual Harassment**.[15]

The Code, issued in 1992, stresses the crucial role of prevention in reducing or eliminating sexual harassment. It recommends to employers that preventive action should be adopted, where appropriate, after consultation or negotiation with trade unions or employee representatives, along the lines contained in the following box:

Commission of the European Communities:
Code of Practice on Measures to Combat Sexual Harassment

Policy statements
As a first step in showing senior management's concern and their commitment to dealing with the problem of sexual harassment, employers should issue a policy statement which expressly states that all employees have a right to be treated with dignity, that sexual harassment at work will not be permitted or condoned and that employees have a right to complain about it should it occur.

It is recommended that the policy statement makes clear what is considered inappropriate behaviour at work, and explains that such behaviour, in certain circumstances, may be unlawful. It is advisable for the statement to set out a positive duty on managers and supervisors to implement the policy and to take corrective action to ensure compliance with it. It should also place a positive duty on all employees to comply with the policy and to ensure that their colleagues are treated with respect and dignity.

In addition, it is recommended that the statement explains the procedure which should be followed by employees subjected to sexual harassment at work, in order to obtain assistance and indicate to whom they should complain; that it contains an undertaking that allegations of sexual harassment will be dealt with seriously, expeditiously and confidentially; and that employees will be protected against victimization or retaliation for bringing a

---

[13] European Parliament, 1986.

[14] "Council Resolution concerning the protection of the dignity of women and men at work", *Official Journal of the European Communities* (Brussels), 90/C 157/02, 29 May 1990.

[15] In *Official Journal of the European Communities*, 24 February 1992, pp. L 49/3-L 49/8.

complaint of sexual harassment. It should also specify that appropriate disciplinary measures will be taken against employees found guilty of sexual harassment.

Communicating the policy

Once the policy has been developed, it is important to ensure that it is communicated effectively to all employees, so that they are aware that they have a right to complain and to whom they should complain; that their complaint will be dealt with promptly and fairly; and so that employees are made aware of the likely consequences of engaging in sexual harassment. Such communication will highlight management's commitment to eliminating sexual harassment, thus enhancing a climate in which it will not occur.

Responsibility

All employees have a responsibility to help to ensure a working environment in which the dignity of employees is respected and managers (including supervisors) have a particular duty to ensure that sexual harassment does not occur in work areas for which they are responsible. It is recommended that managers should explain the organization's policy to their staff and take steps positively to promote the policy. Managers should also be responsive and supportive to any member of staff who complains about sexual harassment; provide full and clear advice on the procedure to be adopted; maintain confidentiality in any cases of sexual harassment; and ensure that there is no further problem of sexual harassment or any victimization after a complaint has been resolved.

Training

An important means of ensuring that sexual harassment does not occur and that, if it does occur, the problem is resolved efficiently, is through the provision of training for managers and supervisors. Such training should aim to identify the factors which contribute to a working environment free of sexual harassment, and to familiarize participants with their responsibilities under the employer's policy and any problems they are likely to encounter.

In addition, those playing an official role in any formal complaints procedure in respect of sexual harassment should receive specialist training, such as that outlined above.

It is also good practice to include information as to the organization's policy on sexual harassment and procedures for dealing with it as part of appropriate induction and training programmes.

Source: Commission of the European Communities, *Official Journal*, 24 February 1992, pp. L 49/5-L 49/6.

In 1997, the Commission's action in this field led to the production of a document entitled **Guidance on the Prevention of Violence at Work**. This publication includes a review of the scientific literature in this area; a survey to identify the prevalence of violence at work as well as existing guidelines; and draft guidance plans for implementation at the level of the EU. The survey findings are summarized in the following box:

Survey on violence at work in the European Union

The findings from the questionnaire suggested the following situation:
- There is considerable difference in awareness of the issues of violence in the context of health and safety between countries.

- The legislative position, with the exception of the Netherlands and Sweden, is that violence at work is generally covered by both framework-type health and safety legislation and by the civil and criminal codes.
- Research into the issue of violence appears to be a relatively recent phenomenon where it occurs. Research seems to be concentrated in the more developed countries in Europe.
- The implementation of legislation was generally reported to take place, both within the general implementation of the requirements of health and safety legislation and, to some extent, using the criminal and civil codes.
- Significant barriers to the implementation in many countries include lack of awareness, difficulties in implementing legislation in SMEs [small and medium-sized enterprises], and limited resources for enforcement of legislation.

The overall impression from the data supplied by the respondents to the survey is that there is limited awareness of the issue of violence at work in many countries, but that legislative provisions appear to exist in general terms and are generally implemented. However, there are grounds for questioning this impression:

Firstly, a major finding from reviewing the literature is that the extent of the problem is usually underestimated. In the absence of specific and comprehensive research on the prevalence and extent of workplace violence, it is difficult to believe that the problem is being adequately dealt with.

Secondly, the existence of guidelines to deal with violence is not uniform across the EU. In their absence, it is unlikely that consistent and comprehensive management of the issue actually takes place.

Thirdly, the situation with regard to the implementation of legislation must be questioned. While the respondents to the survey generally reported good levels of implementation, the precise nature of implementation is, at best, unclear. While there is no doubt that the appropriate agencies dealing with health and safety carry out their duties with regard to the range of health and safety issues, they do so only in the context of the resources provided to them. In practice, this often means that they have limited resources available to them for enforcement, and that SMEs in particular tend not to be subject to high levels of enforcement. Furthermore, in the context of limited awareness of the problem, the extent of actual management activity within enterprises must be questioned.

For these reasons, it is likely that the operation of legislation in the area is somewhat less than optimal.

Source: Wynne et al., 1997, pp. 28-29.

In providing further guidance plans to combat violence at work, the document stresses the importance of the following issues:

- Definition of violence and abuse
- Recording procedures for violent incidents
- Analysis of data on violent incidents
- Need for a balanced approach involving preventive, protective, treatment and security measures
- Need for sensitive and early treatment of victims of violence
- Need to facilitate organizational learning about the issues of violence
- Need for a risk assessment cycle, as shown in table 19.

Violence at work

Table 19.   Risk assessment cycle

Phase of the cycle	Activities
1. Assessing the scope of the problem	– Find out if there is a problem – Accept the existence of the problem – Define violence
2. Assessing the problem	– Develop and implement/improve recording system – Identify hazards – Identify risks – Analyse and classify all incidents
3. Designing interventions	– Search for potential interventions (preventive protective, treatment, security, training) – Decide on interventions in a collaborative way – Develop company policy
4. Implementing the interventions	– Implement measures in a visible way

5. Monitoring the interventions	– Monitor the interventions in terms of process,
	     uptake and outcomes
	– Alter the interventions on the basis of
	     monitoring data
	– Publicize results of the monitoring activity

Source: Wynne et al., 1997, p. 43.

Part III: Future guidance

BEYOND VIOLENCE: LESSONS FOR FUTURE ACTION

7

Workplace violence: A Zero Tolerance Policy, City of El Centro (California)

The City of El Centro has adopted this *Zero Tolerance Policy* for workplace violence because it recognizes that workplace violence is a growing problem nationally that needs to be addressed by all employers. Consistent with this policy, acts or threats of physical violence, including intimidation, harassment, and/or coercion which involve or affect the City of El Centro or which occur on City property will not be tolerated.

Application of prohibition
The City of El Centro's prohibition against threats and acts of violence applies to all persons involved in the City's operation, including but not limited to City personnel, contract and temporary workers, and anyone else on City of El Centro property. Violations of this policy by any individual on City property, or by an individual acting off of City property when his/her actions affect the public interest of the City's business interests, will be followed by legal action, as appropriate. Violation by an employee of any provision of the policy may lead to disciplinary action (up to and including termination, as provided in the City Personnel Rules and Regulations or Memoranda of Understanding). This policy and any sanctions related thereto are to be deemed supplemental to the City's Personnel Rules and Regulations, and Memoranda of Understanding provisions related thereto, and applicable state and federal laws.

Employee obligations
Each employee of the City and every person on City of El Centro property is encouraged to report incidents of threats or acts of physical violence of which he/she is aware.

In cases where the reporting individual is not a City employee, the report should be made to the City of El Centro Police Department.

In cases where the reporting individual is a City employee, the report should be made to the reporting individual's immediate supervisor, a management-level supervisory employee if the immediate supervisor is not available, or to the City's Personnel Division. Each supervising employee shall promptly refer any such incident to the appropriate management level supervisor, who shall take corrective action in accordance with the City's Personnel Rules and Regulations and any applicable Memoranda of Understanding. Concurrently with the initiation of any investigation leading to a proposed disciplinary action, the management level supervisor shall report the incidents of threats or acts of physical violence to the El Centro Police Department, which shall make a follow-up report to the City's Personnel Division.

Nothing in this policy alters any other reporting obligations established in City policies or in state, federal or other applicable law.

Training
The City will provide opportunities for employees to be trained in the risk factors associated with workplace violence, and proper handling of emergency situations in order to minimize the risks of violent incidents occurring in the workplace.

Dissemination of policy
All employees will be given copies of this policy. All new employees will be given a copy of this part of this policy as part of their orientation by the Personnel Division.

Source: El Centro, letter by Douglas G. Detling, 8 May 1996.

REPUDIATING VIOLENCE

This has been a report about violence at work – its scope, causes and how it may be prevented. It is a report which commenced with the description of two tragedies which occurred at workplaces on opposite sides of the globe. Those tragedies revealed in the most brutal and shocking way how acts of extreme violence could impinge on communities and work sites believed to be completely immune from such horrific events. That illusion was shattered, not only for those directly affected by the violence at Dunblane and Port Arthur, but also for countless millions of the world's citizens exposed to the media's coverage of the shootings and their aftermath.

There is no doubt that many lessons have been learned from workplace tragedies like Dunblane and Port Arthur. They are events which have been the catalysts for positive action to deal with both the broader problems of violence which afflict all societies to a greater or lesser degree, and the more specific issues of violence at work. They are also events which reinforce a growing consensus, exemplified by the statement issued by the small city of El Centro in California which commences this chapter, that a *zero tolerance policy* towards violence in the workplace is a response which should be adopted universally.

FROM A HIDDEN TO A DISCLOSED ISSUE

Traditionally, the workplace has been viewed as a quite benign environment where, despite certain levels of robust confrontation and dialogue, people usually manage to resolve their dilemmas in a peaceful and constructive way. Forward-looking employers recognize that the health and well-being of their enterprise is consistent with, if not dependent upon, the health and well-being of their employees. A healthy workforce is a more productive workforce. Thus employer investment in the identification and control of stress, for instance, can be profitable at the same time as contributing to the prevention and control of violence.

Despite such recognition by employers of the negative consequences of violence in the workplace, and the increasing endorsement by them of a zero tolerance policy towards this violence, unwanted and unwarranted aggression can and does emerge in the workplace and may transform it into a hostile and hazardous setting. This book has described the mounting evidence from around the globe which suggests that violence at work is now an issue transcending the boundaries of a particular country, work setting or occupational group. No country, work setting or occupation can claim realistically to be entirely free of this form of violence, although some nations, like some workplaces and occupations, are undoubtedly at higher risk than others of experiencing such violence.

The evidence also shows that a new profile of violence at work is emerging, which gives equal emphasis to physical and psychological behaviour. It is a profile which also gives full recognition to the damaging impact of repeated behaviour of a type that by itself may be relatively minor, but cumulatively can become a very serious form of aggression, such as in the case of **sexual harassment**, **bullying** or **mobbing**.

The damaging impact of repeated acts of psychological aggression

This new profile of violence further recognizes that violence at work is not limited to a specified workplace, like an office, factory or retail establishment. There is a risk of violence occurring during commuting, and in non-traditional workplaces such as homes, satellite centres and mobile locations, which are being used increasingly as a result of the spread of new information technologies.

This report has stressed that the real magnitude of the violence taking place at work is only now being widely disclosed, as is its potential to harm the individual, the workplace and the community. However, a large proportion of the violence at work still remains unreported. Many employees, and in particular women, may feel constrained to remain silent about their victimization because of fear of reprisals being taken against them, including the possibility of losing their job. Reporting behaviours may also be influenced by different cultural sensitivities to violence, and the context in which it occurs. In recent times, for instance, an enhanced awareness that sexual harassment, bullying and mobbing are completely unacceptable behaviours has resulted in higher rates of reporting of such incidents by victims.

Where good statistics are available, the broad reach of violence at work can be seen in its full dimensions. The data on workplace homicides in the United States, for example, indicate that this is the leading cause of occupational death for women and the second most frequent cause of such deaths among the entire working population. Data on non-fatal violence suggest that more than 2 million American workers were assaulted, 16 million harassed and over 6 million threatened at their workplaces during a recent 12-month period.

The far-reaching dimensions of violence at work

Violence at work is of particular concern to women. The global impact of violence on women, both inside and outside the workplace, is dramatic. Women are concentrated in many of the high-risk occupations, particularly as teachers, social workers, nurses and health-care workers, as well as bank and shop workers. It has also been shown that women are more vulnerable to violence, due to their inferior position in the labour market. The continued segregation of women in low-paid and low status jobs, while men predominate in better-paid, higher status jobs and supervisory positions, contributes to this problem.

Another common finding relates to the vulnerability to violence of younger workers. This finding seems to be related to their relative inexperience in dealing with potentially violent situations. Previous experience enables employees to react more wisely and behave with more self-confidence than inexperienced staff. This may in turn reduce aggression and the likelihood of violence.

The special impact of violence on vulnerable workers

Violence in the workplace is to be found in both developing and industrialized nations, although as the report indicates, the information from developing countries about such violence is frequently limited, episodic and ill-defined. Different sensitivities in different contexts and cultures also contribute to variations in the reporting of violence at work, so that comparative data have to be used and interpreted with great caution. For these reasons attention has, until now, been concentrated principally on industrialized countries, where violence at work is better documented and the field of investigation is more homogenous.

The need to encourage reporting from developing countries

Despite these broad findings outlined in the report, violence at work remains a largely unexplored area, with a knowledge base which is often incomplete, imprecise or contradictory. Entire sectors, like mining and agriculture, have received minimal consideration, while certain occupations have been the object of sustained attention. The situation prevailing in entire countries can remain virtually unknown, and comparative analysis is often very limited in both its scope and outcome. Precise definitions and descriptions of the different forms of violence at work still remain in a state of flux, and the causes of this violence remain matters of conjecture.

The deficiencies which have been identified by this report in the information available regarding violence at work point to a pressing need for further and better systems of data collection and analysis. Among the issues which seem to require specific attention are the:

- enhancement of the capacities of most data collection systems to obtain information on violence at work;
- expansion of data gathering concerning countries, sectors, occupations and types of violence that have received insufficient attention to date;
- promotion of comparative analyses on the nature and extent of violence at work, including at the international level;
- development of commonly accepted definitions for the different forms of violence, and particularly for new and emerging types of workplace violence such as bullying or mobbing;
- development of targeted research in areas of particular concern, such as emerging types of violence, occupations at special risk, vulnerable categories of workers, violence against women, young workers and children, and the cost of violence;
- comprehensive analysis of violence at work in specific sectors of industry, services or trade, including the causes of this violence and the remedies experimented with; and
- expansion of networking on the issue of violence at work among researchers and research centres.

FROM A RESTRICTED TO A PUBLIC ISSUE

As this book has emphasized, the level of public awareness and concern about the issue of violence at work has been heightened by the media's reporting of dramatic events like those occurring at Dunblane and Port Arthur. Immediate information on what is known about these and other major incidents of violence at work is almost invariably obtained through "the media's lens". These media sources of information, while sometimes inaccurate and misleading, have done much to sensitize both the community and governments to the damaging consequences of this type of violent behaviour.

There is also a growing awareness that violence at work is not merely an episodic, individual problem but a structural, strategic problem rooted in wider social, economic, organizational and cultural factors; that violence at work is detrimental to the functionality of the workplace, and that any action taken against such violence is an integral part of the organizational development of a sound enterprise. Violence at work is seen increasingly to be a major problem that has to be tackled, and tackled now.

The growing awareness of the need to tackle the problem of violence at work

Workers, trade unions, employers, public bodies and experts across a broad international spectrum are now expressing common concern about the issue of violence at work. This concern is being matched by calls for action to prevent such violence or, when it occurs, to deal with it in a way which alleviates the enormous social, economic and other costs to the victims, their families, employers and the community at large.

In responding to the problem of workplace violence, it is now recognized to an increasing degree that violence can no longer be accepted as a normal part of any job, even where it would seem to be an occupational hazard, such as in law enforcement. As in the case of hazardous manufacturing and allied occupations, where risk-management strategies are put in place to reduce the level of uncertainty and of the possibility of injury, such strategies should be adopted with regard to violence, in order to minimize the possibility of assault, harassment and abuse to employees in the workplace.

There is also a growing recognition that, in confronting violence, it is important to think comprehensively. This means that instead of searching for the single solution good for any problem and situation, the full range of causes which generate violence should be analysed and a variety of intervention strategies applied. A recognition and an understanding of the variety and complexity of the factors which contribute to violence must be a vital precursor of any effective violence prevention or control programme.

The recognition that violence at work is a varied and complex problem

In terms of long-term strategies to tackle the general problem of violence in any society the most significant positive outcomes are likely to be achieved through a concentration on child development programmes linked to the family. It is within the family that aggressive behaviours are first learned. To the extent that families can instil non-violent values in their children, those children are more likely to negotiate life in society at large without resorting to a repertoire of violent behaviours. Meanwhile, there are many ways in which positive micro-level change can be achieved through targeted programmes and actions within a particular society, and the workplaces of that society.

Significant effort has been devoted to predict when an individual might behave in an aggressive manner. There is no doubt that certain identifiable factors do increase the likelihood that certain individuals, and population groups, will behave in such a way. These factors are to be found in both the long-term life experience of the people concerned, and in immediate, situational factors.

The fact remains that – when seeking to predict whether aggressive behaviour will occur – a distinction must be made between predicting at the level of the general population, or at that of the individual. The available evidence does permit statements to be made with some degree of accuracy and reliability about the heightened risk of violence being committed by population groups. The dilemma remains, however, of predicting with sufficient accuracy and reliability that a particular individual within that group may become violent. It is not possible in the current state of knowledge to predict with complete certainty that a specific person will behave in an aggressive way.

The difficulty of predicting where or when violence will occur

A far more promising approach to an understanding of workplace violence is to be found in an interactive analysis of both individual and social risk factors, with particular attention being given to the situational context in which certain types of work task are performed.

The personal characteristics and conditions of the perpetrator and the victim play an important role. However, both the perpetrator and the victim interact at the workplace. Thus the working environment can greatly influence the risks of violence resulting from this interaction.

The physical design features of a workplace can be an important factor in either defusing or acting as a potential trigger for violence. The organizational setting appears to be equally if not more important in this respect. In a broader context, the type of interpersonal relationship, the managerial style, the level at which responsibilities are decentralized, and the general culture of the workplace, must also be taken into consideration.

The interrelationship between the external environment and the working environment also appears significant in terms of predicting violence. Although the "permeability" of the working environment to the external environment is far from automatic, it is evident that violence in the external environment can find its way into the working environment and vice versa.

Interactions among individuals, the work environment and the external environment are the key generators of violence

Any prediction of the possibility of violent incidents occurring at the workplace will thus depend upon a thorough analysis of the characteristics of the working environment, the external environment, and those of the perpetrator and victim in the particular situation. Each situation is unique and thus requires a unique analysis. That is why predicting the occurrence of specific acts of violence is extremely difficult. Nevertheless, it seems possible and useful to identify a number of working situations which appear to be both highly relevant to an understanding of violence at work and to the development of strategies for its prevention or control.

These "situations at risk" include those associated with working alone; working with the public; working with valuables; working with people in distress; working in education; and working in conditions of special vulnerability.

Within this framework, growing evidence indicates the much higher risk associated with working alone in small shops, petrol stations and kiosks; working alone outside normal hours; working alone as a journalist and especially as an investigative reporter; and working as a taxi driver. Among those working with the public, bus, train and subway workers appear at special risk; so are flight attendants, shop workers in the retail sector and workers providing social services. Hotel, catering and restaurant staff are another group at risk.

The importance of identifying situations at special risk, while recognizing that each one is unique

Working with valuables, including handling cash, is a major area of risk. Violence associated with such activity is reported to be a major problem in the postal service, in financial institutions as well as for people employed in the private security industry. Health-care workers employed in emergency care units, psychiatric hospitals, old-age care units and drug abuse rehabilitation centres are also among those at highest risk.

A worrying escalation of violence is also reported in schools in a number of countries, while a disproportionate share of violent incidents is experienced by migrant workers, workers in free trade zones, and certain categories of rural workers.

Despite significant progress in the understanding of the causes of violence at work and of the situations where such violence is most likely to occur, the report shows that analyses and discussions in this area have been largely confined to experts and specialists. The other interested parties, particularly employers and workers, have entered the arena and voiced their concern but have not been involved, at least until now, in a fully participating way, assessing and responding to the problem of violence at work. Such participation by these interested parties is an essential prerequisite for the development of realistic priorities, strategies and policies in this area. Open discussion and extended engagement by all those concerned would seem to be a matter for priority action.

The need to involve all interested parties in understanding and shaping the response to violence

To achieve this goal it is essential that:

- information on violence at work is widely circulated among all interested parties;
- interested parties are offered concrete opportunities for dialogue and orientation on the issue of violence at work, such as workshops, seminars, conferences, etc.;
- awareness campaigns are launched to sensitize responsible bodies, enterprises, workers and the general public to the importance of violence at work;
- public officials, employers and workers' representatives are given easy access to specialized data banks on violence at work, and encouraged to establish integrated networks (including electronic networks) among themselves on this issue;
- individual workers are actively associated in the identification of the risk of violence at their workplace;
- access of the interested parties, including the victims of violence, to the media are facilitated;
- production of joint statements and policy orientation documents by the interested parties are encouraged.

FROM AN ISSUE FOR DISCUSSION TO AN ISSUE FOR ACTION

The approach chosen for dealing with the problem of violence at work is of paramount importance. Most attention is now focused on proactive approaches which utilize the potential of the workplace itself to control and diffuse violence, and emphasize the key role of preventive rather than reactive strategies.

The importance of a systematic approach to violence at work has also been stressed. This involves the application of a "control cycle" based usually on the sequence: risk assessment; design and implementation of the policy; reassessment of the risks; and so on. It is also recommended that a targeted response be provided to violence at work according to the type of "hazardous agent" involved, the type of occupation and situation, and the type of violence being anticipated.

The importance of a preventive, systematic and targeted approach to violence at work

In responding to violence at work, new legislation, guidelines, policies and practices are being introduced and developed. The scope of existing criminal, civil and common law, and of social security, health and safety, labour and environmental legislation is being extended progressively and adapted to deal with the issue of workplace violence.

As a reflection of the growing awareness of the importance of responding directly to violence at work, legislation strengthening traditional controls and sanctions is being supplemented increasingly by legislation that addresses this behaviour in specific terms. Violence at work is emerging as a separate legal issue with legislation and regulations providing for a targeted rather than a diffuse response. This trend has been accompanied by legislation and regulations relating to specific risk factors of violence, special occupations at risk and special types of violence. This trend has been further advanced by a growing number of collective and "model" agreements paving the way for, or supplementing, these legislative and regulatory actions.

The emergence of specific legislation on violence at work

An important body of guidelines on violence is emerging from governments, trade unions, special study groups, workplace violence experts, and employers' groups. Despite different approaches and methods used, such guidelines reveal common themes: preventive action is possible and necessary; work organization and the working environment hold significant keys to the causes and solutions to the problem; the participation of workers and their representatives is crucial both in identifying the problem and implementing solutions; the interpersonal skills of management and workers alike cannot be underrated; there cannot be one blueprint for action but rather the uniqueness of each workplace situation must be considered; and continued review of policies and programmes is needed to keep up with changing situations.

Attention is focusing to an increasing degree on the positive implications of preventive strategies. Experts emphasize the importance of selection, training, information and communication, and the quality of the work environment, work organization and job design in shaping effective preventive responses to violence at work.

The key role of guidelines in shaping an effective response to violence

While prevention is by far the best way to deal with violence at work, and every effort should be made to tackle the causes of prevention rather than its effects, it is important that workers be prepared and procedures established to defuse difficult situations and avoid violent confrontation. There is often, even in the most difficult circumstances, some room for manoeuvre before violence is released. Control of these situations is not easy, but possible, and many guidelines now recommend ways for minimizing the risk of violent incidents at this stage.

Victims of violence can experience a wide range of disturbing reactions such as anxiety, feelings of vulnerability and helplessness, disturbed sleep, difficulty in concentrating, increased fear, irritability, obsessive thoughts and images, feelings of shame, anger, frustration, guilt, changes in beliefs and values, and a desire to retaliate. Experts emphasize the necessity of psychological help for victims of violence, to deal with the distressing and often disabling after-effects of a violent incident and to prevent severe psychological problems from developing later. The quicker the response, the more effective and the less costly it will be.

The importance of both immediate intervention and long-term assistance to victims of violence

Tackling violence at work by preventive strategies and early intervention is becoming recognized as the most effective way to contain and defuse such behaviour. These principles are progressively incorporated in the different responses to violence at work. However – despite the lessons to be learned from forward-looking legislation, innovative guidelines and leading enterprises introducing successful anti-violence programmes based on these principles – their application is far from universal. Reactive responses, based on the use of fear and counter-aggression, still remain prevalent.

These responses concentrate on the effects of violence, rather than on its causes, with consequent waste in terms of the cost-effectiveness of the action undertaken. In too many situations the potential of the workplace itself to defuse violence is underexploited. In too many cases violence is a forgotten issue, and little or no action is taken to deal with it should it arise. The lessons on prevention spelt out in this report need to be transformed into practice.

Early intervention and prevention measures lead to more permanent results, and eventually pay for themselves

To achieve such a goal, the following initiatives might be envisaged:

- disseminating information about positive examples of innovative legislation, guidance and practice in this area, to act as multipliers for other anti-violence initiatives;
- encouraging anti-violence programmes, particularly at enterprise level, specifically addressed to combating violence at work;
- assisting governments, employers and workers' organizations to develop effective policies against violence at work;
- assisting in the elaboration of training programmes for managers, workers and government officers dealing with or exposed to violence at work;
- assisting in the elaboration of procedures to enhance the reporting of violent incidents; and
- assisting in coordinating different anti-violence initiatives at different levels into organized strategies and plans.

FOCUSING INTERNATIONAL ACTION

The rejection of the use of violence as a means of resolving inter- or intra-State conflicts, or disputes between individual groups, has been at the centre of a long-lasting international campaign. A growing body of conventions, recommendations, resolutions, and guidelines have addressed this problem, targeting different forms of violence, including violence in the family, in the community, by the State or at work. Depending on the nature of the international body or agency involved, including the UN, violence at work has been tackled as a human rights, labour, health and safety or criminal justice issue.

For many years the ILO's concern and action in areas closely related to violence at work has materialized in a series of studies and publications, in particular on occupational stress, and drug and alcohol abuse at the workplace. A specific form of violence – sexual harassment – has, for a long time, been high on the action agenda of the ILO.

The long and continuing concern of the ILO about violence at work issues
The ILO has the distinction of being the first international body to adopt an instrument containing an express protection against sexual harassment. The Indigenous and Tribal Peoples Convention, 1989 (No. 169), states that governments shall adopt special measures to ensure that the people concerned "enjoy equal opportunities and equal treatment in employment for men and women, and protection from sexual harassment" (Article 20, para. 3(d)).

Building on this action, the ILO's 1998-1999 Programme of Work targeted violence at work as a key issue within the fundamental scope of safeguarding the dignity and equality of workers.

> Violence at work has complex and interrelated causes, which may include serious problems in the working environment. Left unanswered, it is a serious threat to the safety and health of workers, results in heavy personal, social and economic costs, drains the productive capability of an enterprise and destroys the goodwill necessary to attract clients and workers.[1]

Action undertaken and new action from the ILO in this area finds a firm basis in the spirit and the mandate provided to the Organization by the ILO Constitution and the Declaration of Philadelphia. While the Preamble to the Constitution calls for all nations to "adopt humane conditions of labour", the Declaration affirms the fundamental principles on which the organization is based and, in particular, "that labour is not a commodity..." and that "all human beings, irrespective of race, creed or sex, have the right to pursue both their material well-being and their spiritual development in conditions of freedom and dignity, of economic security and equal opportunity...". Furthermore, as stated by the Director-General of the ILO in his Report to the 85th Session of the International Labour Conference in 1997, the role of the ILO in this area goes beyond the simple protection of fundamental rights:

> There are many other rights which, without being termed "fundamental" (meaning that their implementation is considered a priority), are nevertheless of fundamental – one might even say vital – importance for workers; for an example, one has to look no further than certain occupational safety and health standards, without which there could be a heavy loss of human lives.[2]

---

[1] ILO, *The Director-General's Programme and Budget Proposals for 1998-99*, Geneva, ILO, January 1997, pp. 90-98, para. 90.41.
[2] ILO, *The ILO, standard setting and globalization*, Report of the Director-General, International Labour Conference, 85th Session, 1997, Geneva, p. 20.

The right to a violence-free working environment would appear to fall into the category of "vital" rights as defined above. Thus, the ILO would seem to constitute an unique forum for dealing effectively with violence at work. Its tripartite composition must add greatly to its effectiveness in this area, since dialogue and interaction among the constituent parties are an essential prerequisite to the formulation of policies and the launching of initiatives on violence at work.

The ILO as a unique forum for combating violence at work

A call for action from the ILO in this field has been voiced in the international arena. The International Federation of Commercial, Clerical, Professional and Technical Employees – FIET – has urged that "the ILO should also develop guidelines and/or a Code of Practice [on violence at work]."[3]

As already indicated, in the ILO's 1998-1999 Programme of Work, action is under way in this area, including a compilation of best practices on how to tackle violence at work. Violence at work is also central to the ILO programme on "Safe Work" for 2000-01.

It is essential, and in line with the ILO's vocation, that the above activities be accompanied by a large participatory effort to promote dialogue among representatives of governments, employers and workers on the various issues involved. A networking exercise at decentralized levels would contribute to the search for best solutions according to the particular situation. The creation of electronic data banks would facilitate the exchange of information and opinions in this area.

Without doubt the action of the ILO will be critical in shaping an effective response to the challenge of violence at work in the future. Indeed that challenge is one in which the ILO is already engaged, as the preparation of this report has demonstrated. It is a challenge in which the ILO stands shoulder-to-shoulder with other international bodies, like the WHO, which have expressed their long-term commitment to tackling the growing problem of violence.

The broad lessons which should guide future action have been documented. The path to further progress now lies clearly in the direction of applying these lessons to the task of minimizing or eliminating the heavy toll that violence inflicts on so many of the world's workplaces. The slogan is clear: **Let us repudiate violence and remove it from the workplace now!**

---

[3] FIET, 1994, p. 21.

REFERENCES

Abrera-Mangahas, A.: "Violence against women migrant workers: A Philippine reality check", in *Philippines Labor Review* (Manila, Institute for Labor Studies), Vol. 20, No. 2, 1996.

Adams, A.; Crawford, N.: *Bullying at work: How to confront and overcome it*, London, Virago Press, 1992.

Aeberhard-Hodges, J.: "Sexual harassment in employment: Recent judicial and arbitral trends", in *International Labour Review* (Geneva, ILO), Vol. 135, No. 5, 1996.

Aggarwal, A.P.: "Dispute resolution processes for sexual harassment complaints", in *Canadian Labour and Employment Law Journal* (Scarborough, Ontario, Carswell), Vol. 3, No. 1, 1994.

Allcorn, S.: *Anger in the workplace: Understanding the causes of aggression and violence,* Westport, Connecticut, Quorum Books, 1994.

Alvazzi del Frate, A.; Zvekic, U.; Van Dijk, J.J.M. (eds.): *Understanding crime: Experiences of crime and crime control,* United Nations International Crime and Justice Research Institute (UNICRI) Publication No. 49, Rome, UNICRI, 1993.

American Federation of State, County and Municipal Employees, AFL-CIO: *Preventing workplace violence*, Washington, DC, 1998. (Web site http://www.igc.org/afscme/health/violtc.htm)

Anfuso, D.: "Deflecting violence in the workplace", in *Personnel Journal* (Costa Mesa, California), Vol. 73, No. 10, 1994.

Arnetz, J.E.; Arnetz, B.B.; Petterson, I.L.: *Violence, sexual and psychological harassment toward nurses: Occupational and lifestyle factors*, Stockholm, National Institute for Psychosocial Factors and Health, 1994.

Aromaa, K.: "Survey results in victimization to violence at work", in *OECD Panel Group on Women, Work and Health: National Report,* Helsinki, Institute of Occupational Health, Ministry of Social Affairs and Health, 1993.

—; Haapaniemi, M.; Kinnunen, A.; Koivula, A.K.: *Väkivalta Työtehtävissä: Työssä koettua väkivaltaa koskevan tutkimushankkeen osaraportti: [Violence at work: An interim report on a project concerning violence experienced at work]*, Helsinki, National Research Institute of Legal Policy, 1994.

Violence at work

Backman, R.: *Violence and theft in the workplace: Crime data brief, National Crime Victimization Survey,* Washington, DC, US Department of Justice, 1994.

Banking, Insurance and Finance Union (BIFU): *The hidden cost: A survey of bank and building society robberies,* London, 1992 (April).

Barab, J.: "Workplace violence: How labor sees it", in *New Solutions* (Lakewood, Illinois), 1995 (Spring).

Baron, S.A.: *Violence in the workplace: A prevention and management guide for businesses,* Ventura, California, Pathfinder Publishing, 1993.

Barrier, M.: "The enemy within", in *Nation's Business* (Washington, DC), 1995 (February).

Barth, P.S.: "Workers' compensation for mental stress cases", in *Behavioral Sciences and the Law* (Washington, DC), Vol. 8, 1990.

Bast-Pettersen, R.; Bach, E.; Lindström, K.; Toomings, A.; Kiviranta, J. (eds.): *Research on violence, threats and bullying as health risks among health care personnel: Proceedings of the Workshop for Nordic Researchers, 14-16 August 1994,* Reykjavik, 1995.

Beck, C.; Robinson, C.; Baldwin, B.: "Improving documentation of aggressive behaviour in nursing home residents", in *Journal of Gerontological Nursing,* (Thorofare, New Jersey), Vol. 18, No. 2, 1992.

Becker, M.: "Mobbing in der Führungsetage", in *The Proceedings of the Mobbing Symposium, Zurich, 23 February 1995: Mobbing: Psychostress am Arbeitsplatz,* Zurich, Kaufmännischer Verband and *Tagesanzeiger,* 1995.

Beermann, B.; Meschkutat, B.: *Psychosocial factors at the workplace: Taking account of stress and harassment,* Dortmund, Federal Institute for Occupational Safety and Health, 1995.

Black, M.: *Report on the Innocenti Global Seminar on Street and Working Children,* Florence, UNICEF/ICDC, 1993 (October).

Boom, E.V.; et al.: "Violence and aggression: Not just a problem for the individual worker", in *Janus* (Luxembourg), No. 20-II-1995.

Bowie, V.: "May I shake you by the throat? Dealing with difficult clients", in *Criminology Australia* (Canberra), Vol. 3, No. 4, 1992.

—: *Coping with violence: A guide for human services,* London, Whiting and Birch Ltd., 1996.

Boxer, P.A.: "Assessment of potential violence in the paranoid worker" in *Journal of Occupational Medicine* (Arlington Heights, Illinois), Vol. 35, No. 2, 1993.

Brooks, C.; Cross, C.: *Retail Crime Costs 1994/95 Survey,* London, British Retail Consortium, 1996.

Bureau fédéral de l'égalité entre femmes et hommes: *Harcèlement sexuel: la réalité cachée des femmes au travail,* Geneva, 1993.

Bureau of Labor Statistics (BLS): *Work Injuries and Illnesses by Selected Characteristics 1992,* US Department of Labor, Washington, DC, 1994.

Bush, D.F.; O'Shea, P.G.: "Workplace violence: Comparative use of prevention practices and policies", in G.R. VandenBos and E.O. Bulatao: *Violence on the job,* edited by American Psychological Association, Washington, DC, 1996.

California. Department of Industrial Relations (CAL/OSHA): *Guidelines for security and safety of health care and community service workers,* San Francisco, Division of Occupational Safety and Health, State of California, 1993.

—: *Guidelines for workplace security,* San Francisco, Division of Occupational Safety and Health, State of California, 1994.

Canadian Union of Public Employees (CUPE): *Stopping violence at work* (Health and Safety Guidelines Series), Ottawa, Ontario, 1994.

Castillo, D.N.: "Trends, risks, and interventions in lethal violence. Nonfatal violence in the workplace: Directions for future research", in C. Block and R. Block, (eds.): *Proceedings of the Third Annual Spring Symposium of the Homicide Research Working Group,* Washington, DC, National Institute of Justice, 1995.

—; Jenkins, E.L.: "Industries and occupations at high risk for work-related homicide", in *Journal of Occupational Medicine* (Washington, DC), Vol. 36, 1994.

Center for Personnel Research: *Personnel practices: Workplace violence,* Research Series, Vol. 1, No. 5, Alexandria, Virginia, 1994.

Chappell, D.; Egger, S.: *Australian violence: Contemporary perspectives,* Canberra, Australian Institute of Criminology, 1995.

Claiborne, Inc., Liz: *Addressing domestic violence: A corporate response,* New York, 1997 (10 March).

Colatosti, C.; Karg, E.: *Stopping sexual harassment: A handbook for union and workplace activists,* Detroit, Michigan, Labor Education and Research Project, 1992.

Coleman, J.: "Corporate bullying on the rise at Japan's troubled companies", in *The Japan Times* (Tokyo), 1996 (14 December).

Collinson, M.; Collinson, M.: "It's only Dick: The sexual harassment of women managers in insurance sales", in *Work, Employment and Society* (London), Vol. 10, No. 1, 1996.

Commission of the European Communities: *How to combat sexual harassment at work: A guide to implementing the European Commission Code of Practice,* Brussels, 1993.

Commission on Crime Prevention and Criminal Justice: *Report of the Secretary-General,* Sixth Session, Vienna, 28 April-9 May 1997, E/CN.15/1997/11, 1997 (4 March).

Conference Clearing House (CCH) International: *Workplace health and safety manual,* North Ryde, New South Wales, 1991.

Conlon, K.: "Sexual harassment: An American judicial perspective", in *Labor Law Journal* (Chicago), Vol. 48, No. 1, 1997 (January).

Cornish, M.; Lopez, S.: "Changing the workplace culture through effective harassment remedies", in *Canadian Labour and Employment Law Journal* (Scarborough, Ontario), Vol. 3, No. 1, 1994.

Cullen, W.D.: *The Public Inquiry into the Shootings at Dunblane Primary School on 13 March 1996,* CM. 3386, Edinburgh, Scottish Office, 1996.

Department of Employment: *Sexual harassment in the workplace*: *A guide for employers*, London, 1992 (June).

Department of Labour, Occupational Safety and Health Service, Government of New Zealand: *Guidelines for employers and employees on dealing with violence at work*, Wellington, 1995(a).

—: *Guidelines for the safety of staff from the threat of armed robbery*, Wellington, 1995(b).

Department of Transport: *Protecting bus crews*: *A practical guide*, London, 1995 (July).

Desjardins, Lucie: "Violence en milieu de travail: Les victimes sont rarement indemnisées", in *Le Journal du Barreau* (Québec), Vol. 29, No. 6 – 1 April 1997, Web site: http://www.barreau.qc.ca/journal/vol29/no6/.

Dibattista, R.A.: "Forecasting sabotage events in the workplace", in *Public Personnel Management* (Alexandria, Virginia), Vol. 25, No. 1, 1996 (Spring).

Dickson, R.; Cox, T.; Leather, P.; Beal, D.; Farnsworth, B.: "Violence at work", in *Occupational Health Review* (London), 1993 (November/December).

Dietrich, S.; Emsellem, M.; McNeil, S.: "Violence in the workplace: Exploring employee rights and remedies", in *Clearinghouse Review* (Chicago), Vol. 28, No. 4, Special Issue ("Do you know the effects of violence on your clients?"), 1994.

Di Martino, V.: "Télétravail: A la recherche des règles d'or", in *Technologies de l'Information et Société,* (Paris), Vol. 8, No. 4, 1996.

—: *The high road to teleworking*, Geneva, ILO, forthcoming.

—; Wirth, L.: "Telework: A new way of working and living", in *International Labour Review* (Geneva), Vol. 129, No. 5, 1990.

Dobrin, A.; Wiersema, B.; Loftin, C.: *Statistical Handbook on Violence in America*, Phoenix, Arizona, Oryx Press, 1996.

Easteal, P.W.; Wilson, P.R.: *Preventing crime on transport: Rail, buses, taxis, planes,* Canberra, Australian Institute of Criminology, 1991.

Educational Institute of Scotland: "Discipline breakdown: Teachers dare to speak out", in *Scottish Educational Journal* (Glasgow), Vol. 75, No. 3, 1992.

Edwards, P.K.; Scullion, H.: *Social organization of industrial conflict: Control and resistance in the workplace,* Oxford, Basil Blackwell, 1982.

—; —: *Organización social del conflicto laboral: Control y resistencia en la fábrica*, Madrid, Ministerio de Trabajo y Seguridad Social, 1987.

Ekblom, P.: *Preventing robberies at sub-post offices: An evaluation of a security initiative*, London, Home Office Crime Prevention Unit, 1987.

Elliott, R.H.; Jarrett, D.T.: "Violence in the workplace: The role of human resource management", in *Public Personnel Management*, (Alexandria, Virginia), Vol. 23, No. 2, 1994.

Equal Opportunities Commission: *Sexual harassment at work: Consider the cost*, London, 1994 (October).

Erdreich, B.L.; Slavet, B.S.; Amador, A.C.: *Sexual harassment in the Federal workplace*, Washington, DC, United States Merit Systems Protection Board, 1996.

European Foundation for the Improvement of Living and Working Conditions: *First European Survey on the Work Environment (1991-92)*, Dublin, 1993.

—: *Second European Survey on Working Conditions (1995-96)*, Dublin, 1997.

European Parliament: *Resolution on violence against women,* Doc. A.2.44/86, Strasbourg, 1986 (11 June).

—: *Measures to combat sexual harassment at the workplace: Action taken in the Member States of the European Community,* Women's Rights Series, Working Paper No. 2, Luxembourg, 1994.

European Trade Union Confederation (ETUC): *Tackling violence at work*, Background Report for the ETUC Health and Safety Forum, London, 1993 (February).

Evers, G.; van der Velden, P.: "Aggression and violence at work recognized as a problem at long last", in *Janus* (Luxembourg), No. 14, 1993.

Feliu, G.: "Workplace violence and the duty of care: The scope of an employer's obligation to protect against the violent employee", in *Employee Relations Law Journal* (Washington, DC), Vol. 20, No. 3, 1994.

FIET (International Federation of Commercial, Clerical, Professional and Technical Employees): *Tackling violence at work: EURO-FIET/ETUC seminar on violence to workers, London, February 1993*, Geneva, 1994.

Fried, N.E.: *Sex, laws and stereotypes: Authentic workplace anecdotes and practical tips for dealing with sexual harassment, workplace violence and beyond*, Dublin, Ohio, National Press Publications, 1994.

Gibson, D.: "Assaults on bus crews", in *Urban Transport* (London), No. 1, 1995.

Giuffre, P.A.; Williams, C.L.: "Boundary lines: Labelling sexual harassment in restaurants", in *Gender and Society* (New York), Vol. 8, No. 3, 1994 (September).

Gopalen, P.: *A situational analysis of violence in the working conditions of domestic helpers in Metro Manila,* Manila, ILO-IPEC, 1996.

Violence at work

Grainger, C.: "Occupational violence: Armed hold-up – A risk management approach", in *International Journal of Stress Management* (New York), Vol. 2, No. 4, 1995.

—. "How controllable is occupational violence", in *International Journal of Stress Management* (New York), Vol. 3, No. 1, 1996.

—; Kerr, S.L.: *Violence: A risk management handbook for dealing with violence at work*, Everton Park, Queensland, Australia, Mintinta Press, 1994.

Grund, U.: "Mobbing – Prävention: Gewerkschaftlicher Handlungsauftrag und betriebliche Lösungsansätze" [Prevention of mobbing: The trade unions' mandate and emerging solutions at the workplace level], in *The Proceedings of the Mobbing Symposium, Zurich, 23 February 1995: Mobbing: Psychostress am Arbeitsplatz*, Zurich, Kaufmännischer Verband and *Tagesanzeiger*, 1995.

Health and Safety Commission (HSC): *Violence to staff in the education sector*, London, 1990.

Health and Safety Executive (HSE): *Violence to staff*, London, HMSO, 1991.

—: *Prevention of violence to staff in banks and building societies*, London, HMSO, 1993.

—: *Preventing violence to retail staff,* London, 1995.

—: *Violence at work – A guide for employers*, London, 1997.

Health Services Advisory Committee: *Violence to staff in the health services*, London, 1987.

Hebden Lindsay Limited: *Personal harassment: Harassment and bullying in the workplace* Burnley, Lancashire, 1995.

Hoad, C.D.: "Violence at work: Perspectives from research among 20 British employers", in *Security Journal* (London), Vol. 4, 1996.

Holzbecher, M.; Braszeit, A.; Mueller, U.; Plogstedt, S.; Bundesministerium für Jugend, Familie, Frauen und Gesundheit: *Sexuelle Belästigung am Arbeitsplatz*, Stuttgart, Kohlhammer, 1991.

Homel, R.; Tomsen, S.; Thommeny, J.: "Public drinking and violence: Not just an alcohol problem", in *Journal of Drug Issues* (Tallahassee, Florida), Vol. 22, 1992.

—; Clark, J.: "The prediction and prevention of violence in pubs and clubs", in *Crime Prevention Studies* (New York), Vol. 3, 1994.

Horenstein J.-Mario, et al., *Les pratiques du harcèlement en milieu éducatif*, Paris, Mutuelle Générale de l'Education Nationale, 1998.

House of Representatives Standing Committee on Employment, Education and Training: *Sticks and stones: Report on violence in Australian schools* (Canberra), Australian Government Publishing Service, 1994.

Incomes Data Services Ltd.: *Violence against staff*, IDS Study 557, London, 1994.

—: *Violence at work*. IDS Study 628, London, 1997 (June).

Industry Commission: *Work, Health and Safety: Inquiry into Occupational Health and Safety*, Report No. 47, Canberra, Australia Government Publishing Service, 1995.

International Air Transport Association (IATA): *Guidelines for handling disruptive/unruly passengers*, Geneva, 1999.

International Confederation of Free Trade Unions (ICFTU): *Trade Union Action Programme on Violence Against Women,* Brussels, 1995.

International Federation of Journalists: *IFJ Directline* (Brussels), December 1996/January 1997.

International Labour Office (ILO): *Psychosocial factors at work: Recognition and control*, Occupational Safety and Health Series, No. 56, ILO, Geneva, 1986.

—: *Conclusions and Recommendations: Tripartite Symposium on Equality of Opportunity and Treatment for Men and Women in Employment in Industrialized Countries: Report,* SEEIC/1990/2, Geneva, 1990.

—: "Alcohol and drugs", *Conditions of Work Digest*, Vol. 6, 1/1987.

—: "Telework", *Conditions of Work Digest* (Geneva), Vol. 9, 1/1990.

—: "Combating sexual harassment at work", *Conditions of Work Digest,* Vol. 11, 1/1992.

—: "Preventing stress at work", *Conditions of Work Digest,* Vol. 11, 2/1992.

—: "Workers' privacy – Testing in the workplace", *Conditions of Work Digest,* Vol. 12, 2/1993.

—: *Estudios de caso y educación obrera en zonas francas y empresas maquiladoras en países del istmo centroamericano y de la República dominica – El caso de Costa Rica*, Geneva, 1995 (February).

—: *Child labour: Targeting the intolerable,* Report VI (1), International Labour Conference, 86th Session, 1998, Geneva, 1996.

—: *Equality in employment and occupation,* General Survey by the Committee of Experts on the Application of Conventions and Recommendations, International Labour Conference, 83rd Session, 1996, Report III (Part 4B), Geneva, 1996.

—: *The Director-General's Programme and Budget Proposals for 1998-99,* Geneva, ILO, January 1997.

—: *Decent work*, Report of the Director-General, International Labour Conference, 87th Session, Geneva, 1999.

—: Governing Body, Committee on Employment and Social Policy: *International migration and migrant workers*, GB 265/ESP/2, 265th Session, Geneva, 1996 (March).

—: *The ILO, standard setting and globalization*, Report of the Director-General, International Labour Conference, 85th Session, 1997, Geneva.

— Manila Office: *Welfare cases 1994 from overseas workers welfare administration*, Manila, 1995 (February).

Violence at work

Japanese Trade Union Confederation (JTUC): *The spring struggle for a better life 1997,* Rengo White Paper, Tokyo, 1997.

Jenkins, E.L.: *Violence in the workplace: Risk factors and prevention strategies,* National Institute for Occupational Safety and Health (NIOSH), Publication No. 96-100, Washington, DC, US Government Printing Office, 1996.

Johnson, P.R.; Indvik, J.: "Workplace violence: An issue of the Nineties", in *Public Personnel Management* (Alexandria, Virginia), Vol. 23, No. 4, 1994 (Winter).

—: "Stress and workplace violence: It takes two to tango", in *Journal of Managerial Psychology* (Bradford, West Yorkshire), Vol. 11, No. 6, 1996.

Joint Parliamentary Group: *Report of the Special Commissioner for Port Arthur, Mr. Max Doyle, into Matters Affecting the Port Arthur Historic Site and other Associated Matters,* Bellerive, Tasmania, 1997.

Kelleher, M.D.: *New arenas for violence: Homicide in the American workplace,* Westport, Connecticut, Praeger, 1996.

—: *Profiling the lethal employee. Case studies of violence in the workplace,* Westport, Connecticut, Praeger, 1997.

King, A.; Peart, M.: *Teachers in Canada: Their work and quality of life,* Kingston, Ontario, Queen's University, 1992.

Kinney, J.A.: *Violence at work: How to make your company safer for employees and customers,* Englewood Cliffs, New Jersey, Prentice Hall, 1995.

Koss, M.P.; et al.: "Violence in the workplace", in *No safe haven: Male violence against women at home, at work, and in the community,* Washington, DC, American Psychological Association, 1994.

Kuzmits, F.E.: "When employees kill other employees", in *Journal of Occupational Medicine,* (Arlington Heights, Illinois), Vol. 32, No. 10, 1990.

Laabs, J.J.: "HR puts its sexual harassment questions on the line", in *Personnel Journal* (Costa Mesa, California), Vol. 74, No. 2, 1995 .

Lamplugh, D.: "Personal safety at work", in *Health and Safety Data File* (London), 1994 (May).

Lamplugh Trust, Suzy: *Violence and aggression at work: Reducing the risks. Guidance for Employers,* London, 1994(a) (November).

—: *Personal safety at work. Guidance for all employees,* London, 1994(b).

—: *Personal safety for social workers,* London, 1994(c).

—: *Personal safety for health-care workers,* London, 1995.

—: *Personal safety for schools,* London, 1996.

—: *Personal safety in other people's homes,* London, 1998.

La Van, H.; Katz, M.; Hochwarter, W.: "Employee stress swamps workers' compensation", in *Personnel* (New York), Vol. 67, No. 5, 1990.

Le Figaro (Paris): "Les dix-neuf mesures arrêtées. Le plan de prévention de la violence à l'école se présente en trois grands axes et dix-neufs mesures", 1996 (21 March).

Levi, L.: *Stress in industry – Causes, effects and prevention,* Occupational Safety and Health Series, No. 51, ILO, Geneva, 1984.

Leymann, H.: "Mobbing and psychological terror at workplaces", in *Violence and Victims* (New York, Springer), Vol. 5, No. 2, 1990.

—: *Mobbing: Psychoterror am Arbeitsplatz und wie man sich dagegen wehren kann,* Reinbek bei Hamburg, Rowohlt, 1993.

—; Lindell, J.: "Social support after armed robbery in the workplace", Offprint from *The victimology research handbook,* Garland Publishing, New York, 1990.

Lim, L.L.: *More and better jobs for women: An action guide,* Geneva, ILO, 1996.

Lippe, K.: "Compensation for mental-mental claims under Canadian law", in *Behavioral Sciences and the Law* (Washington, DC), Vol. 8, 1990.

Liss, C.M.; McCaskell, L.: "Violence in the workplace", in *Canadian Medical Journal* (Ottawa), Vol. 154, No. 4, 1994.

Littler, Mendelson, Fastiff, Tichy and Mathiason, Inc.: *Combating workplace violence: The new California requirements task force report,* San Francisco, California, 1994(a).

—: *Terror and violence in the workplace,* San Francisco, California, 1994(b).

MacDermott, T.: "Duty to provide a harassment-free work environment", in *Journal of Industrial Relations* (Sydney), Vol. 37, No. 4, 1995.

MacKinnon, C.A.: *Sexual harassment of working women. The case of sex discrimination,* New Haven and London, Yale University Press, 1979.

Mantell, M.; Albrecht, S.: *Ticking bombs: Defusing violence in the workplace,* Burr Ridge, Illinois, Irwin Professional Publishing, 1994.

Manufacturing, Science, Finance Union (MSF): *Prevention of violence at work: An MSF guide with model agreement and violence at work questionnaire,* Bishop's Stortford, Hertfordshire, 1993.

—: *Bullying at work: Confronting the problem,* London, 1994.

—: *Working alone: Guidance for MSF Members and Safety Representatives,* London, 1994.

Martine, M.S.: *La situación de las mujeres, docentes en centroamerica: hacia la igualdad de oportunidades y de trato,* ILO, Geneva, 1994.

Mattman, J.W.; Kaufer, S.: *Complete workplace violence prevention manual,* Newport Beach, California, Workplace Violence Research Institute, 1995.

Violence at work

Mayhew, C.; Peterson, C.: *Occupational health and safety in Australia: Industry, public sector and small business,* Sydney, Allen and Unwin, 1999.

Mayhew, P.; Aye Maung, N.; Mirrlees-Black, C.: *The 1992 British Crime Survey,* Home Office Research Study, No. 32, London, HMSO, 1993.

McClure, L.F.: *Risky business: Managing employee violence in the workplace,* New York, Haworth Press, 1996.

McDonald, D.; Brown, M.: *Indicators of Aggressive Behaviour: Report to the Minister for Health and Family Services from an Expert Working Group,* Research and Public Policy Series, No. 8, Canberra, Australian Institute of Criminology, 1997.

McMattis, M.C.; Resnick, J.: *Cracking the glass ceiling: Strategies for success,* New York, Catalyst, 1994.

Minor, M.: *Preventing workplace violence: Positive management strategies* (50-minute series), Menlo Park, California, Crisp Publications, 1995.

Ministère de l'Education Nationale, Inspection Générale de l'Education Nationale, (Rapporteur G. Fotines): *La violence à l'école – Etat de la situation en 1994: Analyse et Recommandations*, Paris, 1995.

Monahan, J.: "Dangerous and violent behaviour", in *Journal of Occupational Medicine* (Arlington Heights, Illinois), Vol. 1, 1986.

Morin, W.J.: *Silent sabotage: Rescuing our careers, our companies, and our lives from the creeping paralysis of anger and bitterness*, New York, AMACOM, 1995.

Mukherjee, S.: *Crime trends in twentieth century Australia,* Sydney, Allen and Unwin, 1981.

National Association of Letter Carriers (NALC) USA: "Safeguarding the mail and the messenger: LA residents rally around carriers", in *Postal Record* (Washington, DC), Vol. 17, No. 5, 1994 (May).

National Clearinghouse for Legal Services, Inc.: "Do you know the effects of violence on your clients?", special issue of *Clearinghouse Review* (Chicago), Vol. 28, No. 4, 1994.

National Committee on Violence (NCV): *Violence: Directions for Australia,* Canberra, Australian Institute of Criminology, 1990.

Nogareda Cuixart, C.; Nogareda Cuixart, S.: "Valoración de la carga mental en el servicio de urgencias de un hospital", in *Salud y Trabajo* (Barcelona), No. 2, 1990.

Nordin, H.: *Fakta om våld och hot i arbetet*, Solna, Occupational Injury Information System (ISA), Swedish National Board of Occupational Safety and Health, 1995 (28 August).

Northwestern National Life Insurance Company: *Fear and Violence in the Workplace: A Survey Documenting the Experience of American Workers,* Minneapolis, Minnesota, Northwestern National Life, Employee Benefits Division, 1993.

Nowosad, M.: "Was kostet Mobbing?" [*How much does mobbing cost?*], in *The Proceedings of the Mobbing Symposium, Zurich, 23 February 1995: Mobbing: Psychostress am Arbeitsplatz*, Zurich, Kaufmännischer Verband and *Tagesanzeiger*, 1995.

Occupational Safety and Health Administration (OSHA): *Guidelines for preventing workplace violence for health care and social service workers,* OSHA 3148, Washington, DC, 1996(a).

—: *Draft guidelines for workplace violence prevention programs for night retail establishments,* Washington, DC, 1996(b) (28 June).

—: *Recommendations for workplace violence prevention programs in late-night establishments,* Washington, DC, 1998.

Pater, R.: *Organizational self defense: Preventing violence at your workplace,* Portland, Oregon, Society for Human Resource Management, 1994.

Pérez, N.C.; Valera, C.A.: *Impacto socio-económico de las maquiladoras y las zonas libres en Honduras,* Geneva, ILO, 1995 (January).

PERSEREC, Defence Personnel Security Research Center: *Guidance for employers,* Washington, DC, 1995.

Piper, C.: *The hidden cost: A survey of bank and building society robberies,* London, Banking, Insurance and Finance Union, 1992.

Pizzino, A.: *Report on CUPE's (Canadian Union of Public Employees) National Health and Safety Survey of Aggression Against Staff,* Ottawa, 1994 (January).

Postal, Telegraph and Telephone International (PTTI): *Study Report on Health, Safety and the Environment,* 22nd European Congress, Rome, 1992 (13-16 October).

Poyner, B.; Warne, C.; Tavistock Institute of Human Relations: *Preventing violence to staff,* London, Health and Safety Executive, 1988.

Reiss, A.; Roth, J. (eds.): *Understanding and preventing violence* (4 volumes), Washington, DC, National Academy Press, 1993.

Robertson, D.: *Violence in your workplace: How to cope,* London, Souvenir Press, 1993.

Robinson, R.K.; Fink, R.L.; Allen, B.M.: "Unresolved issues in hostile environment claims of sexual harassment", in *Labor Law Journal* (Chicago), Vol. 45, No. 2, 1994 (February).

Rosch, P.J.: "Job stress violence epidemic", in *Newsletter of the American Institute of Stress* (New York), No. 6, 1994.

Royal College of Nursing: *Violence and community nursing staff: A Royal College of Nursing survey,* London, 1994(a).

—: *Violence and community nursing staff: Advice for managers,* London, 1994(b).

Roy-Loustaunau, C.: "Droit du harcèlement sexuel: Un puzzle legislatif et des choix novateurs", in *Droit Social* (Paris), No. 6, 1995 (June).

Rubenstein, M.; Commission of the European Communities: *Dignity of women at work: Report on the problem of sexual harassment in the Member States of the European Communities,* Brussels, 1987.

Violence at work

Saskatchewan Teachers' Association: "Survey finds teacher abuse growing", in *Saskatchewan Bulletin*, 1994 (13 May).

Scottish Office: *The Public Inquiry into the Shootings at Dunblane School on 13 March 1996: The Government Response*, CM.3392, Edinburgh, Scottish Office, 1996.

Schmitt, H.: *Kein Kavaliers-Delikt? Sexuelle Belästigung im Arbeitsleben*, Bonn, Bundesministerium für Frauen und Jugend, 1993.

Schwarz, E.D.; Kowalski, J.M.: "Malignant memories: Effect of a shooting in the workplace on school personnel's attitudes", in *Journal of Interpersonal Violence* (Newbury Park, California), Vol. 8, No. 4, 1993.

Seligman, P.J.; Newman, S.C.; Timbrook, C.; Halperin, W.E.: "Sexual assault of women at work", in *American Journal of Industrial Medicine* (New York), No. 12, 1987.

Serna Calvo, M.M.: *Acoso sexual en las relaciones laborales*, Montevideo, Relasur, 1994.

Sheikh-Hashim, S.: *Occupational hazards of working women*, Dar es Salaam, ILO, 1990 (May) (unpublished working paper).

Smith, L.J.F.: *Crime in hospitals: Diagnosis and prevention*, London, Crime Prevention Unit, Home Office, 1987.

Smith, N.M.: "Staff harassment by patrons: Why administrators flinch", in *American Libraries* (Chicago), Vol. 25, No. 4, 1994.

Solomon, C.M.: "Talking frankly about domestic violence", in *Personnel Journal* (Costa Mesa, California), 1995 (April).

Sprouse, M.: *Sabotage in the American workplace: Anecdotes of dissatisfaction, mischief and revenge*, San Francisco, Pressure Drop Press, 1992.

Steinmetz, C.H.D.: "Contacts with a violent public: Profit and non-profit organizations", in *Security Journal* (Amsterdam), No. 6, 1995.

Stuart, P.: "Murder on the job", in *Personnel Journal* (Costa Mesa, California), 1992 (February).

Suively, S.: *The New Zealand Economic Cost of Family Violence*, Summary produced by the Department of Social Welfare, Wellington, New Zealand, 1995 (December).

Swanton, B.: "Violence and public contact workers", in *Violence Today* (Canberra), No. 5, Australian Institute of Criminology, 1989.

—; Webber, D.: *Protecting counter and interviewing staff from client aggression,* Canberra, Australian Institute of Criminology, 1990.

Toohey, J.: *Corporate culture and the management of violence*, unpublished conference paper presented at the "Occupational Violence: Were you threatened at work today?" seminar series held at the University of Queensland, Australia, 10-12 February 1993, Brisbane, 1993.

Toscano, G.; Weber, W.: "Violence in the workplace: Patterns of fatal workplace assaults differ from those of non-fatal ones", US Department of Labor, in *Compensation and Working Conditions* (Washington, DC), No. 47, Vol. 4, 1995.

—; Windau, J.: "Changing character of fatal work injuries", in *Monthly Labor Review* (Washington, DC), Vol. 117, No. 10, 1994.

Trades Union Congress (TUC): *Guidelines. Sexual harassment at work,* London, 1992 (June).

—: *Racial harassment at work: A guide and workplace programme for trade unionists*, London, 1993.

—: *Violent times*, London, 1999.

Trident Consultants Ltd.: *Report to Staff Assaults Working Group (London Underground Ltd.): Quantitative analysis of staff assaults*, Report J. 2909, London, 1997 (March).

Turnbull, J.: "Hitting back at the bullies", in *Nursing Times* (London), Vol. 91, No. 3, 1995.

UNISON: *Violence in the National Health Service*, London, 1992.

—: *Working alone in safety – Controlling the risks of solitary work*, London, 1993.

—: *Bullying at work: Guidance for safety representatives and members on bullying at work and how to prevent it*, London, 1996.

—: *Violence at work. A guide to risk prevention for UNISON branches, stewards and safety representatives*, London, 1997.

United Nations: Report of the Committee on the Elimination of Discrimination against Women: Eleventh Session, General Assembly, *Official Records*, 47th Session, Supplement No. 38, A/47/38, New York, 1992.

—: *Report of the Fourth World Conference on Women*. Beijing, 1995 (4-15 September).

—: *Report of the Special Rapporteur on violence against women, its causes and consequences, Ms. Radhika Coomaraswamy*, Commission on Human Rights, Geneva, E/CN.4/1997/47, 1997 (12 February).

—: *Report of the Special Rapporteur on violence against women, its causes and consequences, Ms. Radhika Coomaraswamy*, Commission on Human Rights, Geneva, E/CN.4/1999/68, 1999 (10 March).

United States Departments of Education and Justice: *A guide to safe schools*, Washington, DC, 1998. (Web site http://www.ed.gov/offices/OSERS/OSEP/earlywrn.htm)

United States Office of Personnel Management: *Dealing with workplace violence: A guide for agency planners*, Washington, DC, 1997 (Oct.).

VandenBos, G.R.; Bulatao, E.O. (eds.): *Violence on the job*, Washington, DC, American Psychological Association, 1996.

Violence at work

Van Dijk, J.J.M.; Mayhew, P.; Killias, M.: *Experiences of crime across the world: Key findings of the 1989 International Crime Survey,* The Hague, Ministry of Justice of the Netherlands, 1989.

—; —; —: *Experiences of crime across the world,* Deventer, Kluwer, 1990.

—; —: *Criminal victimization in the industrialized world,* The Hague, Ministry of Justice of the Netherlands, 1992.

Vartia, M.: "Psychological harassment at work", in *OECD Panel Group on Women, Work and Health: National Report,* Helsinki, Institute of Occupational Health, Ministry of Social Affairs and Health, 1993.

Wainwright Industries: "Creating a violence-free company culture", in *Nation's Business* (Washington, DC), 1995 (February).

Weisinger, H.: *Anger at work: Learning the art of anger management on the job,* New York, 1978.

Windau, J.; Toscano, G.: "Workplace homicides in 1992", in *Compensation and Working Conditions* (Washington, DC), 1994 (February).

Woods, M.; Whitehead, J.; Lamplugh, D.: *Working alone: Surviving and thriving,* Corby, United Kingdom, Institute of Management, 1993.

WorkCover Authority of New South Wales: *Armed hold-ups and cash handling: A guide to protecting people and profits from armed hold-ups,* Sydney, 1994.

WorkCover Corporation of South Australia: *Guidelines for aged care facilities,* Adelaide, 1996.

Workers' Compensation Board of British Columbia: *Take care – How to develop and implement a workplace violence programme – A guide for small business,* Vancouver, Canada, 1995.

Working Women's Centre: *Stop violence against women at work,* Adelaide, 1994 (June).

WorkSafe Western Australia Commission: *Working alone,* West Perth, 1999.

World Health Organization (WHO) – World Health Assembly: *Prevention of violence: A public health priority,* Resolution WHA 49.25, 25 May 1996, Geneva, 1996.

Wynne, R.; Clarkin, N.; Cox, T.; Griffiths, A.: *Guidance on the prevention of violence at work,* Brussels, European Commission, DG-V, Ref. CE/VI-4/97, 1997.

Yamaji, N.: "Victims of white-collar bullying speak out", in *Mainichi Daily News* (Tokyo), 1997 (29 January).

Yamakawa, R.: "'Personal rights' in the workplace: The emerging law concerning sexual harassment in Japan", in *Japan Labor Bulletin* (Tokyo), Vol. 36. No. 9, 1997 (1 September).

Yassi, A.: "Assault and abuse of health care workers in a large teaching hospital", in *Canadian Medical Association Journal* (Ottawa), Vol. 151, No. 9, 1994.

Younger, B.: "Violence against women in the workplace", in *Employee Assistance Quarterly* (New York), Vol. 9, No. 3/4, 1994.

Zabala, C.A.: "Sabotage at General Motors' Van Nuys Assembly Plant, 1975-83", in *Industrial Relations Journal* (Oxford), Vol. 20, No. 1, 1989.

Zegers de Beijl, R.: *Combating discrimination against migrant workers: International standards, national legislation and voluntary measures. The need for a multi-pronged strategy,* Paper prepared for the Seminar on Immigration, Racism and Racial Discrimination, held in Geneva, 1997 (May).

Zvekic, U.; Alvazzi del Frate, A. (eds.): *Criminal victimization in the developing world,* UNICRI Publication No. 55, Rome, UNICRI, 1995.